Thinking
in Henry James

Thinking
in Henry James

Sharon Cameron

The University of Chicago Press

Chicago and London

PS
2127
.T53
C3
1989

SHARON CAMERON, William R. Kenan, Jr., Professor of English at The Johns Hopkins University, is the author of *Lyric Time: Dickinson and the Limits of Genre* (1979), *The Corporeal Self: Allegories of the Body in Melville and Hawthorne* (1981), and *Writing Nature: Henry Thoreau's "Journal"* (1985).

The University of Chicago Press, Chicago 60637
The University of Chicago Press, Ltd., London

© 1989 by The University of Chicago
All rights reserved. Published 1989
Printed in the United States of America
98 97 96 95 94 93 92 91 90 89   54321

⊗The paper used in this publication meets the minimum requirements of the American National Standard for Information Sciences—Permanence of Paper for Printed Library Materials, ANSI Z39.48-1984.

Library of Congress Cataloging-in-Publication Data
Cameron. Sharon.
  Thinking in Henry James / Sharon Cameron.
    p.   cm.
  Bibliography: p.
  Includes index.
  ISBN 0-226-09230-5 (alk. paper)
  1. James, Henry, 1843–1916—Criticism and interpretation.
2. James, Henry, 1843–1916—Knowledge—Psychology. 3. Thought and thinking in literature. 4. Consciousness in literature.   I. Title.
PS2127.T53C3 1989
813'.4—dc19   89–4707
                                                                      CIP

Contents

Acknowledgments

The writing of this book was facilitated by resources from the National Endowment for the Humanities and the American Council of Learned Societies. I am especially grateful to The Johns Hopkins University, whose support for faculty research has often seemed incomparable, and to the Department of Psychology and Social Relations at Harvard University, which has repeatedly extended its hospitality to me in the renewed appointment of Visiting Scholar. The office at William James, which I have, with some regularity, preferred not to leave, has been made available to me with the rare institutional and personal generosity of that building's occupants. For his overseeing, and enabling, of this, I thank Roger Brown.

The reading of this book, chapter by chapter, and then the whole manuscript, was done several times over by Walter Benn Michaels and Garrett Stewart. Their thoughts about revision inform every page of the book that follows, at times significantly redetermining the shape of its argument. Large portions of the manuscript were read by Jerome Christensen, Jonathan Crewe, Elizabeth Falsey, Jonathan Goldberg, Albert Gilman, Allen Grossman, Deborah Kaplan, Richard Poirier, Peter Sacks, Eric Sundquist, Barry Weller, and Larzer Ziff. Again, the manuscript is changed many times over in large and small ways by the suggestions of these readers and by conversations with Roger Brown. To acknowledge a more general but pervasive debt: for the students and colleagues I have had at Johns Hopkins over the past ten years, I count myself fortunate.

Finally, I am grateful to Roxanne Rhodes for preparing the manuscript.

O N E

Introduction by Way of
The American Scene

I

Central to Anglo-American analysis of the novel is the assumption that what is being examined is the representation of a psychology which is an account of consciousness; that a concern with consciousness is a concern with psychology; or, in slightly different terms, that consciousness can be explained with reference to a psychology. Henry James's work has come to epitomize this assumption, and his interest in, even obsession with, the workings of consciousness taken to exemplify the fact that he writes the psychological novel par excellence.[1] In the following three chapters, in quite different contexts—those of the externalizing, the empowering, and the reversing of thought[2]—I question the identification of consciousness with psychology. The major texts I use in doing this are the late Prefaces (and three of the early novels they revise) and the late novels. I want to anticipate my discussion of the novels by looking at *The American Scene* to clarify what I mean by asserting that James dissociates consciousness from psychology.[3]

There is another reason to look immediately at *The American Scene*. In the following pages I shall be arguing that James's attempts to reconceive consciousness are neither single nor continuous. They cannot be seen to develop from each other, notwithstanding the Prefaces' compulsive attempts to describe the novelistic endeavor as unitary. The Prefaces may even be understood as those documents that, written late in James's career, postulate the predictively uniform definitions of consciousness that the novelistic project itself repudiates. In fact if the novels have a single project, it might rather be viewed in light of *The American Scene*, another late work, in which, as in the Prefaces, James com-

1

ments on his writing, but here from a vantage that is answerable only to the truth of momentary perceptions. In *The American Scene* James wants to disseminate consciousness, showing how much diverse territory it can be made to cover. Travel through the country, the opportunity for spreading consciousness around, is even more the occasion for celebrating the versatility of consciousness—its defiance of a consistency to which, as James declares, he will not have it bound:

> I would take my stand on my gathered impressions, since it was all for them, for them only, that I returned; I would in fact go to the stake for them—which is a sign of the value that I both in particular and in general attach to them. . . . My cultivated sense of aspects and prospects affected me absolutely as an enrichment of my subject, and I was prepared to abide by the law of that sense—the appearance that it would react promptly in some presences only to remain imperturbably inert in others.[4]

It could even be argued from a passage like this that James is finally less concerned with how consciousness looks (whether it is consistent) than with what it can do, less concerned with any single way it might function than with the fact that it cannot be bound by the singleness of function.

II

I shall press further on *The American Scene*—in this section moving back and forth between it and *The Golden Bowl*—to elicit concretely how James isolates consciousness from realistic considerations of it. *The American Scene* tells the story of consciousness empowered as a subject outside of psychological confines: able to have life, to be as if embodied, divorced from the strictures of situation and character, made sufficient independently of these. And this extraction of consciousness from character or event, this pure consideration of it, more than any other feature of *The American Scene*, gives that work its signature, identifying it as James's. The journey across the country is less the occasion for exploring aspects of places than it is for examining aspects of consciousness. Or rather it is the occasion for identifying instances of consciousness which proliferate as if endlessly. One way to look at the travelogue as a form is to see it as generating an ostensible randomness of impressions which suffuse the book. But another way to look at the genre James chooses is to see it as *licensing* this randomness, providing James the opportunity to disengage his considerations of consciousness from anything but the most immediate context. Thus travel through the land becomes the occasion for, rather than the cause of, that dissociation of impressions from extrinsic impositions (as of story, for example) to which these impressions would otherwise be answerable.

James would, of course, take exception to my characterization, describing his observations in *The American Scene* as instead occasioned by what he sees. He declares himself victimized by the scene: disempowered, disenfranchised, marginalized, and made a spectator to a new kind of power—to the vulgar materialism that is the antithesis of consciousness, a power against which his own consciousness records repeated protests, attempting to obliterate, even as it registers, the vulgarity it views. And, at one level, consciousness cannot be pure in that there is always a dialectic between the specific thought and what occasions it. This is another way to say that consciousness cannot be pure in that there is always a *content* governing its workings. Thus one way to read *The American Scene* is to see James, as he says he sees himself, at the mercy of a present that doesn't value value, doesn't value consciousness. Against this present, he asserts the value of the past, which is his consciousness of its significance. But, as I shall argue, another way to experience James's position—polemical, embattled—is to see it as embracing its embattlement so as to free itself of the given, effectively to banish it, and to substitute for what is there what is *wanted* to be there. For to read this book, with its reiterated designations of the self as cast out—the "restless analyst" (11), the "homeless wanderer" (168), the "restored absentee" (235)—is to see James as intoxicated by his newfound alienation, sent forth to propagate his interpretations of it. It is to see the power of the homeless, of the unconfined, vantage from which everything can be seen and anything can be said. In fact, in *The American Scene*, James, as if recoiling from what he sees, almost, it seems, stops seeing at all. Thus seeing becomes the occasion for blanking out what is there and for reconceiving the devastation.

In *The American Scene*, then, consciousness has authority because it determines meanings. Determines, not reflects them. Or, in James's words, "We capture . . . nothing; we merely project . . ." (330). The world deprived of our responses to it is not simply undiscriminated, but, more, devoid of meaning: "The day . . . [is the] frame of an interesting picture—interesting above all from the moment one desire[s] with any intensity to find it so" (408). The point of distinctions like these is not the capriciousness of being conscious but rather the power of being so. Specifically, it is the power to confer meaning by changing, relocating it, as it were, from "the day" to "the desire," from the so-called reality to the perceptual designation of it. Thus James, in the midst of a New Hampshire landscape, begins by talking about the beauty of wild apples, which quickly come to look to him like "strange-coloured pearls" (17). And this appropriation of the landscape, the making of it exotic—seeing the "scattered wild apples [which] were like figures in the carpet" (16)—is less a means of aestheticizing the natural than it is a means of making good on the claim that what is of value is not the apprehended object but the transforming apprehension. What is of value is the complexity of perceived pattern for which the "figure in the carpet" is so completely the right emblem. Finally, although James repeatedly deplores the emptiness of the American scene, that emptiness is a necessity or a strategy, whatever its status as a fact. The "resounding voids" (167) James laments (or celebrates) are not simply a consequence of the absence of structures. They are also a consequence of the absence of persons. James is not talking for the people, and he is not talking about them. People are dismissed so that, socially unencumbered, consciousness is free to converse with itself.

Conversations that occupy the vacuum from which all else has been cleared—conversations between one part of James's consciousness and other, discordant parts, which are variously identified with the air, with Fifth Avenue, with the newspapers, with Saint-Gaudens—are, nonetheless, not made fantastic. Even the memorable passage in which

James, rebuking Saint-Gaudens for his monument to Sherman, recasts Sherman thus: "I would have him deadly and terrible, and, if he be wanted beautiful, beautiful only as a war-god. . . . I would have had a Sherman of the terrible march . . ." (173)—even this impassioned declaration with its grammatical optatives working like grammatical threats is made to seem commonplace, not associated with the fanciful but with matters of fact. It is also made conciliatory, as James, on Saint-Gaudens, turns soft or benign: "It is not one's affair to attempt to teach an artist how such horrors may be monumentally signified; it is enough that their having been perpetrated is the very ground of the monument" (174).

Here one might be misled by a temptation to psychologize. For one way to understand these conversations, which articulate differences only to disregard them, so the horror that is wanted becomes the horror that is there ("the very ground of the monument"), is in a psychological context. James, it might be said, clears the scene so that nothing will occupy it but his own conflicted points of view, which still issue from one consciousness. In the explanatory apparatus of the psychological context, ambivalence is externalized as ventriloquism so that James can voice both sides of the dispute. But another explanatory context—one that better accounts for the book's obsessive impulse to make James's consciousness all-pervasive—reverses the causality I have just described. Disparate points of view are not significant because they exemplify conflicts in consciousness. Rather, they are significant because they exemplify the omnipresence of consciousness, identifying it with all points of view, even those in opposition, demonstrating thereby that there is no place in the book where consciousness has not been made to penetrate. Thus by light of the latter explanation (which doesn't hold *The American Scene* to an interest in the psychological that the book doesn't have), conflicts become occasions for consciousness to proliferate, as in a dialogue which would keep going, or keep exchanging, not so much viewpoints held by consciousness as, more simply still, diverse manifestations of it.

Thus James has rebuked New York—for the "pitch of all the noises," for the "February blasts," for the "character of the traffic," for its buildings, and its values—only himself to be rebuked: "'It's all very well,' the voice of the air seemed to say . . . 'to "criticize," but you distinctly take an interest and are the victim of your interest.'" And the air (still talking after two pages) expansively registers both its "own" point of view, "'New York . . . is always forgiven,'" *and* James's challenge to it: "'On what ground "forgiven"? of course you ask.'" Finally, the air is not simply projected *by* James. Nor does it simply anticipate James. But, more vertiginous still, the air, as represented, corrects James: "'but note that you ask [on what grounds forgiven] while you're in the very act of forgiving.'" Finally the air is represented as bullying by disputing a disclaimer James has not yet spoken: "'you're in the very act of forgiving. Oh yes, you are; you've as much as said so yourself'" (108–9). It is precisely the point that in this cacophony of voices, we be unable to say which voice is James's.

One could of course say that it is easy to answer the question "Which voice is James's?" in that James's alliance to old New York seems wholly unambiguous. But what happens in the process of James's critique is that the voice that is speaking against what it abhors discovers a residual affection, surviving the condemnation, for what is being condemned and, as much to the point, is taken to task by the thing it is condemning *for* the condemnation. Moreover, because the voice condemning the condemnation is made progressively more audacious, more impertinent in its questions, and more insistent in its rebukes, James's ostensibly clear position is progressively undermined. This is not represented as a psychological phenomenon, since the repartee points to manifold aspects of consciousness rather than to ambivalent aspects of it. Thus what might be experienced as a conflict, even superficially depicted as such, does not function as one. In fact, as in other similar conversations in the book, James's obvious relish for the rectitude of the so-called other side and, more generally, his pleasure in consciousness's ability to shift the sides taken make it difficult for the reader to continue to see the passage as focused by the initial, and I would say enabling, disagreement that generates it.

In *The American Scene*, then, James empties the landscape,

marginalizes the people, so that consciousness, a pure subject, becomes empowered outside the structures of psychological realism whose limits and conditions it is free to disregard. Here power is a consequence of the ability of consciousness to dominate objects, which are repeatedly subordinated to its interpretive reassessment. But power is also a consequence of consciousness's skill in *dispensing* with objects, so that what is being contemplated by consciousness is something like itself. This proprioception has as its corollary the book's ventriloquism, where, as in the passage above, the voice being listened to is the voice that is speaking. Finally, power is a consequence of the fact that, as *The American Scene* is not determined by a psychologically realistic context, it is free of that context, not bound by its restrictions, not delimited to a self in conventional terms. And it is more radically free in the sense that since consciousness as represented has nothing to do with consciousness as psychologized, the two have no categorical as well as no operational bearing on each other (consciousness being implicitly defined in relation to other criteria, as I shall further explain). Thus a law of genre enables James to assert a different law of consciousness. The travelogue provides the generic conditions for the disengagement of consciousness from psychological realism, conventionalizing the dissociation in terms that make it falsely recognizable.[5] In view of James's attempt to redefine consciousness in *The American Scene*, what kind of preliminary account can be given of James's attempt to redefine consciousness in the novels?

•

To identify the kind of question that requires such an account I take up an example elaborated in the third chapter. It is generally acknowledged that in part 2 of *The Golden Bowl* what Maggie Verver is willing to think is opposite to what she is willing to say. To put this in other terms: while Maggie Verver is conscious of (haunted by) her husband's adultery, she barely speaks of it at all. Why is this the case?

The conventional explanation for the discrepancy between Maggie's thinking and speaking is that Maggie can't speak of the adultery because to speak of it would be to rebuke Amerigo, and so further risk losing her hold over him. From a different explanatory vantage, Maggie can't speak of the adultery because to do so would be to reify it. If Maggie spoke of the adultery, she would acknowledge it existed. But these explanations for Maggie's not speaking are manifestly illogical. Maggie *does* rebuke Amerigo. She has, moreover, an extensive repertoire for doing so. She establishes the fact that in a contest of wills hers will be dominant. She arranges for Amerigo to witness Charlotte's suffering and to appreciate her engineering of it. During a carriage ride, she disabuses Amerigo of the belief that he still has sexual power over her. So the claim that Maggie doesn't speak to Amerigo because to do so would be to rebuke him disregards the multiple humiliations with which she wordlessly castigates him. Nor is Maggie's not speaking explained by her not wishing to reify the adultery, since her knowledge of the adultery is completely demonstrated in her repeated reprisals for it.

It is equally illogical that Maggie's not speaking of the adultery is a consequence of the wish *herself* to assume blame for it. That explanation is interpretively pinned on the moment when Maggie ostensibly makes Charlotte feel that *Maggie* has wronged Charlotte, so that the latter will be the agent in separating Adam Verver from his daughter. In that moment Maggie, or James on her behalf, says with approbation, "Yes, she had done all" (2.318). Yet grounds for this approval are contested by the evidence that Charlotte perfectly understands her own culpability as well as that Maggie is accusing her. Because a prior scene in which Charlotte defends herself ("Charlotte looked at her splendidly hard. 'You're perfectly sure it's *all* my mistake?'" [2.249]) and the scene in question, in which Charlotte attacks Maggie, are verbally as well as psychologically connected ("It was a repetition more than ever then of the evening on the terrace . . . allowing . . . for the difference of the intention" [2.309]), the magnanimous approval afforded Maggie by James, "Yes, she had done all," is belied. For the very scene meant to illustrate Maggie's assumption of the blame instead illustrates her failure to assume it. In any case, it indicates Charlotte's perception that Maggie *has* accused her, since Charlotte responds, as to an accusation, with a counterattack.

Nor does it make sense that Maggie doesn't speak so that Amerigo, kept blind to his wife's intentions, will admire an inscrutability he is helpless to penetrate. Contradicting that explanation, Maggie speaks enough to certify she knows completely and unmysteriously what Amerigo has done and that, as I have noted, she will refuse further to tolerate it. When, in the scene in which the bowl is broken, she also informs Amerigo that he must himself discover if Adam Verver knows of his adultery, this has less to do with making the question of her own knowledge enigmatic than with informing her husband that he may no longer consider her as her father's spokesman.

In these various ways—Maggie doesn't speak so as not to chastise Amerigo; Maggie doesn't speak so as not to reify the adultery; Maggie doesn't speak so that she may be seen to assume rather than to ascribe blame; Maggie doesn't speak so that, in her inscrutability, she can make herself interesting, hence desirable—the novel represents an action, or (since Maggie does not speak) it represents the negation of an action, for which it seems to propose psychologically realistic explanations that do not explain the phenomenon purportedly being accounted for. This is the case because questions raised in realistic terms cannot be addressed in realistic terms. The questions "Why doesn't Maggie speak?" and "Why does Maggie think instead of speak?" (why, in other words, are consciousness and speech juxtaposed to each other as if they were alternative?) are made all the more disturbing for being inadequately addressed by the kinds of explanations described above. For such explanations are both instigated by the novel and invalidated by a scrutiny of its actual, rather than manifest, logic. In fact the explanations, so poorly equipped to withstand scrutiny, almost appear designed to give way. They seem to push us to consider an issue raised realistically by the novel—that, in the second half of the novel, Maggie, to reclaim Amerigo, predominantly thinks rather than speaks—in a context completely dissociated from realistic features of the plot. What other context?

In the novel "not speaking," which is not satisfactorily contextualized or explained by the plot, in the ways enumerated above, *is* contextualized by thinking. For "thinking" is the most immediate other context in which we see "not speaking." Yet to explain "not speaking" in terms of "thinking" is to imply that the problem posed by the relation between thinking and speaking could be lifted out of the novel, that it could be understood without primary reference to the plot. The consequence of this dissociation is that James seems to be connecting consciousness with power outside of the realistic contexts that tell stories about it. (Here it is as if James were producing a different, barely recognizable depiction of consciousness in the novel and therefore imposing the requirement for a different, commensurately unrecognizable account of consciousness in the novel.)

Moreover, to consider questions of consciousness and power with reference to the plot is to have one understanding of them. To consider questions of consciousness and power dissociated from the plot is to have another understanding of them. What is at issue is not different explanations, but different kinds of explanations. In light of the plot, we are asked to consider whether Maggie Verver is justified in what she does. Is the power of her manipulations, whose success is represented as directly proportionate to the degree of her felt consciousness, to be admired or abhorred? But in a categorically different context, questions about the empowering of consciousness are not associated with evaluation. They are rather associated with James's attempt to investigate, or dictate, the conditions whereby consciousness gains power over speech and other minds.

In the latter context, the novel attempts to establish a phenomenology of the asymmetrical relations between thought and speech in which meaning is shifted back and forth from one to the other, often by one person for the other. The adultery, itself a model of asymmetrical relations, is the *occasion* for our viewing this second asymmetry.* But that sec-

---

*It could of course be claimed that the subject of otherness is specifically raised by the issue of the adultery. For adultery is a topos that underlines the problem of the other in two specific ways. First, in adultery the other, it is seen, cannot be stably fixed by the self. Second, that displacement involves a displacement of the self by the other to whom the other has turned. Thus, losing the other as a stable entity, you yourself are then displaced as a stable entity by the other with whom the other has replaced you. Yet if in these two ways the adultery in *The Golden Bowl* might occasion the meditation on otherness (emblematized by the asymmetry between thinking and speaking), it is, as I argue above, finally not shown to do so. That it "might" in some non-Jamesian context "do so" is what has permitted the actual dissociation to be for so long unremarked.

ond asymmetry, between thinking and speaking, is not shown to be produced by the first asymmetry of the adultery. Nor can it be disposed of when the relations in the marriages are righted. Thus, understanding the empowering of consciousness in a psychologically realistic context, which is also an evaluative one, differs radically from understanding the empowering of consciousness in that operational context in which James is predicating how the relations between speech and thought, between one consciousness and another, hence between consciousness and power, are to be discovered. For in this second context James seems to be deducing what might be called a grammar of the relation between thought and speech. Here it must be added that James's attempt to anatomize consciousness is inseparable from his attempt to invest it with power: for James a phenomenology of consciousness is a phenomenology of its domination.

Questions raised by the empowering of consciousness in the second phenomenological context—What does it mean for one person to speak for another? Or to be spoken for by another? To see the thoughts of another? To conceal thoughts from another?—suggest that what is being represented in the novel is not a deviant case, but a paradigm for how consciousness operates. What is thus being considered in the context of such questions is a normative or ordinary case which the exaggerated case produced by the adultery opens up for our consideration. What is oppositely being considered in the different context of questions raised by the realistic plot—How does the adultery require Maggie to exercise power so terrible that under less extreme circumstances it would be deemed illegitimate?—is the *transgression* of the ordinary case. Thus in the context of psychological realism, the empowering of consciousness is only provisionally sanctioned. Only events this terrible could justify Maggie's mental reprisals. In the countercontext of the normative case, the attempts to conceal, deny, evade, shift meaning around from speech to thought are not strictly associated with reprisal. They are rather viewed as accommodations to the categorical discrepancy between thought and speech and between one mind and another, as a consequence of which consciousness must empower itself or be victimized by another. In this light, dominance is not associated with the problem of whose consciousness is most moral, but rather with a different standard that involves the quantification of consciousness, with the need to assess who has more of it.

To separate completely the categories and explanations I have invoked is impossible. But their dissociation is implied, because, as indicated above, the context of psychological realism fails to explain why Maggie does not speak, or, in broader terms, why thinking and speaking are played off against each other with such definitive and, with reference to the plot, inexplicable antagonism. Moreover, while the moral questions do not trivialize the novel, they do misrepresent the source of its power. This is not to suggest that the subject of adultery is insufficient to explain the passion the novel generates over it. But it is to say that power seems, in addition, "purely" vested in the novel's exchanges, in what characters speak to each other and what they think in manifest opposition to what they speak. These exchanges, while in one sense absurd without reference to the plot, are, in another sense, perfectly contained by the structural opposition of thinking and speaking which itself seems to generate them, as I elaborate in the third chapter. I do not, however, mean here to invoke a structuralist or semiotic model. For, as I shall argue, the implicit meditation on consciousness depends on a particular opposition between thinking and speaking, not on opposition per se.

Finally, the context of psychological realism seems inadequate to explain why the victory of the novel, as experienced by the reader of it, is less associated with retrieving Amerigo (who has never, to most readers, seemed worth it) than it is associated with the fact that, as if outside the story—outside any story—consciousness, for a moment, is made unequivocal. That it is *Maggie's* consciousness which is made definitive seems less the point of the novel's final paragraph than does the stark imperialism of consciousness's domination. Such domination, absolute, can't quite be owned, can't even quite be identified with. This is the fact I take Maggie to appreciate when she, like Amerigo, perceives herself victimized by it. Thus one way to explain what happens in the novel is to say not that Maggie rearranges the quartet and gets Amerigo back, but rather that consciousness (as it happens, hers) is made adequate in the sense of made ultimate; in the sense of empowered; in the sense of made to have the last, the only, word.

•

When James returned to America in 1904 he conceived the idea for *The American Scene*. In those pages of a notebook where he planned the part on Cambridge, he jotted notes for what would represent his sense of the place:

> the *Stadium*, the foot-ball (Dartmouth) match, and the way the big white arena *loomed* at me, in the twilight, ghostly and queer, from across the river, during the ½ hour, the wonderful, the unforgettable, that after-noon's end that I spent in C[ambridge] C[emetery]. Do that (the picture) with the pink winter sunset and the ghosts, the others, Lowell's, Longfellow's and Wm. Story's.[6]

In the notebook, three months later, now writing in California, he elaborates the assignment. What is to epitomize the thought of Cambridge is his recollection of an afternoon when, standing in the Cambridge cemetery by the graves of both parents and of Alice, his sister, he notes:

> the Cambridge *tendresse* stands in the path like a wait-ing lion—or, more congruously, like a cooing dove that I shrink from scaring away. I want a little of the *ten-dresse*, but it trembles away over the whole field—or would if it could. Yet to present these accidents is what it is to be a *master*; that and that only. Isn't the highest deepest note of the whole thing the never-to-be-lost memory of that evening hour at Mount Auburn—at the Cambridge Cemetery when I took my way alone— after much waiting for the favouring hour—to that un-speakable group of graves. It was late, in November; the trees all bare, the dusk to fall early, the air all still (at Cambridge, in general, *so* still), with the western sky more and more turning to that terrible, deadly, pure polar pink that shows behind American winter woods. But I can't go over this—I can only, oh, so gen-tly, so tenderly, brush it and breathe upon it—breathe upon it and brush it. It was the moment; it was the hour, it was the blessed flood of emotion that broke out

at the touch of one's sudden *vision* and carried me away. I seemed then to know why I had done this; I seemed then to know why I had *come*—and to feel how not to have come would have been miserably, horribly to miss it. It made everything right—it made everything priceless. The moon was there, early, white and young, and seemed reflected in the white face of the great empty Stadium, forming one of the boundaries of Soldiers' Field, that looked over at me, stared over at me, through the clear twilight, from across the Charles. Everything was there, everything *came;* the recognition, stillness, the strangeness, the pity and the sanctity and the terror, the breath-catching passion and the divine relief of tears. William's inspired transcript, on the exquisite little Florentine urn of Alice's ashes, William's divine gift to us, and to *her,* of the Dantean lines—

> *Dopo lungo exilio e martiro*
> *[Venne] a questa pace*—

took me so at the throat by its penetrating *rightness,* that it was as if one sank down on one's knees in a kind of anguish of gratitude before something for which one had waited with a long, deep *ache.* But why do I write of the all unutterable and the all abysmal? Why does my pen not drop from my hand on approaching the infinite pity and tragedy of all the past? It does, poor helpless pen, with what it meets of the ineffable, what it meets of the cold Medusa-face of life, of all the life *lived,* on every side. *Basta, basta!* x x x x x (*Notebooks,* 239–40)[7]

In the notebook, where the entry seems definitively to say what James hinted he had wished it to, it is hard to imagine any revision left to execute. This sense of "finish" is reiterated by the fact that James the witness is made James the participant. Completing the picture by seeing it from all vantages, James misremembers Dante so as to write himself into the scene he is memorializing. The lines from the *Paradiso* (10:128–29) are: *"ed essa da martiro / e da essilio venne a questa pace."* By light of the misrecollection James is not just reading the words. He is also being represented by them:

"After long exile and martyrdom, [he/she] came to this peace."*

In *The American Scene*, however, James does rewrite the notebook passage, specifically revising the content of the recollection. This revision of the passage, which in effect reverses everything significant about it, depends first on obscuring the identity of those dead:

> I walked . . . occupied with the sight of the old Cambridge ghosts. . . . My small story would gain infinitely in richness if I were able to name them, but they swarmed all the while too thick, and of but two or three of them alone is it true that they push their way, of themselves, through any silence. . . . (68)

And then on turning away from the deaths:

> Just opposite, at a distance, beyond the river and its meadows, the white face of the great empty Stadium stared at me, as blank as a rising moon—with Soldiers' Field squaring itself like some flat memorial slab that waits to be inscribed. I had seen it inscribed a week or two before in the fantastic lettering of a great intercollegiate game of football, and that impression had been so documentary, as to the capacity of the American public for momentary gregarious emphasis, that I regret having to omit here all the reflections it prompted. (68–69)

In the notebook passage the encounter, though prepared for, cannot be prepared for, as James is—so he describes it—accosted by recognition. In *The American Scene*, there is no encounter, only "documentary" seeing. In the notebook passage the moon illuminates the stadium, which reflects onto the gravesite ("through the clear twilight . . . everything *came*"). In *The American Scene* the stadium is "blank as a

---

*In the context of the *Paradiso*, "*essa*," a feminine demonstrative pronoun, refers to the soul delivered from the flesh. In William James's epitaph, "*essa*" refers to William's sister, Alice. (The tombstone, and presumably the urn, essentially reproduces Dante's Italian.) In Henry James's recollection, "*essa*" drops out, and through the subsequent ambiguity of gender James makes himself also into the object of the lines' reference. This is more the case since in Dante "exile" and "martyrdom" receive equal weight, whereas in James's rewriting of the lines the words "*Dopo*" and "*lungo*" shift the stress to exile by marking it temporally.

rising moon"; nothing illuminates and nothing is to be seen. In the notebook passage there is a half-implied union of brother and sister in the elision of gender, and a proleptic blurring of James's life (and death) with that of his sister. For the following sentence, with its subordinate allusion to James's years in Europe, is also self-reflexive: "it was as if one sank down on one's knees in a kind of anguish of gratitude . . . [at] all the life lived on every side." In *The American Scene* "one" becomes "I," there being no passion, and no confusion, left to objectify.

In other substitutions of the passage—the playing ground for the burial ground; the inscription of the football game for the inscription on the urn; the emphasized for the ineffable; the ground of Soldiers' Field, which the man turns to stone by imagining it as such to avert the "Medusa-face of life" that turns the man to stone—we see what it is for a thought to be translated. For, contrary to the last sentence, "reflections" are not exactly omitted; they are rather being transformed. The pen "dropped" in the notebook passage before "the Medusa-face of life" is missing, differently "dropped," in that from *The American Scene*. In a corollary displacement, the grief occasioned in the notebook passage by the writing of the transcript becomes incredulity first at the absence of writing and then at its triviality. If the field is like "some flat memorial slab that waits to be inscribed" (from which writing is omitted), then what is being done away with, and awaited, is the epitaph, the kind of writing on memorial slabs. In these various ways the lament of the notebook is transmogrified. Or rather the subject to be mourned is a subject to be ironized: "the capacity of the American public for momentary gregarious emphasis." In a central conversion the letters on the urn become the football players—themselves read as letters by James—inscribing Soldiers' Field. This transposition parodies whatever particular meaning (whether Dante's, or William's for Alice, or James's, as appropriated to pertain to himself) the letters might have had. So emblematic letters become incidental ones.

My point is not that James rewrites the scene of the notebook into a scene of writing. What is oppositely at stake here is a parody of writing that leads to its erasure—making writing transitory by construing the players themselves as letters gone off the text/field/slab—as if this might facilitate, by analogy, the vanishing of other letters (those in the epitaph) and the obliteration, as well, of what the epitaph signifies. My point is rather that the scene-of-writing topos, with the Master thematizing writing, much as he does in the Prefaces to the novels, becomes, with reference to the revision, almost a cover for the half-suppressed issue of the radical rethinking of this passage. One could in fact argue that James is not only rewriting so as to rethink the episode. He is, in the ways enumerated above, fundamentally reconceiving what rethinking and rewriting are.

Here one could elaborate. For when in *The American Scene* James displaces the writing on the urn to that on Soldiers' Field across the river, the letters, as noted, no longer refer to persons. Rather, conversely, the persons (the players) are represented as letters, which then vanish, leaving the slab/field/text blank. Also across the river, the stands too are blank, so that the crowd—the readers of the text/field (with James a week ago among them)—are gone at the same time. Thus the readers and the writing are made to disappear simultaneously. This matters, for inasmuch as James depicts himself as a reader of that writing ("I had seen [the field] inscribed"), he is implicitly, in his own image, a reader who is annihilated. This annihilation of the writing, and subordinately of the reader, is the antithesis of the represented experience of reading letters on the urn. For in the notebook, on this side of the river, James comes into Alice's presence through the reading of the letters, though she herself is dead. Alice is made present because William's transcription of Dante not only speaks of Alice (the transcription being "William's divine gift to us") but in a sense reembodies her (the lines being also "William's divine gift . . . to *her*"). I take embodiment, James's as well as Alice's, to be at issue here. For at this point in the notebook, James is caught at "the throat," as if the lines had summoned up a too corporeal sense of her. Thus if the notebook passage represents a central experience of the life that is "given" in reading a text, *The American Scene* represents the inversion of that experience, of life that is deadened. Letters read as bodies—letters that embody—in the notebook passage are in *The American Scene* converted to bodies read as letters and then peremptorily dismissed. If in the revision what is done away with is the deliverance (the peace), what is also done away with is the occasion that would necessitate it. Such transformations suggest that if one could alter consciousness not only in the sense of changing its content, but more fundamentally in the sense of changing its function—could associate consciousness not with awareness but rather with conversion, much as the passage above demonstrates—that would be mastery.

Mastery by conversion, specifically the working on consciousness until it has transformative power, characterizes James's writing, not just this instance of it. Thus in *The American Scene* consciousness is moved around from the day to the desire, from New York to the baroque back talk it is thought to generate, subordinating the objects being contemplated to consciousness itself, until consciousness attends only to its own workings.* Thus in *The Golden Bowl* consciousness is made transformative in that Maggie's consciousness comes to dominate that of the other characters, from one explanatory vantage, and to dominate the very idea of character, from another. Thus in *The Wings of the Dove* to write about death, to "do that (the picture)," is equivalent to getting death out of the picture, much as *The American Scene*, in relation to the initial notebook passage, does. How are we to understand these repeated conversions or revisions?

In the Preface to *The Golden Bowl* James introduces the subject of revision, variously referred to as "re-reading," "re-writing," "re-penetrating," "re-acting," "re-perusing," "re-asserting," and I have not exhausted the number of gerunds, not quite identical, but also not clearly distinguished,

---

*Here one could argue that this is also true in the notebook, but it is not true there in the same way, or for the same reasons. In the notebook what is being attended to is the pain registered on consciousness, which is passive. Thus if in the notebook passage consciousness is attending to its own workings, it is also at the mercy of them. Hence James backs away, "I can't go over this." In *The American Scene*, consciousness, being double, is at once agent and thing acted on. It discriminates among its impressions, omitting some while according others "emphasis" that is called "gregarious." In *The American Scene*, then, consciousness attending to its workings means working on consciousness, working it up, until it is transformed.

which make the notion being propounded opaque, almost senseless. Thus in the Preface to *The Golden Bowl* "revision" is not being explained; it is rather being obscured. The obfuscation is accomplished in a number of ways, not just by the assault of these same-prefixed words whose unclear relation to each other we could presumably bypass were they the only source of confusion. But other unclarities follow. For example, James says that a revision is implicit in a text's initial rendering *or* that the revision later undertaken is implicitly executed so that the reader can't deduce it, and these possibilities, imperceptibly there or imperceptibly executed, are importantly undiscriminated. The point of the ambiguity is that what is being done, or *whether* something is being done, remains unclear. (For if the possibility of revision is already implicit in the work, nothing new is being done, something already there is only being seen.) In a further equivocation, James, though talking about *his* revisions, advises us that "no revisionist I can recall has ever been communicative" (xix–xx). Finally we are informed that there are two kinds of revisionists: the "inconsequent and insincere" (xx), who is defined by only revising piecemeal, and the kind epitomized by Balzac but blankly characterized by James as the "illusive, the inscrutable, the indefinable" (xxi). In a number of ways, then, what is not being communicated by James's Preface is what is being revised or what James thinks revision is. The specific way in which James's thoughts about revision are not being communicated is by a torrent of words and images which contradict, complement, overlap each other—words *about* revision. In the following pages I shall argue in several contexts that what is most ambitiously being revised by James is conceptions of consciousness.

When in the Preface to *The Golden Bowl* James connects rewriting, re-reading, and re-seeing, that association has been understood, much as James appears to mean us to understand it, in an aesthetic context. What Maggie does in part 2 of *The Golden Bowl* is like what James does when he rewrites *The Golden Bowl*, or like what he does when he rewrites his novels for the New York Edition. There would be other terms in which to interpret revision. To resee or to revise is not just differently to be conscious. It is also (as I argue in

the second chapter with reference to the late Prefaces and
the early novels) differently to understand what consciousness is. In Maggie's case this means that in part 2 of *The
Golden Bowl* she does not simply see something different;
she also equates seeing (consciousness) with power.

Mastery (psychic, artistic, ultimately political) lies in transforming the objects of consciousness, as *The American Scene*
demonstrates—whether with respect to a rereading of the
memorial statue of Sherman ("I would have him deadly and
terrible") or with respect to a rereading of the "memorial
slab" in Cambridge Cemetery ("I had seen it inscribed . . .
in the fantastic lettering of a great intercollegiate game of
football"). For these seemingly noncomparable examples
that translate the personal into the "documentary," and vice
versa, are perfectly analogous in that they translate what is
there into what is desired, revising the meanings of the
deaths or, rather, the interpretation of those meanings, respectively monumentalized. "And monuments," James tells
us in the passage on Saint-Gaudens, "should always have a
clean, clear meaning" (174). Executing that clarity by offici-
ating over its changes, consciousness exercises its uncon-
ceded, hence uncontested, hence illicit, authority. Mastery
lies in determining the rules which govern the power behind
consciousness's transformative procedures, as *The Golden
Bowl* demonstrates. Mastery lies not only in investigating the
phenomenology of that domination, on the one hand, and
that conversion, on the other, but finally, as I argue
throughout, in attempting to master consciousness itself, to
rethink or to revise what thinking is.

In this context Henry's letter to William of November 23,
1905, is pertinent:

> I mean (in response to what you write me of your
> having read the *Golden B.*) to try to produce some un-
> canny form of thing, in fiction, that will gratify you, as
> Brother—but let me say, dear William, that I shall be
> greatly humiliated if you *do* like it, and thereby lump it,
> in your affection, with things, of the current age, that I
> have heard you express admiration for and that I
> would sooner descend to a dishonoured grave than
> have written. Still I *will* write you your book, on that
> two-and-two-make-four system on which all the awful
> truck that surrounds us is produced, and *then* descend

to my dishonoured grave. . . . I see nowhere about
me done or dreamed of the things that alone for me
constitute the *interest* of the doing of the novel—and
yet it is in a sacrifice of them on their very own ground
that the thing you suggest to me evidently consists. It
shows how far apart and to what different ends we
have had to work out (very naturally and properly!) our
respective intellectual lives.[8]

The passage has conventionally been taken to illustrate
James's acknowledgment of how disparate his conception of
consciousness is from that of his psychologist brother. This
is also how I take it. Although at the end of the second
chapter I briefly investigate the differences in their respective understandings of consciousness, I here anticipate that
discussion. In the above passage, James is not only denying
a certain logic to the terms in which he represents consciousness or to the power he imputes to it. He is also disparaging
the conventions of that logic. He is conversely claiming for
his work not simply originality, but in the terms of his hyperbole ("nowhere about me done or dreamed of . . .") also
something like transcendent power for it. The declaration to
William can be read as a promissory note on what Henry
James's works actually demonstrate: what it means for consciousness not to add up in realistic ways. For consciousness
in James's novels is differently mapped—this is how *The
American Scene* literally conceives of it—and so defies the
very representational boundaries (specifically the boundaries
that restrict thoughts to minds) that up to that point had
characterized the novel and, more fundamentally, ordinary
understandings of it.

III

I have been discussing Henry James in terms that dissociate
consciousness from psychology,[9] but these terms are not
themselves derived from Henry James. They are, of course,
phenomenological, and they are in fact associated with a
particular form of phenomenology that developed in Edmund Husserl's writing from *Logical Investigations* through
The Crisis of the European Sciences. My point is not that James
was influenced by Husserl (though Husserl was influenced
by William James). Nor do I mean to read James through
Husserl. Yet although I am dealing specifically with James's

representations, and the literary and critical problems they generate, the issues raised therein are not entirely sui generis but have an affinity with Husserl's roughly contemporaneous philosophy.[10] Thus it seems appropriate and even necessary to say something about what is at stake for Husserl and phenomenology in the attempt not only to dissociate psychology from consciousness, but also to think about what kind of thing consciousness or thinking is.

In *Cartesian Meditations* (1929), elaborating notions formulated in his initial writings, Husserl historicizes the idea of transcendent consciousness—transcendent because it extends beyond itself to "constitute" the world. Specifically, he redefines Descartes's *cogito* so that, however oxymoronically, the very sense of an ontology is shown to depend on an "egology,"[11] on the mind's constitution of the objective world. I want to examine this notion of thinking as "constituting" or "productive,"[12] as it is pertinent to my discussion of James (specifically, the notion that thoughts produce objects or things), and to do so at a length that may initially seem digressive, for it anticipates James's even more radical notion of the relation between thoughts and things, discussed in the fourth chapter.

First, Husserl disavows the idea of a psychology, for a psychology is predicated on a distinction between the mind and the world. He dismisses the conceptual dichotomy of "inner" and "outer," arguing that the error of psychology is to posit a whole out there which the part "in here" experiences (38). Therefore, as Gaston Berger summarizes, "nothing is farther from phenomenology than a philosophy of internal experience."[13] Second, the dichotomy between internal and external, between the psychological and the factual, is made to disappear because Husserl posits a "phenomenological reduction" in which "the natural world" (where those dichotomies operate) is bracketed. When, through this "reduction," the world is bracketed, it is seen to exist not in itself but as a consequence of our intuitings of it. What remains is "not nothing," but a world of phenomena which "derives its whole sense . . . *from me as the transcendental Ego*" (26). In other words, the reduction of the world to pure consciousness illustrates, in the words of René Le Senne, that "the thing in itself" is really only "the thing-in-itself-as-thought."[14] If it seems extreme to reduce understanding of the constitution of the world to under-standing of the constitution of one's consciousness of it, we have just to remember that only through consciousness are we "given" the world. (In the Jamesian corollary of *The American Scene,* where, through another kind of reduction, the world is ventriloquized, made a dummy for the voicings of consciousness, the analysis of the world is, also necessar-ily—through a necessity that has also been created—equiv-alent to the analysis of one's consciousness of it.)

Third, the consequence of this hyperbolic claim that the constitution of consciousness and of the world is one and the same is, extraordinarily, not solipsism. In fact it is the reduction of the world to a constituting consciousness that allows you the sense of others. The logic goes like this: you imagine others by first imagining yourself as others. The ego becomes not only a "de facto ego"; you have the ability to "phantasy" yourself as if you "were otherwise" (72). This imagining yourself as other without imagining another self is nonetheless the ground for imagining true otherness. Thus for Husserl empathy is a consequence of imagining yourself as an object (other than you are) and then subse-quently of being able to imagine that object as if it were a subject.

Fourth, the ability to imagine another self amounts to the ability to imagine an objective "natural" world. When the self has the "experience of something alien (something that is not I . . . non-Ego in the form: other-Ego)," it, as a conse-quence, experiences "a world *'external' to my own concrete ego,*" an "immanent transcendency," "an Objective world . . ." (106). In fact, "by means of the alien constitutings con-stituted in my own self, there becomes constituted for me . . . the common world for 'all of us' " (87).* Thus the ideal-

---

*Just how alien this imagining of others is will be revealed by the lan-guage of the following passage, in which the capacity to imagine others is first self-referential and then analogic. You perceive the other by analogy to your own body, which "appresents the other Ego, by virtue of the pairing association with my bodily organism": "In so doing, it appresents . . . the other Ego's governing in this body, the body over there, and mediately his governing in the Nature that appears to him perceptually—identically the Nature to which the body over there belongs, identically the Nature that is my primordial Nature. It is the same Nature, but in the mode of ap-pearance: 'as if I were standing over there, where the Other's body is' " (123–25).

ism we might have presumed inevitable to Husserl's position seems to—or rather, is said to—fall away. It is said to
because the objective world, in Husserl's case, like the social
world, in James's, is not apparently put into jeopardy by the
transcendence of consciousness, but rather comes into existence as a consequence of it.

In touching on points of *Cartesian Meditations* which are
suggestive for reading James, I am especially struck by the
belief that the self-referentiality of consciousness does not
call into question the existence of the objective world, but
specifically creates it. This is nowhere more apparent than in
a passage from the Fifth Meditation when Husserl illustrates
that the "possible experience *of* what is other, is wholly un-
affected by screening off what is [actually] other" (98). Thus
through a "primordial reduction" the objective world is
"made to vanish," and the self alone remains, a mere "own-
ness," not yet an experienced body, below called an "animate organism," but still able to have sensations. Even in
this state, however, consciousness can distinguish between
itself and the external world:

> As an initial problem concerning the psychological ori-
> gin of the experiential world, there emerges here the
> problem concerning the origin of the "thing-phantom,"
> or "thing pertaining to the senses," with its strata (sight
> thing, ⟨touch thing,⟩ and so forth) and their synthetic
> unity. The thing-phantom is given (always within the
> limits set by this primordial reduction) purely as a unity
> belonging to modes of sensuous appearance and their
> syntheses. The thing-phantom, in its variants as "near
> thing" and "far thing," all of which belong together
> synthetically, is not yet the "real thing" of the primor-
> dial psychic sphere. Even in this sphere the "real
> thing" becomes constituted at a higher level, as a causal
> thing, an identical substrate of causal properties (a
> "substance"). Obviously substance and causality indi-
> cate constitutional problems of a higher level. The con-
> stitutional problem of the thing pertaining to the
> senses, along with the problem of the spatiality and
> temporality that are fundamentally essential to it, is
> precisely the problem just now indicated. It is a prob-
> lem of descriptive inquiry that concerns only the syn-
> thetic complexes of thing-appearances (apparencies,

perspective aspects). Moreover, it is one-sided. The other side concerns the relation of the appearances back to the functioning animate organism, which in turn must be described in respect of its self-constitution and the signal peculiarity of its constitutive system of appearances. (145)

The initial distinction between the phantom and real thing is understandable in general terms with reference to the idea of the constituting consciousness that informs all of Husserl's work. The "thing-phantom" of the world which is declared "not yet the 'real thing' of the primordial psychic sphere" is temporally invalidated because to posit a world without yet positing a mind constituting the world is to posit a phantom.

But there is a more context-specific way of understanding the temporality of the "thing-phantom" as not yet the "'real thing' of the primordial psychic sphere." For *Cartesian Meditations* predicates a temporality to the constitution of the thing. In what Husserl calls "passive genesis"—which refers to the rudimentary levels of constituting that precede categorical judgment—there are first sensations; then the extension of those sensations into the external spatial world, where, not yet codified, they have the status of phantoms; then the solidification of those phantoms into concrete identity, into the "real [material] thing" of consciousness (77–81). The process of passive genesis is especially pertinent to the primitive state of solipsism described in the passage. For sensations are perceived "out there" as phantoms because they are not yet owned or incorporated by consciousness. Only in consciousness (only conferred materiality, hence otherness, *by* consciousness) do thing-phantoms become real things. Moreover, if one side of the reifying process concerns how I constitute visual or tactile phantoms into the real things of consciousness, the other side concerns the fact that by the very act of constituting these "real" things, my body is itself constituted as an experienced, biological body. For in Husserl, the subject, when it is constituting the object, also constitutes itself.

The question of where to locate the object or otherness, here called a "thing"—as initially in the mind or initially in the world—is really a question of perspective, as the conclusion of the paragraph acknowledges in raising the issue of two sides. If you saw consciousness constituting the object from both sides, you would be seeing yourself doing the constituting as well as seeing the thing being constituted. From the vantage of one side, you would be fully aligned with the object you, as subject, have constituted. From the vantage of the other side, you would be fully aligned with the process of constituting it. Moreover, the subject must in turn be understood in terms of its self-constitution. Although this term, "self-constitution," may seem to have broken out of the subject-object prison that defines the apparently inseparable, if opposite, "sides" here referred to, in fact, as I have implied, it is caught up in them. For earlier in the *Meditations* Husserl has defined the ego not simply as a stable "pole of identity" but in terms of "habitualities" (66), which indicate that the way we initially see objects deposits a sense and has an effect on the way we *continue* to see them. Since only subjects can constitute objects, and since, with reference to the habitualities, subjects are themselves constituted only by this process, what else would it mean to see "from the other side" but that you would see yourself doing the thing you're doing: self-constitution defined by constitution of the thing, from whichever side regarded.

But what I have described here is, as I have been implying, problematic, for reasons enumerated in the next few pages. The strategy of the passage, for example, like that of the book as a whole, is to introduce oppositions (ostensibly two sides) which don't function as oppositions, though they have the structure of oppositions. And this is nowhere more clearly demonstrated than in the circularity of the passage's last sentence, which gestures toward a description in which the constitution of the self (and of its consciousness) and the constitution of the thing would be possible to understand as if from one perspective—as it almost is here in the passage's rapid oscillations.

This problem of whether otherness is to be understood as actual or constituted, which is fundamentally a matter of *where* otherness is *initially* placed (in the world or in the mind) lies at the heart of the representations of consciousness at the turn of the century. For Husserl, who internalizes otherness in the name of consciousness, there is no tension between the mind and the world because in the phenomenological reduction the self is always connected to the otherness which it, in fact, constitutes. In addition, its own existence is inconceivable except with reference to that otherness which—as in the thing-phantom/real thing passage—is imaged as its own "other side." The "other" side in Husserl's typology is therefore a side you can see, whereas the other side in Freud's typology (not counting symptoms of it) is one you cannot. Thus for Husserl proof of otherness does not require real others; only in consciousness does the phantom become the real thing; if there is dualism it will be located in the mind; finally there isn't dualism, there is only reflexivity. One consequence of this is that for Husserl consciousness not only constitutes the object; it also constitutes the separateness of the object.

In the passage discussed above, thing-phantoms become real things in the mind's constitution of them, and this inverting of the terms of an empirical psychology (which reifies things in the world as it dematerializes thoughts in the mind) indicates the lengths to which phenomenology goes to convert questions of being into questions of meaning. Henry James goes further. For it is one thing to say that thoughts are things in the sense that only in consciousness are things "constituted" as material. It is another to equate thoughts with things by an inverse spatial movement which moves thoughts out of the mind and into the world, where they have the palpable existence that things would have. Yet this is precisely what I illustrate in my fourth chapter. Moreover, however exasperating the extremity of Husserl's reduction, as a consequence of which consciousness is imperialized as omnipresent, the point of the reduction, like the point of the passage, is to illustrate that as a result of the process being explained there is a common world for all of us in which real things and real others (albeit ones I have constituted) also exist. Although one can ask what perspective enables these operations, as, for example, Derrida does,[15] there is a simple, if not a satisfactory, answer to that question. These reductions are taking place as propositions of what I "can" or "cannot" "do." They are not taking place with reference to actual others. They are not taking place in what Husserl calls the "natural" world.

In James's novels, on the other hand, within the fiction of the natural world, that is precisely where they are taking place. The contrast is of interest. For this predication of a world of characters, of others whom we, as readers, are supposed to regard as represented by James as actual in the "natural" world, not as constituted in some reduced bracketed world, allows us to ask what it would mean for consciousness to dominate, not in the presence of others we hypothesize ("as if I were standing over there, where the Other's body is," in the spooky analogy of the Fifth Meditation), but rather what it would mean for consciousness to dominate in the presence of actual others.* We see the meaning of this difference (of others represented as actual without being represented, in Husserl's terms, as being constituted as such) not only by contrasting James's representations of consciousness with Husserl's representations of consciousness. We see it also by contrasting consciousness as represented in *The American Scene* with consciousness as represented in James's novels. For in the former something analogous to Husserl's bracketing of the "natural" world is executed before the book begins. Thus in *The American Scene* others as represented are *like* others as constituted. This is because in *The American Scene* others count only through James's impression of them.

If they count at all. To put this in the terms that James in the section on Cape Cod does: what is seen "interfere[s] no

---

*Here I am interested in how others are represented in the philosophical rather than the mimetic sense. In other words, I am not interested in how Henry James is representing the consciousness of his "I" but rather in how consciousness as represented, or, say, as formulated, is shown to behave. Moreover, implicit in the discussion above are two kinds of idealism. In the first, the very act of writing is a bracketing of the natural world. As this form of idealism is not specific to James, I'm assuming it, and I'm assuming I can assume it. It is not, for my argument, a point to be marked.

In the second, the bracketing is not associated generally with the act of writing but is associated specifically with the content of what is written in James's novels. It is, as I argue above, associated with consciousness's domination over, or conversion of, those ostensible others, so that, though they are said to be other—though they are personified as characters—consciousness treats those others as if their otherness could be mastered, contested, or differently, often violently, overcome.

whit, for all its purity of style, with the human, the social question always dogging the steps of the ancient contemplative person and making him, before each scene, wish really to get *into* the picture, to cross, as it were, the threshold of the frame" (35). That transgressive crossing of the frame—the getting of the human into the picture—is just what James says the American scene prohibits. In any case it is what *The American Scene* prohibits for the reason, on that same page, James specifies as follows: "the constituted blankness was the whole business, and one's opportunity was all, thereby, for a study of exquisite emptiness."

But if in *The American Scene* the representation of consciousness, as having to contend with constituted blankness, is, in one sense, the test of its power, there is another sense in which it is no test at all, since there are no others (no people in the frame) and no phenomena distinguished *as* other against which consciousness can exercise its authority, at least not after the book's initial establishing of its terms. The performance of consciousness in *The American Scene* is sheer virtuosity. If it takes work, there is no resistance to the work. That is not the case in the novels I consider in the following chapters, where I am concerned with the question of how single consciousnesses, represented as actual, come to have autonomy and to dominate in the presence of other consciousnesses, also represented as actual.

To reiterate the distinction one last time: In *The American Scene* others are gotten out of the way. That is the book's enacted, if not stated, premise. James's novels, on the other hand, are ostensibly about others as actual, in the sense of being about others as discrete characters. To get others out of the way—as Husserl in the *Meditations* does, or as James in *The American Scene* does—constitutes a reduction *before* the fact. Others are either never there to begin with, or they are dismissed at the beginning. But it is one thing for a single consciousness to dictate its impressions as James does in *The American Scene*, where he is the sole consciousness. It is another, more complicated issue when in the novels James represents supposedly separate characters with supposedly separate consciousnesses, which then dominate each other much the way he dominates with impunity the entirety of *The American Scene*. Not to acknowledge that you have got-

ten others out of the way—to reify them as there in the per-
sonification of discrete characters, while at the same time
problematizing their existence by, in effect, denying it, or in
The Wings of the Dove even annihilating it—is a more aggressive reduction. It is a reduction of a different order, which in
effect constitutes a mastery of others by the overt contesting
of their otherness. Moreover, to make the annihilation of
otherness the subject of the novel, as in quite different ways
Roderick Hudson, The Golden Bowl, and *The Wings of the Dove*
do, underscores the meaning of this difference. In this respect, what is bracketed in the fiction is not others but their
otherness. Or, in terms more congenial to the violence of
this phenomenon, James posits otherness so it can then be
bracketed by his characters and so that we can be made to
bear witness to the consequences of that bracketing. (In *The
American Scene* the bracketing at issue is a consequence of
the first-person singular. In the novels the bracketing occurs
by virtue of the *absence* of the first-person singular. Although, as I have noted, James predicates ostensible others,
ostensible discrete characters, he does so only in order to
master this so-called otherness, often by a single consciousness, with which James's own consciousness often seems,
after all, allied.)[16]

Yet to define consciousness in relation to others who are
categorically other, categorically external, has consequences:
James remains ambivalent about the outcome he desires.
This is the case because consciousness desires to be sover-
eign in a world where other persons, represented as actual,
are therefore also represented as resisting that desire. In
James's fiction the conflict between consciousness and the
otherness it would appropriate isn't resolved and it isn't
turned away from. It isn't resolved because nothing would
count as resolving it. This is what we knew all along, for
how could there be a way, outside the reduction, for consciousness to constitute the world? But it is what James's
characters never seem to know, for how could there be a
way for consciousness *not* to? Thus James's fiction records
the outrageous triumph in which the mind and the world,
the self and the other, consciousness and the things it appropriates—or however these oppositions are rhetorically
formulated—converge or are even interpenetrated.

Consciousness always triumphs in that the objects it appropriates are gotten to be in the same place. But unlike that moment in Husserl's passage where the thing-phantom and the real thing are miraculously brought together—when, in effect, the two have discrete identities by virtue of the fact that, in effect, they don't (the thing in itself not ever separable from the thing in itself as thought)—in James's fiction consciousness and its object are never permitted to be the same *thing*. That disparity, defying, as it does, certain extreme efforts to conciliate the two, would indicate demonstrable limits to the efficacy of these efforts. Or, from another, Jamesian, perspective, it would indicate a demonstrable incentive simply to escalate them.

TWO

The Prefaces, Revision, and Ideas of Consciousness

It is a well-known fact that in 1897, after he developed severe writer's cramp, Henry James began to dictate his novels. His first amanuensis was William MacAlpine, a shorthand reporter, but James quickly learned to dictate to MacAlpine directly at the typewriter. James's departure from his customary mode of composition inevitably calls into question in a perfectly mundane way the site or location of consciousness. For in the process under consideration consciousness occurs in the mind, but its content is then immediately spoken to another who writes it down, or types it out, a practice which in effect exteriorizes thought and moves it between persons. James claimed there was no difference between the writing of his novels and dictation of them to his Remington:

> The value of [dictating] is in its help to do over and over, for which it is extremely adapted, and which is the only way I can do at all. It soon enough, accordingly, becomes *intellectually,* absolutely identical with the act of writing—or has become so, after five years now, with me; so that the difference is only material and illusory—only the difference . . . that I walk up and down. . . . (To Mrs. Cadwalader Jones, *Letters,* October 23, 1902, 4:247)

It is difficult, however, to credit that disclaimer, especially as the practice begins in the middle of the composition of *What Maisie Knew,* just at the time when James is investigating (as in a conversation between Maisie and Sir Claude which I shall examine at the end of this chapter) to what extent consciousness (in *Maisie* it is sometimes designated as "knowledge") is "inside" persons and to what extent it is "between" them. In calling attention to the fact that James in 1897 implicitly poses questions about consciousness as a double phenomenon, one that is "in" persons and that is also "between" them, at the same time that the dictation of the novels replaces the writing of them, I want to postpone elaborating a connection between the practice of dictation and the phenomenological confusion about where consciousness "is." But as this preliminary description indicates, I nonetheless suppose the occurrences are related. In fact, when Eugene O'Neill, who had been writing for thirty years, developed Parkinson's disease, which exacerbated a possibly familial tremor that had afflicted him since childhood, it prevented him from holding a pencil, and he could not make the transition between writing and dictating his plays. As a consequence he stopped writing them entirely:

> O'Neill attempted to dictate his thoughts to Carlotta [his wife] but found it impossible. Thinking that perhaps the mere presence of another person . . . was the stumbling block, Carlotta bought him a recording machine. They experimented . . . O'Neill reading passages . . . into the machine from different distances, and playing back the results; but, though he mastered the technique of the machine, his mind could not function creatively when he was left alone with it. An electric typewriter was tried but that, too, proved useless. His thoughts, he told Carlotta, flowed from his brain, through his arm and into his pencil; there was no other process by which he could write.[1]

For O'Neill, as presumably for James, the work in the mind and the means of externalizing it are not, then, separable; how one has been thinking motorically, or rendering one's thinking, does not simply affect consciousness; it is part of that consciousness.[2] In O'Neill's case the necessity for motoric change meant he could no longer commit his thoughts to paper. In James's case the conversion from writing to dictation raises the question of the mediation of consciousness or, to situate the question as James's work does, of its externalization. The question of how consciousness is placed, and of where conceptually it is thought to reside, is pertinent to the concerns raised centrally by James's writing. For what consciousness is deemed to be in James's novels is fre-

quently a question of where it is thought to be located—
whether, for example, it is supposed to be within the mind,
as in awareness, or between selves, as exemplified by the idiom of the exchange of minds through conversation, or outside the mind, in the sense of free of the mind's possession
of its own workings.

Such questions about consciousness, its location, and its
topography, at the end of the nineteenth century were not
Henry James's alone.[3] In 1890, William James published his
two-volume *Principles of Psychology*, with its analysis of mental states in general and, particularly memorable, its chapters "The Stream of Thought" and "The Consciousness of
Self," which anatomize the *felt* qualities by which transitory
states are apprehended. William James's investigations of
consciousness were themselves not contextless. In 1882 the
Society for Psychical Research, an outgrowth of a movement
to investigate the unknown aspects of mind, had been
founded. Also in the 1870s and 1880s in Paris, Jean-Martin
Charcot did pioneering work on hysteria, hypnosis, and
dual personality, which was later to become virtually identified with the exploration of these phenomena. Morton
Prince, in America, was at roughly the same time conduct-
ing research on multiple personality, a subject William
James had also explored in an essay of 1890, "The Hidden
Self," published in the then popular *Scribner's* and later incorporated in part in *The Will To Believe*. In 1886 Robert Louis
Stevenson fictionalized the subject of split personality in *Dr.
Jekyll and Mr. Hyde*. Differently popularized, this time in an
academic setting, the *Harvard University Catalogue* for 1874–
75 announced the topic for the Bowdoin prize by asking its
applicants to address themselves to the question, "How
much is Unconscious or seemingly Unconscious in mental
Action and what is the proper Theory for such Unconsciousness?" Again contemporaneously, Pierre Janet, in his book
Psychological Automatism, introduced distinctions between
conscious and subconscious that conceptually paved the
way for more sophisticated Freudian ones. Between 1887
and 1904, in Freud's letters to Fliess, the former anticipated
his own future theories, at times almost telegraphically.
Thus Freud to Fliess on October 20, 1895:

Now listen to this. During an industrious night last week, when I was suffering from that degree of pain which brings about the optimal condition for my mental activities, the barriers suddenly lifted, the veils dropped, and everything became transparent—from the details of the neuroses to the determinants of consciousness. Everything seemed to fall into place, the cogs meshed, I had the impression that the thing now really was a machine that shortly would function on its own. The three systems of n[eurones]; the free and bound states of [quantity]; the primary and secondary processes; the main tendency and the compromise tendency of the nervous system; the two biological rules of attention and defense; the characteristics of quality, reality, and thought; the state of the psychosexual group; the sexual determination of repression; finally, the factors determining consciousness, as a function of perception—all that was correct and still is today![4]

What is of interest to me in this completely superficial glance at some of the explorations of consciousness in the last two decades of the nineteenth century is that ideas about consciousness pervade the writing of the time; that conceptions about the phenomenon, despite the certitude in the last sentence of Freud's letter to Fliess, are hardly codified propositions, but explicitly present themselves as evolving discoveries; that often they do so according to a given researcher's reassessments of his own prior suppositions. This is true of William James's writings, and it is especially true of Freud's, whose changing theories of the mind are conventionally regarded as "revisions" of his earlier ideas about it.

It is in this double context of investigations of consciousness and of revisions of earlier conceptions of it, that Henry James's reconceptions of his prior representations of consciousness may seem like positive contributions in the same field as that of the scientific investigators. Yet in situating Henry James's revised conceptions of consciousness in the framework of his brother's (with which he was familiar) and of Freud's (with which probably he was not),[5] I mean at least initially to suggest a failed analogy between the scientific context and the literary one, for Henry James's revisions of consciousness are neither systematic nor signposted.

Moreover, as they develop, they remain in conflict with each other. One could observe their instability by examining how consciousness is differently represented from one novel to another. Or one could chart James's wayward conceptions of consciousness by considering the statements he made about it in the critical Prefaces he thought out and dictated between 1906 and 1908 to precede the novels he would reprint for the series of his collected (and textually revised) works, the New York Edition.[6]

It is a commonplace that James's Prefaces, almost without fail, point out that the story being told is that of a character's consciousness of it.* The formulaic claims about consciousness in the Prefaces suggest that if the story changes from novel to novel, James's conception of consciousness remains static. This is not so, if for no other reason than that consciousness, which connotes awareness (as it would have for William James and Freud), is sometimes defined in opposition to knowledge, or to unconsciousness, or to what James abstractly calls relations. The framework in which consciousness assumes meaning does not remain stable, then, from one novel to the next. It also does not remain stable with respect to a single novel and its preface. For how the Prefaces *describe* the novel's consciousness and, more to the point, "where" they locate it differ from how the novel *represents*

---

*From the Preface to *The Golden Bowl*: the various narratives are "not . . . my own impersonal account of the affair in hand, but . . . my account of somebody's impression of it—the terms of this person's access to it and estimate of it" (v). From the Preface to *The Ambassadors:* "Strether's sense of things and Strether's only should avail me" (xv). In *What Maisie Knew* we are told that an event will matter "only as it might pass before [Maisie] and appeal to her, as it might touch her and affect her, for better or worse, for perceptive gain or perceptive loss" (x). From *The Portrait of a Lady:* "Place the centre of the subject in the young woman's own consciousness . . . and you get as interesting and as beautiful a difficulty as you could wish" (xv). From *Roderick Hudson:* "The centre of interest throughout *Roderick* is Rowland Mallet's consciousness, and the drama is the very drama of that consciousness" (xviii). From *The Spoils of Poynton:* "appreciation, even to that of the very whole, lives in Fleda. . . . Fleda almost demonically both sees and feels, while the others but feel without seeing" (xiv–xv). From the Preface to *The American* (about Christopher Newman): "the interest of everything is all that it is *his* vision, *his* conception, *his* interpretation: at the window of his wide, quite sufficiently wide, consciousness we are seated" (xxi).

that same consciousness. I shall therefore be suggesting that the Prefaces attempt to revise, in the sense of redetermine, the reader's understanding of the central consciousness in the novel that follows. James himself uses the word "revise" to indicate *textual* transformation:[7]

> To revise is to see, or to look over, again—which means in the case of a written thing neither more nor less than to re-read it . . . the act of revision, the act of seeing it again, caused whatever I looked at on any page to flower before me as into the only terms that honourably expressed it; and the "revised" element in the present Edition is accordingly these terms, these rigid conditions of re-perusal, registered. . . . (*GB*, xvi)

Yet there is an incommensurability between the minute textual revisions, however quantitatively impressive, and the actual reconceptualization of the novels undertaken by the Edition considered in its totality. For the novels in the New York Edition are not just reprinted with textual variants; they are also selected and arranged by James, as well as introduced by his prefatory interpretations of them.[8] In light of such substantial recontextualizations, the revision of a novel is tantamount to its reconception, as James acknowledges, vaguely, in the following passage:

> I could but dream the whole thing over as I went—as I read; and, bathing it, so to speak, in that medium, hope that, some still newer and shrewder critic's intelligence subtly operating, I shouldn't have breathed upon the old catastrophes and accidents, the old wounds and mutilations and disfigurements, wholly in vain. (*GB*, xxi–xxii)

The most unrestricted space in which to "dream the whole thing over" is in the critical Prefaces. To invoke the word "revise," then, as I do, is to echo James's term in the Prefaces to the New York Edition for textual emendation.[9] It is to reiterate his notion that although the revision he concedes is on any page, it is, in addition, more extensive than the tinkering with individual words. But it is also to deviate from James's usage: first, by particularizing the object of revision, as he chooses not to, since the revision on which I focus occurs in James's *unacknowledged* attempts to manipu-

late our sense of the consciousness in the novel that follows;
and second, by understanding that this particular form of revision takes place not textually in the novels but rather pre-
scriptively in the Prefaces to them. Thus the description of a
novel, as James offers it up for our scrutiny in the Preface,
changes the comprehension of it we would have without the
benefit, or interference, of a preliminary, dictating perspective.[10] Although in the following pages I mean "revision" to
designate James's purposeful reassessment of the conception of consciousness, this does not mean that the Prefaces
themselves are free of the conflict of which, I shall argue,
they try to rid the novels. For precisely in contrast to evolving scientific theories of consciousness, which depend on
successiveness for their purported achievement, James's corrected descriptions of consciousness depend on (presume)
the initial conception's remaining *actively* opposed to the revision that would reconstrue it.

It is the early novels especially that require the redefini-
tional ingenuity of the Prefaces. About *Roderick Hudson*, *The
American*, and *The Portrait of a Lady*, James writes Charles
Scribner's Sons:

> These *three* early books thus dealt with, the worst will
> be over; nothing else in the series will demand (or re-
> ceive) so much re-manipulation. (*Letters*, May 9, 1906,
> 4:403)
>
> Have a little more patience with me over these first
> three productions, which have been on a different foot-
> ing, as regards the quantity of re-touching involved,
> from any of those to follow. . . . (*Letters*, June 12,
> 1906, 4:408)

The Prefaces to *Roderick Hudson* and *Portrait* are considered
in detail below. *The American* is tangential to my concern, for
in its Preface consciousness is not so much resituated as it is
more fundamentally *introduced*. I speak briefly about it here,
however, because it exemplifies the way in which even in
works to which the following analysis is not directly pertinent, the Preface's understanding of the phenomenon of
consciousness effectively alters the interpretive framework
of the novel it precedes.

The central problem in *The American* revolves around understanding the relation between what Christopher Newman *initially* does (when he decides not to revenge himself on an American businessman who "'had once played me a very mean trick'" in which "'There was a matter of some sixty thousand dollars at stake'" [25]) and what he *ultimately* does (when he decides not to revenge himself on the Bellegardes, the European, aristocratic family who forbid him to marry Claire de Cintré because his values are those of a "commercial person" [239]). One way to comprehend Newman's repeated renunciations of revenge is to say they are an inevitable consequence of his "remarkable good nature," or of the fabled innocence of the American type. This is how Mrs. Tristram insists that the Bellegardes understand Newman's letting them go free. But another way to understand Newman's aversion to revenge is to see it as having nothing to do with his nature or type and everything to do with his shifting consciousness of his position.[11]

In line with the two possibilities, in some parts of the Preface James appears to be concerned with "types" and "fabled characters" (of American versus European characteristics statically construed), in the context of which he defines the "romance" of *The American*. But in other parts of the Preface "romance" is rather defined in terms of power and its reversibility:

> (It is as difficult, as I said above, to trace the dividing-line between the real and the romantic as to plant a milestone between north and south; but I am not sure an infallible sign of the latter is not this rank vegetation of the "power" of bad people that good get into, or *vice versa*. It is so rarely, alas, into *our* power that anyone gets!) (xx)

Although the sentences are parenthetical, the concerns they voice are central. For the "vice versa" or reversibility of position applies not only to the ultimate transfer of power from the Bellegardes to Newman. It more immediately applies to Newman's multiple vacillations each time he, in possession of the letter by which he would incriminate the Bellegardes in murder, changes his mind about whether to use it. In the last of these shifts he tosses the letter into the fire because,

he tells Mrs. Tristram, he has already enjoyed his advantage
("'they *were* frightened . . . and I have had all the ven-
geance I want'"). But when Mrs. Tristram challenges this
analysis ("'they believed . . . you would never really come
to the point'" [349]), Newman, in the early editions, turns to
the flames presumably to try to retrieve the letter in order to
enjoy his revenge. In the revised text of 1907 James rewrites
the novel's ending, making Newman unambiguously turn
away from the fire. Yet Newman's action's being made decisive in the second of the two texts does not alter my point,
since the reversibility associated with romance in the Preface to the novel is operative specifically with respect to the
consciousness that determines Newman's action. In line
with Newman's shifting sense of what constitutes his power
(exercising it or refusing to do so), the parenthetical definition of romance, cited above, associating power with reversibility, dominates the novel. We are to see Newman's
enjoyment of his power as contingent upon its sacrifice; as
contingent upon the illusion of sacrifice; as *contingent* per se:
as having meaning only with reference to Newman's *understanding* of the Bellegardes' interpretation of his action.

The two interpretive frameworks—one concerned with a
particular opposition between Europeans and Americans,
the second with the *principle* of opposition, by which particular oppositions are not in fact fixed—are unequal. Although they are interlineated, one can be read as a critique
of the other. For in the Preface questions of typicality, of
how Americans and Europeans differently behave (which
would dominate our understanding of the novel if there
were no Preface), are subordinated to questions of power
volatilely conceived and to Newman's apprehension of that
instability. Whether Newman enjoys his advantage must be
understood in terms of how he sees his shifting relations to
the Bellegardes. In terms of how he sees them, and believes
they see him, not in terms of who he is. It is in the context
of how Newman sees the Bellegardes that consciousness
becomes an issue, the one on which the Preface to *The American* closes: "the interest of everything is all that it is *his*
vision, *his* conception, *his* interpretation." Thus, insisting
implicitly that it takes a central consciousness to register
shifts of power, James introduces as contingent two primary

conceptions—of consciousness, of power—that reassess the novel purportedly being described.

In the following pages I consider "re-manipulation[s]" of consciousness that are more extreme than that in the Preface to *The American*, for these remanipulations depend not on the *introduction* of consciousness as a subject, but more radically, on its *redefinition*. Specifically, in sections II and III of this chapter I examine the Prefaces to *Roderick Hudson* and *The Portrait of a Lady*. The argument in these sections is that the Prefaces to the early novels propose the centrality, isolation, and sufficiency of consciousness, which the novels contest. In section IV I consider *What Maisie Knew*, whose conclusions about consciousness require clarifications and codifications related to those in the Prefaces to the earlier novels. In *Maisie* James's placing of consciousness is not stable but rather shifts. I shall, in fact, be suggesting that the Prefaces, too, consistently reconceive consciousness by respatializing it. One can only conclude from the operations to which consciousness is subjected in the Prefaces and the later novels that James finds consciousness, as he himself has previously represented it to be, in need of such revision or correction. In section V, the conclusion, I address the question of why it is difficult for James, in the Prefaces, to normalize the representations of consciousness recorded in the novels, for these representations have been aggrandized and made formidable in their own alien right. It is against the backdrop of the progressively magical claims about consciousness made by the late works—that a self could hear another's thoughts *(The Golden Bowl)*, could produce another's thoughts *(The American Scene)*, could immortalize thoughts ("Is There a Life after Death?")—that I here consider the *covert* attempts to empower consciousness in the Prefaces to *Roderick Hudson, The Portrait of a Lady*, and *What Maisie Knew*. Thus I see the present chapter as providing a context for the more aggressive reconceptions of consciousness in James's other writings, discussed elsewhere in this book, even as the chapter undertakes its own task: to scrutinize James's alternative spatializations of consciousness, first, between the Prefaces and the novels and, second, within particular novels.

In the discussion that follows, I shall be assuming that

there is no single conception of consciousness in the novels and also, as the relation between Prefaces and novels
suggests, that there is no *developing* sense of a Jamesian consciousness. The tension between the empowering of consciousness in magical or hypothetical ways and the disputing of that power exists both between the Prefaces and the
novels and within individual novels. And, notwithstanding
the chronological progression of the novels, *continues* to do
so. James's representations of consciousness have always
been understood to be the central concern of the novels,
even as most considerations have conventionalized their
scrutiny by immediately thematizing it. In the following
pages I assume that something is to be gained by declining
to do that. For the novels and Prefaces do not simply represent characters thinking; they also raise the question of what
thinking is, of how it can be made to register, and albeit
disconcertingly, of *where* it might do so.

II

In the Preface to *Roderick Hudson*, James enumerates a series
of dissatisfactions with the novel he wrote thirty-five years
earlier, though each inadequacy has its balancing justification: Mary Garland is not the appropriate antithesis to Christina Light, but perhaps such antitheses do not exist. Although the novel's title is wrong, nonetheless the "centre of
interest" is clearly "Rowland Mallet's consciousness," and
the drama of the novel "is the very drama of that consciousness." Although Hudson goes to pieces too fast, people do
go to pieces. It is equally impressive that, following a caveat
about America's being erroneously typified by Northamp-
ton, James's litany of errors is prefaced by a rebuke to his
criticisms that all but preempts them: "The thing escapes, I
conceive, with its life" (xiv). *Roderick Hudson* does escape
with its life, and not because critique is balanced by justification for which it may even be the occasion, but more co-
gently, I think, because James chooses to remain silent about
an aspect of the novel which is centrally problematic: how to
confine a psychological dilemma to the consciousness of a
single character.

  Rowland Mallet, the character whose consciousness James
designates in the Preface as the novel's center of interest, is

a critic who lives vicariously, through Roderick Hudson, the artist. Mallet manages Hudson's career, and he oversees Hudson's dealings with the novel's three women: Cecilia, Mallet's cousin and confidante; Mary Garland, Hudson's fiancée; and Christina Light, Hudson's lover. Yet Rowland Mallet's self-effacing relation to Hudson is ambiguous. It is not clear whether what Rowland Mallet fears and desires is sexual in nature (having to do with the relation between self and others) or is identic in nature (having to do with the self's ambivalent acceptance of aspects of its own person—in this case, the connection between the critical faculty and the creative one). The creative faculty is externalized for Rowland Mallet by the person of Roderick Hudson. To the extent that *being* Hudson would involve *having* Christina Light as well as Mary Garland, Mallet's wish to be Hudson, and to have what Hudson has, suggests that relations in the novel are asymmetrical (in René Girard's term, "triangulated") and incomplete.[12] Relations are incomplete because, with respect to the question of identity, only together do Rowland and Roderick make a whole person. They are asymmetrical because, with respect to the question of passion, there is always an extra, third person, whether that third person be the lover, Christina Light, whose presence calls into question Hudson's engagement to Mary Garland, or whether it be the fiancée, Mary Garland, the pledge to whom threatens Hudson's passion for Christina Light. In the economy of Mallet's psychic scheme, which would save him from satisfaction, would keep him from, in Lambert Strether's terms, "wanting more wants," there is always an incomplete person (himself or Hudson), an extra person (Christina Light), or an absent person (Mary Garland).

That sexual and identic relations are confused for Mallet is, as James implies, the subject of the novel. Why, however, are all the other characters whom we would suppose to be disengaged from the Rowland-Roderick split equally afflicted by the same confusion? Mary Garland, loved by Mallet, is engaged to Roderick Hudson, though her intercourse with Hudson primarily concerns the witnessing of Hudson's unrequited passion for Christina Light, who, not incidentally, wishes to be like Mary Garland. Christina Light flirts with Rowland Mallet, makes love to Roderick Hudson,

but marries Casamassima. Mrs. Light wants Christina to be
a princess so that Mrs. Light can exchange her former lover,
and present servant, the Cavaliere, for Christina's husband,
Casamassima. Augusta Blanchard and Mr. Leavenworth are
"going to make a match" (3.16), although Madame Grandoni
tells Mallet, "'when she accepted Mr. Leavenworth she
thought of you'" (3.17).

The failure to differentiate the plights of the novel's characters is further illustrated by Mallet's odd relation to Mrs.
Hudson and Mrs. Light, both of whose ambassadors Mallet
becomes, for when Hudson is recklessly destroying himself
by his infatuation with Christina Light, Mrs. Hudson assumes a "clinging confidence in Rowland['s]" (2.230) ability
to rescue Hudson, and when Christina breaks off her plans
of marriage with Casamassima, Mrs. Light engages Mallet to
make Christina come to her senses. Both mothers in the
novel are defined only in terms of their custodial relation to
their children and—calling the efficacy of that role into
question—by their virtual inability to make those children
do what they want. If Rowland Mallet supplants Mrs. Hudson and Mrs. Light in their supervisory role, he is similarly
unsuccessful in its execution. Thus Mallet is like the novel's
mothers, whose places he assumes. But he is also like the
novel's father, the Cavaliere. Both repudiate their passivity
at crucial moments of intervention: the Cavaliere, to tell
Christina that if she fails to marry Casamassima, the Cavaliere will reveal Christina to be his daughter; Rowland Mallet, to tell Christina Light that Hudson is engaged to Mary
Garland, information that has the desired effect of making
her flirt with Hudson. Thus although Rowland says to the
Cavaliere, "'I don't understand double people . . . I don't
pretend to understand you'" (3.87), Mallet's only ostensibly
passive relation to the novel's action is virtually identical to
the Cavaliere's. Yet however apparently telling these com-
parisons, they are in fact insignificant. Rowland Mallet is
like the novel's mothers and he is like the Cavaliere, but he
is no less like Cecilia (because Cecilia, Mallet's cousin and fe-
male counterpart, only oversees other people's wants, never
admitting her own); and, to the extent that Mary Garland is
like "a person who is watching at a sick-bed" (3.144), Mallet
is also "like" her. When Mary Garland asks Mallet, "'What

is your part supposed to have been?'" (2.269), there is only a superficial answer to that question, for characters' parts in this novel are not appreciably different.

"'I am incomplete'" (2.131), Roderick Hudson tells Christina Light, and that assessment, though Rowland is not privy to it, is echoed by Rowland when he writes to Cecilia: "'The poor fellow is incomplete, and it is really not his own fault'" (2.184). But despite repeated insinuations that, privy to each other's minds, the two characters are counterparts, what this might mean is not in fact clear.* In *Roderick Hudson* what we most wish to understand is how desire that is unfulfilled (Mallet's) and desire that is unfulfillable (Hudson's), which seem perfect complements, are bequeathed to characters who behave toward each other—specifically with respect to the manifestation of desire—as if they embodied antithetical states. Although the final conversation between Mallet and Hudson promises a disclosure of what binds the two together, it only confesses what the reader has known all along. While Hudson explains Mallet from Hudson's point of view ("'There is something monstrous in a man's pretending to lay down the law to a sort of emotion with which he is quite unacquainted . . .'" [3.230]) and while Mallet explains Hudson from Mallet's point of view ("'It's a perpetual sacrifice to live with a transcendant egotist!'" [3.234]), no explanation is provided which would acknowledge that the inability to fulfill one's desires and the inability to tolerate the frustration of not always fulfilling them are two characteristics dynamically connected to each other. In fact, it half seems as if the function of the schematization is to represent desire so that it cannot be understood in terms of psychological integrity. For if one reason the self in *Roderick Hudson* is incoherent as an entity is that traits are called

*The connection between Roderick and Rowland is made even more vexed by the novel's end, since Mallet's dream of Hudson's death ("a vision of Roderick, graceful and beautiful as he passed, plunging like a diver into a misty gulf" [2.216]) anticipates the cause of that death as well as its fact. Roderick dies by falling over a cliff, so that, looking down into a gorge in the "Alpine void," Rowland sees Roderick's face, which "stared upward open-eyed at the sky" (3.256, 258). Because the plot prohibits us from seeing causality between what Mallet imagines and what Hudson experiences, we are thrown back to entertaining an identic connection between what happens in Mallet's mind and what happens to Hudson's body.

persons, a second reason is that in *Roderick Hudson* these
traits, once individuated, seem reproductions of each other
in that they share not only the same desires but also comparable ways of manifesting them. Thus fragments are embodied as if they were wholes, but the externally different traits,
once embodied, nonetheless behave like each other. Because
selves are fragments or incompletions and because they are
also repetitions, it makes sense that James, the young man,
should have gotten the title of the novel wrong. Since the
novel prohibits the narrative of an integrated or differentiated self, the story can only arbitrarily be designated as one
character's rather than another's.*

According to this logic, of course, neither title for the
novel would ever be right. One could protest the extremity
of such a diagnosis, arguing the story is indisputably more
Mallet's than Hudson's. That assessment would be correct if
the criterion were point of view. Yet although James invokes
consciousness in the Preface to *Roderick Hudson* to designate
Mallet's perspective, or awareness, as presiding over the
novel's narrative, and although Mallet is technically different from the other characters (we see through his eyes), he

---

*The language of the 1879 edition reveals the very problematic connection
between Rowland and Roderick which the later text, as well as the Preface
to it, attempts to "revise," obscure, or correct. Thus, for example, while the
1879 text echoes Roderick's "'I am incomplete'" with Rowland's independent assessment that he "'is incomplete,'" the New York Edition recognizes, and avoids, the questions of characterological fusion raised by the
unexplained verbal echo. Specifically, it averts the questions of that fusion
by changing Rowland's words from "'[he] is incomplete'" to "'He isn't
made right'" (217), so that Rowland's description of Roderick is no longer
identical to Roderick's description of himself. Thus on page 366 of the New
York Edition James obscures the reflexivity of characters' relations to each
other by revising the sentence about Augusta Blanchard from "'when she
accepted Mr. Leavenworth she thought of you'" to "'when she surren-
dered to Mr. Leavenworth she was thinking of quite another gentleman,'"
making the relation between the characters substitutive instead of reflexive.
Thus in the New York Edition, Rowland's words to the Cavaliere, "'I don't
understand double people . . . I don't . . . understand you,'" are simply
deleted. In these various instances the New York Edition is not randomly
revising the 1879 text. It is specifically revising the unexplained characterological incompletions, fusions, and doublings of that text, much as the Preface tries to do.

is not dynamically different from them.* As I have been arguing, *all* of the characters understand desire only in mimetic or imitative terms. While consciousness and desire are obviously not equivalent, an integrated consciousness would presumably experience desire in ways that were fundamentally discrete, even if the idea of a completely individuated or original desire were correctly understood to be nonsensical. Thus in *Roderick Hudson* undifferentiated mental states that will be sanctioned in *The Wings of the Dove* and ostensibly forbidden in *The Golden Bowl* are rendered neutrally or accidentally. In this sense *Roderick Hudson* presents the quintessential Jamesian dilemma apparently without understanding it to be a dilemma—naively presents the situation which will be either contested or endorsed in all of the late novels.

But James's awareness of the central difficulty in *Roderick Hudson* is indirectly conceded elsewhere in the Preface to the book, although James displaces his admission from the formal criticism of that novel. In fact it is clear that James's listing of the novel's errors is a strategy for deflecting the reader's attention from a quandary which cannot be quantified by any castigating itemization because, like the following passage which addresses the dilemma, the difficulty on which *Roderick Hudson* founders is not reductive:

> Really, universally, relations stop nowhere, and the exquisite problem of the artist is eternally but to draw, by a geometry of his own, the circle within which they shall *appear* to do so. He is in the perpetual predicament that the continuity of things is the whole matter, for him, of comedy and tragedy; that this continuity is

*One could argue that the characters are confused because Mallet *sees* them as such. But this explanation fails to account for why the other characters represent themselves as experiencing desire only as Mallet and Hudson do. From this vantage, then, "consciousness," denoting "awareness," is not Mallet's alone, or, if it is so, then only in the most cursory sense. For while we do not see through anyone else's eyes, Mallet's way of seeing is so much like that of the other characters as to rupture the narrative distinction only formally kept intact. Here one thinks of Poe's *Narrative of Arthur Gordon Pym* (which James had read), where characters, though antipathetic, are also partial without each other and therefore to be understood as a split but compound single identity, as one psychically *un*integrated personality.

never, by the space of an instant or an inch, broken,
and that, to do anything at all, he has at once intensely
to consult and intensely to ignore it. All of which will
perhaps pass but for a supersubtle way of pointing the
plain moral that a young embroiderer of the canvas of
life soon began to work in terror, fairly, of the vast ex-
panse of that surface, of the boundless number of its
distinct perforations for the needle, and of the tendency inherent in his many-coloured flowers and figures to cover and consume as many as possible of the
little holes. The development of the flower, of the figure, involved thus an immense counting of holes and a
careful selection among them. That would have been, it
seemed to him, a brave enough process, were it not the
very nature of the holes so to invite, to solicit, to per-
suade, to practise positively a thousand lures and
deceits. The prime effect of so sustained a system, so
prepared a surface, is to lead on and on; while the fas-
cination of following resides, by the same token, in the
presumability *somewhere* of a convenient, of a visibly-
appointed stopping-place. Art would be easy indeed if,
by a fond power disposed to "patronise" it, such con-
veniences, such simplifications, had been provided. We
have, as the case stands, to invent and establish them,
to arrive at them by a difficult, dire process of selection
and comparison, of surrender and sacrifice. The very
meaning of expertness is acquired courage to brace
one's self for the cruel crisis from the moment one sees
it grimly loom. [Preface, vii–viii]

The immediate subject to which the embroidery passage refers is the young author's concern about how to determine
which developments are *"indispensable* to the interest" (an
anxiety elaborated in the paragraph preceding that cited
above). Yet it is not with respect to developments of plot
that continuousness appears so arbitrarily in *Roderick Hudson*. Rather it is the "sameness" of the novel's characters
which leads us to believe that in *Roderick Hudson* relations
"stop nowhere." Thus although the thematic of continuousness (taken up by the embroidery passage) and the thematic
of a single consciousness (taken up unsuccessfully by the
novel) are not explicitly related, they are implicitly so, since
it is in terms of the inadequate differentiation among osten-

sibly discrete characters that continuousness in the novel manifests itself.

Moreover, while the passage espouses the importance of executing discriminations, its own metaphoric complexity reproduces the very confusion ostensibly to be warded off. Confusion is replicated in several ways. For example, to the extent that the passage repeatedly presents double terms (points to be consulted/those to be ignored; the figure of the flower/the ground on which it is embroidered), it suggests that at stake here are central dichotomies. We could designate the primary one as the necessity for the artist to distinguish what he will appropriate as integral to his subject from what he will ignore as alien to his subject. Yet to denominate this dichotomy as primary is already descriptively to extricate it from significant considerations which are not, in the passage, affectively separable from it. These may be specified incompletely as follows: the sacrifice which attends those aspects of life from which the artist turns away; the achievement of maturity which vouchsafes such a sacrifice; the terror which nonetheless permeates the passage, as if no expertness will avert the experience of loss not only retrospectively identified as such. In the play of these several subjects for dominance, the passage enacts the relational confusion also being described, and James's anxiety is transferred to the reader, who is disabled from knowing in any stable way the hard edges of what he is being asked to "take in." In addition, if the vehicle of the metaphor in the embroidery passage comprises too many, unclearly differentiated parts, the clarity of its tenor is similarly jeopardized, for, as I have noted, the referent for the metaphor—developments of plot—is irrelevant to the novel's actual confusion, the one that victimized its author when, first in serial publication, and then in novel form, he got its title wrong. Finally, the meditation on relations' stopping nowhere *itself* continues in the Preface to *The Golden Bowl*, twenty-two volumes later:

> as the whole conduct of life consists of things done, which do other things in their turn, just so our behaviour and its fruits are essentially one and continuous and persistent and unquenchable, so the act has its way of abiding and showing and testifying, and so,

> among our innumerable acts, are no arbitrary, no
> senseless separations. (xxiv)

In these various ways—the multiplicity of parts of which
the vehicle in the embroidery passage is composed; the unclear tenor to which the vehicle refers; the repetition of the
subject of continuousness from the Preface of one novel to
that of another—the embroidery passage does not simply
express terror at the difficulty of separations; it also demonstrates their apparent impossibility.

The imperative for separations (described by the embroidery passage) and the subversion of that imperative (enacted by the passage) excepts it from other paragraphs in the
Preface to *Roderick Hudson* which consider the novel in
ultimately unconflicted terms. Again in distinction to the
Preface as a whole, in which emotion is reflected upon, here
it seems experienced. It erupts in the last sentence, where
James sees himself at the mercy of a crisis that is not past
tense, and that, by definition, cannot ever be so. Even the
sustained metaphoric density of the prose distinguishes this
paragraph from the texture of the surrounding writing. Most
to the point, the passage concedes, however obliquely, the
trouble in the novel that acutely afflicts it, trouble to which
James elsewhere seems oblivious. For if the Preface in its
entirety makes distinctions the novel fails to (most notably
between Rowland and Roderick), the embroidery passage
replicates fusions related to those of the consciousnesses in
the novel.

The anxiety in the embroidery passage seems to be, How
can what confers identity ("the visibly-appointed stopping-
place") *also* be arbitrary? And—to anchor the observation
overtly to the novel, as James chooses not to—Is what separates Mallet from Hudson, and both from the other characters, really differentiating, or is it only said to be so? In such
questions as these, which the passage presses on us if we
try to connect it to the novel that follows, one can only wonder whether James is obliquely conceding that he initially
failed to make these separations, or whether he is rather jus-
tifying his inability to make them. If in posing these alternatives for understanding the passage I seem to be vacillating
between two contradictory points of view—James acknowl-

edges the trouble with the novel/James corrects the trouble
in the novel by refusing to acknowledge it, except perhaps
evasively—the contradiction in my argument (my wanting
it both ways) directly reflects what the Preface itself wants.

Let me reiterate this doubleness in a slightly different context. In the Preface to *Roderick Hudson* the correction of inadequately differentiated characters manifests itself in James's
unambiguous attribution of consciousness to Mallet ("the
centre of interest throughout 'Roderick' is Rowland Mallet's
consciousness, and the drama is the very drama of that consciousness"). When the Preface disagrees with this proposition—with the idea of a "centre" and with the idea of its
containment—when, that is, it suggests that relations may
extend infinitely (hence be impossible to contain and so center), it does this by generalizing, metaphorizing, and *relegat-
ing* the subsequent unclarity to a passage which at once
applies to *every* novelistic phenomenon and therefore to no
specific one. Thus one could say that the "revision" of an inadequately circumscribed consciousness in *Roderick Hudson*
is undertaken by the Preface by omission (in the enumera-
tion of the novel's faults, as it leaves out the primary one);
by counterstatement (in the aggressive assertion "My subject, all blissfully, in face of difficulties, had defined itself—
and this in spite of the title of the book" [xvi]); and, finally,
by deflection (in converting a problem of particular relations
to a general philosophic reflection, the point of which seems
to be to disable the very applicability of reflection to the
novel).

These revisions by evasion are italicized with reference to
The Ambassadors, which correctly denominates its subjects as
plural, and which could be understood as James's overt, if
silent, rewriting of *Roderick Hudson*. In linking *Roderick Hudson* to *The Princess Casamassima*, the later novel in which
some of the same characters reappear, rather than to *The
Ambassadors*, the later novel in which, more interestingly,
some of the same problems reoccur and are addressed (Is
Strether his own person, or is he Chad's or Mrs. New-
some's, in service to one and refusing the lover of the
other?), James, at the close of the Preface to *Roderick Hudson*,
connects it to its sequel trivially conceived rather than to its
sequel substantively conceived. For in deflecting the latter

connection James also deflects acknowledgment of what in his "first" novel (vi)—not in fact his first novel—requires substantive correction.

Yet what is wrong with the novel is also what is interesting about it. Whatever James's other reasons for wishing to include *Roderick Hudson* in the collected series of his works, I expect he also chose the novel for his Edition because it raises the issue of a single consciousness inadequately delineated (if one accepts my account) and inadvertently delineated (if one accepts James's). In a sense these characterizations add up to the same analysis. For not to know what you are representing—Roderick's story or Rowland's—is also not to be able to tell these characters clearly apart. It is to be disabled from narrating the drama of a single consciousness in any way but technically.

In the novels that follow *Roderick Hudson*, questions about a finite consciousness are not absent from James's consideration, nor are they unrelated to the concerns expressed abstractly in the embroidery passage. But they may be said less ambiguously to invite particularization as follows: Where does consciousness end? What is truly alien to it? If consciousness is, after all, seen to be delimited, can prestige be conferred rather than subtracted by the limits that constrain it? (In this formulation, consciousness would have value not because it extends infinitely, but oppositely because it is circumscribed and inaccessible.) Say the delimiting of consciousness is equated with its sufficiency, hence its superiority (and James says just that in the Preface to *The Portrait of a Lady*), then what might threaten that equation? Finally (this question is pertinent to *What Maisie Knew*) what are the criteria for delimiting consciousness, for arbitrating *where* it ends? If my analysis of *Roderick Hudson* has insistently converted the general philosophic question of "relations stop-[ping] nowhere" to the particular dilemma of one mind's relation to another, this is not only because it is with reference to that subject that James's later work positions itself. It is also because the novel *Roderick Hudson* primitively acts out its own inadvertent drama in just these terms. The Preface to *Roderick Hudson* is itself divided on the question of what separations of consciousness might in fact mean. Most of the Preface blithely treats the separation of consciousness as if it were a technicality, a matter of technique or of narrative craft. The embroidery passage catches a glimpse—or betrays one—of what would be at stake in acknowledging otherwise.

III

In the Preface to *The Portrait of a Lady*, James insists that the center is to be placed in "the young woman's own consciousness," a strategy that will differentiate his novel from those of his fictional predecessors: Scott, Dickens, and, most especially, George Eliot. Yet Eliot, not unlike James (and, significantly, prior to him), speculates on the value of her heroines' consciousnesses. She does so in a passage from *Daniel Deronda*, which in the Preface to *The Portrait of a Lady*, ostensibly acknowledging Eliot's interest in her heroines, James miscites: "George Eliot has admirably noted it—'in these frail vessels is borne onward through the ages the treasure of human affection'" (xiii). "Delicate," not "frail," is Eliot's adjective. The substitution is trivial, but not so the fact that James chooses to quote only the last line of the following passage from *Daniel Deronda*, leaving out the sentences in which Eliot underscores, as James will, the significance of her heroine's consciousness:

> Could there be a slenderer, more insignificant thread in human history than this consciousness of a girl, busy with her small inferences of the way in which she could make her life pleasant? . . . What in the midst of that mighty drama are girls and their blind visions? They are the Yea or Nay of that good for which men are enduring and fighting. In these delicate vessels is borne onward through the ages the treasure of human affections.[13]

The skewed reference to the Eliot passage—skewed because James omits that portion of the passage which locates the source of a heroine's importance for Eliot in the heroine's visions—implies that James's novelistic feat arises from his unique representation of Isabel Archer's consciousness.

But unique in what sense? By light of the passage in which James alludes to Eliot, the innovation of *Portrait* arises from the sufficiency of Isabel Archer's consciousness, whereby she becomes, unlike Eliot's heroines, the "sole

minister of . . . appeal" (xiv), to be attended to instead of
the male characters and commanding attention apart from
her interest in them. By light of other passages the claim is
more extreme. Her consciousness is to require attention independent of *all* other characters and of anything that happens to her. So, James says, it first engaged him, when he
conceived it as yet free of the concrete aspects of the novel's
story. It was

> vivid, so strangely, in spite of being still at large, not
> confined by the conditions, not engaged in the tangle,
> to which we look for much of the impress that consti-
> tutes an identity. (xi)

A paragraph later: "she stood there in perfect isolation" (xii).
In protected isolation, too, for although James speaks of the
plot he will erect around her, and the other characters he
will engage for her, she is at least initially to be safeguarded
from these. She is a "treasure," or "precious object [to be]
locked up indefinitely rather than commit it, at no matter
what price, to vulgar hands" (xii). In the testimony of that
metaphor Isabel Archer is immediately removed until James
can invent the right circumstances in which to place her. By
light of other assertions in the Preface she is also ultimately
removed from these. While James talks about the isolation of
Isabel Archer's "character," not her consciousness, my ex-
trapolation from his wording is invited by his then defining
her character solely in terms of her consciousness construed
as a framed phenomenon. Just to the extent that James in
the Preface imagines moments of consciousness extricated
from the "tangle" of other phenomena, he leads us to believe that such a separation is possible. Thus although the
thematic of the novel corrects Isabel Archer's belief that she
could be "free" of her circumstances so as to imagine them,
the Preface expresses a nostalgia for that same freedom, associating it even with the value of her character.

Although the two claims I have been examining (the one
introduced by James's comparative reference to Eliot, the
other self-referential) are related, they are not identical. In
one case what is at issue is the comparative sufficiency of Isabel Archer's consciousness, its adequacy to be represented
apart from that of a male character. In the other case, what

is at issue is a categorical sufficiency, one which removes consciousness from everything else in the novel that could be equal to and hence engage with it. By light of this latter claim, James's depiction of consciousness is legitimately to be differentiated from Eliot's representation of it. For what James enumerates repeatedly in the Preface is the "possibilities of [consciousness's] importance to itself" (xv). How does the novel defer to such formulations? And if we grant Isabel Archer the true separation from male characters and even from *other* characters that it is difficult to grant Rowland Mallet, what, in the novel, are the consequences of such a separation?

When James in the Preface calls attention to Isabel Archer's vigil of meditation, he insists upon its typicality, on the fact that "it is obviously the best thing in the book, but it is only a supreme illustration of the general plan":

> I might show what an "exciting" inward life may do for the person leading it even while it remains perfectly normal. And I cannot think of a more consistent application of that ideal unless it be in the long statement, just beyond the middle of the book, of my young woman's extraordinary meditative vigil. . . . It was designed to have all the vivacity of incident and all the economy of picture. She sits up, by her dying fire, far into the night, under the spell of recognitions. . . . It is a representation simply of her motionlessly *seeing*, and an attempt withal to make the mere still lucidity of her act as "interesting" as the surprise of a caravan or the identification of a pirate. It represents, for that matter, one of the identifications dear to the novelist, and even indispensable to him; but it all goes on without her being approached by another person and without her leaving her chair. It is obviously the best thing in the book, but it is only a supreme illustration of the general plan. (xx–xxi)

In that vigil there is no life but that of the mind wholly absorbed in the complexity of its vision. Yet significant moments in the novel contest the autonomy of Isabel Archer's consciousness. In one such moment we are shown Isabel's contemplation disrupted and broken into, as if her vision (the "inward life" whose story is being recorded) were first forced outward and second, thereby, threateningly made contingent. The scene occurs directly after the Countess Gemini has informed Isabel that Osmond and Madame Merle have been lovers. Still gripped by this thought Isabel sees Merle:

> The effect was strange, for Madame Merle was already so present to her vision that her appearance in the flesh was like suddenly, and rather awfully, seeing a painted picture move. Isabel had been thinking all day of her falsity, her audacity, her ability, her probable suffering; and these dark things seemed to flash with a sudden light as she entered the room. Her being there at all had the character of ugly evidence, of handwritings, of profaned relics, of grim things produced in court. (2.375)

This moment is important because, in distinction to James's typical passage, the life in the mind and the life outside of it suddenly come together as Isabel sees animated what the Countess Gemini has made her think. While the scene of Isabel's meditative vigil harks back to the stasis of the novel's title, the passage just cited presents in "dark things" that "flash" a portrait antithetical to the earlier "motionless" one. Thus, for example, Isabel's thought about Merle, registered in the sequence of nouns that characterize her "falsity, her audacity, her ability, her probable suffering," does not imply a single or sustained picture but rather connotes associations that make the image a disjunctive one. "Ability" is a word whose position in the series is especially unsettling, for Merle's capacity is oppositely associated with falsity and with suffering. Her suffering is what her ability covers over, even as the same ability also obscures her doubleness.

Other disturbing conjunctions punctuate the chapter, for I think we are being asked to contemplate not simply the connection between the picture and the woman but also the connection between the two women. Thus the indeterminate picture of Merle pertains as well to Isabel. The chapter's insistence on identifying the two women is illustrated most elementally by their designations for each other. When Isabel first sees Merle in the parlor of the convent where she goes to visit Pansy, she thinks "she had absolutely nothing to say to . . . this lady" (2.375). But Isabel's impulse to dissociate herself from Merle by the impersonality of designation is itself disallowed in the next paragraph, where Merle refers to Isabel with the same neutral demonstrative, indicating to the portress: "'in five minutes this lady will ring for you'" (2.376). Finally, James repeats the locution in the narrator's voice, the last time with reference to Merle: "'Will you let me remain a little?' this lady asked" (2.381). The point of the examples is the unclarity of their antecedents (completely atypical in the novel as a whole), for at a moment when James is insisting on relations that his characters would repudiate—relations that, as I have noted, he himself eschews acknowledgment of in the Preface—"this lady" sometimes indicates Merle and sometimes indicates Isabel, who, James suggests in the novel, are not clearly separable.

It is Merle's "thought," specifically, that Isabel contemplates in the chapter. In fact Isabel's vision of the depth of Merle's reverie recalls an earlier moment in the novel, that of Isabel's meditation during her midnight vigil. Although Isabel's night of seeing is *ultimately* distinguished from anything that might be consonant with it, it is *immediately* brought to mind at the moment when Isabel, returning from her visit with Pansy, pushes open the door of the parlor to see Madame Merle "sitting just as Isabel had left her, like a woman so absorbed in thought that she had not moved a little finger" (2.387). The chapter's emphasis on vision as unoriginal and interactive, as anything but "motionless" and as anything but self-contained, is underscored in passages like the following one, in which *Isabel* registers Merle's discovery that their relations are changed:

> This subtle modulation marked a momentous discovery—the perception of an entirely new attitude on the part of her listener. Madame Merle had guessed in the space of an instant that everything was at an end between them, and in the space of another instant she had guessed the reason why. The person who stood there was not the same one she had seen hitherto, but was a very different person—a person who knew her secret. (2.378)

Vision in the passage, and in the chapter as a whole, is double. It is double because Isabel sees Merle as Merle sees Isabel—in the same way as (with the sense of discovery) and
at the same time as. But it is also double because the way in
which Isabel sees Merle is by looking at as well as away
from her. Hence the quotation which highlights the palpable
reality of the woman in front of Isabel is coupled with that
which obliterates Merle's physical presence, as if only apart
from actual presences can one see their meaning: "Isabel
saw it all as distinctly as if it had been reflected in a large
clear glass." But a moment later, half turned away and looking out the window, "she saw nothing of the budding plants
and the glowing afternoon. She saw . . . that she had been
an applied handled hung-up tool, as senseless and convenient as mere shaped wood and iron" (2.378–79). The point
to be remarked upon with respect to vision associated with
reflection which connotes realistic mirroring and vision associated with reflection which connotes thought is that the
alternate kinds of seeing, kept rigorously apart through earlier portions of the novel, are coterminous. This twofold coincidence, of Merle's vision with Isabel's, of introspection
with sight, is here eventually found unbearable, Isabel re-
marking, "'I think I should like never to see you again'"
(2.389).

That James wishes to portray the coincidence of thoughts
as violative is emblematized in the same chapter by a
thought Isabel ascribes to Pansy when the former, momentarily leaving Merle, visits her stepdaughter. What occasions
the image in the passage that follows is Isabel's supposition
that Pansy will imagine only as improbable, or as beyond
the capability of her assessment, an intimacy between her
father and stepmother that is less than it should be:

> Her heart may have stood almost as still as it would
> have done had she seen two of the saints in the great
> picture in the convent-chapel turn their painted heads
> and shake them at each other. (2.383)

Yet this thought of Pansy's is not Pansy's thought, but is
rather Isabel's surmise of Pansy's conception. If earlier in the
chapter Isabel "sees" Merle's thoughts, in the passage I am
considering she only imagines Pansy's. Still, by light of the

Preface's proposition that thoughts are ideally autonomous, hence rebuke others' intrusions, Merle's breaking
into Isabel's thought of her, Isabel's "discovery" of Merle's
thought, and, in the present scene, Isabel's fantasy of
Pansy's thought, have the same status. For these insights
or intrusions connect the outer scene with the inner in a
way which categorically questions the separation between
them.

The relations Pansy refuses to contemplate are those of
Osmond and Isabel. Yet they seem rather to apply to Isabel
and Merle. They do so because this is not after all Pansy's
thought but is rather Isabel's picture of it, and because Isabel's immediate conflict is with Merle, not with Osmond.
Thus the image reads like a gloss on the chapter's and the
novel's redescriptions of seeing—seeing become interactive,
fleeting, and ultimately interpenetrated—which I have been
describing. In this context it makes sense that in Pansy's image the identity of the particular figures is immaterial. It is
relativized, even obliterated (in any case, made unrecognizable), *by* their animation. In addition, although menace is
explicit in the image of the saints who "shake [their heads]
at each other," it is more primitively generated by their first
being made to "turn their painted heads," hence, presumably, to *look* at each other. For looking *out*, and then *at* each
other, in the chapter as a whole—and in distinction to the
encapsulated moments in the Preface "which go on without
[Isabel's] being approached by another person"—is itself
associated with aggression. Hence when, returning to the
parlor, Isabel sees that Merle's "own eyes covered [her]
face" (2.379), the verb poses a threat, as if Merle's vision
could envelop as well as pass over her countenance. That
Isabel remains at the mercy of Merle's vision—putatively
comprehensive here—is reiterated when Isabel's dismissal
of Merle is itself dismissed by the fact that only a moment
earlier Merle has had something still to tell her: that Isabel
owes her fortune to Ralph as well as to Merle; that two de-
ceptions rather than one have been practiced on Isabel. Although the scene I have been considering forcibly challenges
the assumptions implicit in the exemplary chapter of the
midnight vigil, consciousness is similarly undermined in
other significant contexts in the novel.

Consciousness has nothing to do with what happens in
the novel. It does not take Osmond away from Isabel, and it
does not give her Goodwood. Its value is intrinsic. Moreover
it is not simply that consciousness does not materialize in action. It more disturbingly leads nowhere, even on its own
terms. Thus, although in the following passage, Isabel will
imagine a future in which her integrity can survive Osmond's attempts to annihilate it, she will ultimately conclude that such confidence is vain. More fundamentally,
thinking seems vain because it has no consequences:

> Deep in her soul—deeper than any appetite for renun-
> ciation—was the sense that life would be her business
> for a long time to come. And at moments there was
> something inspiring, almost enlivening, in the convic-
> tion. It was a proof of strength—it was a proof she
> should some day be happy again. It couldn't be she
> was to live only to suffer; she was still young, after all,
> and a great many things might happen to her yet. To
> live only to suffer—only to feel the injury of life re-
> peated and enlarged—it seemed to her she was too
> valuable, too capable, for that. Then she wondered if it
> were vain and stupid to think so well of herself. When
> had it even been a guarantee to be valuable? Wasn't all
> history full of the destruction of precious things?
> Wasn't it much more probable that if one were fine one
> would suffer? It involved then perhaps an admission
> that one had a certain grossness; but Isabel recognised,
> as it passed before her eyes, the quick vague shadow of
> a long future. She should never escape; she should last
> to the end. Then the middle years wrapped her about
> again and the grey curtain of her indifference closed
> her in. (2.392–93)

It is not, I think, clear how the sentence at the passage's
turning point is disjunctive. "It involved then perhaps an
admission that one had a certain grossness; but Isabel recognised, as it passed before her eyes, the quick vague shadow
of a long future." By light of the whole paragraph, "but"
contradicts the surmise that, as all of history is "full of the
destruction of precious things," Isabel will be sacrificed. Yet
the two parts of the sentence are more immediately at odds,
and with respect to a different contradiction. If "it" refers

vaguely to Isabel's inchoate sense that she is complicit in her destruction ("it involved then . . . an admission"), what is being contested locally is the idea that admission and recognition (whose order here seems backward) will *change* what they acknowledge, purchasing not just endurance but a sense of its significance. What the "but" gainsays is that expectation. In Isabel's calculation, where "being destroyed" and "lasting" are synonymous, discrimination is superfluous. Because recognition leads not to revelation but rather to psychic blackout, James is again reversing the traditional conception of consciousness as beneficial, as he and George Eliot have in their respective ways defined it. Life may ultimately be given to sustain "the quick vague shadow of a long future," but here consciousness rather takes things away and is itself taken away in the stupor to which all vision cedes.

In addition, consciousness, whatever its value, is not the primary means through which the novel delivers meanings. Thus we know Isabel's feelings about Warburton, when he proposes to marry Pansy, not from what Isabel thinks, but rather from the picture James gives us of the two characters as they regard one another:

> Not for an instant should he suspect her of detecting in his proposal of marrying her step-daughter an implication of increased nearness to herself. . . . In that brief, extremely personal gaze, however, deeper meanings passed between them than they were conscious of at the moment. (2.221)

The description exemplifies no point of view (not Warburton's and not Isabel's). Alternatively put, it renders James's point of view of what an "understanding" looks like when it is simultaneously shared and seen at a distance. In the passage cited above meanings are *below* consciousness and *between* persons.

What is being revised in the Preface to *Portrait* is our conception of how consciousness operates in the novel, for the representation of consciousness and the claims made on its behalf differ from each other specifically with respect to its privileged status—whether privilege be conferred by James's assertion that he has assigned it more prominence than that previously afforded it in novelistic tradition; whether it be conferred by testimony, contradicted by the representation in the novel that follows, which suggests that consciousness, independent of knowledge or sight, can achieve a transcendent status; or whether, as a corollary of the preceding point, it be conferred by the explicit claim that meanings in the novel are primarily contingent on Isabel's introspection conceived as an enclosed phenomenon. Consciousness might even be a neutral term for *The Portrait of a Lady* were it not otherwise charged by James's dictates in the Preface.

In those moments when consciousness is not enclosed, its essence is blurred and so disputed, though not in the primitive terms that register indiscriminately in *Roderick Hudson*. *How* then? As they regard each other, Isabel's thought of Merle and Merle's thought of Isabel are not clearly separable, even if only because what preoccupies each is the thought of the other. In the image of the "saints in the great picture," Pansy's thought of Isabel and Osmond is not Pansy's thought. And it is not, as I have argued, most immediately about Isabel and Osmond. Then what is challenged in those moments when consciousness is not completely inner is identity itself: to whom thought *belongs* (which "lady"— Isabel or Merle?) and to whom it *refers*. One could of course claim that the identity of thought is not disputed in any actual sense. Isabel and Merle are obviously differentiated, and Isabel's fantasy is not in fact her stepdaughter's. But identity is absolutely disputed in an affective sense. In the chapter I have been focusing on, James overwhelms the reader with a series of epithets that undermine the determinate conception of identity on which the very value of the novel, as understood by the Preface, has been predicated. Thus, standing before Merle, Isabel witnesses herself only, if momentarily, as Merle sees her, as "the phantom of [Merle's] exposure" (2.379). Thus, visiting Pansy, Isabel observes that the strictures of the convent exact "the surrender of a personality" (2.382), presumably Pansy's. Thus, looking away from Merle in a passage cited in part earlier, Isabel sees the woman's betrayal of her:

> On the other side of the window lay the garden of the convent; but this is not what she saw; she saw nothing

of the budding plants and the glowing afternoon. She
saw, in the crude light of that revelation which had already become a part of experience and to which the
very frailty of the vessel in which it had been offered
her only gave an intrinsic price, the dry staring fact that
she had been an applied handled hung-up tool. . . .
(2.379)

"Frail vessel" is James's phrase (or "Eliot's") in the Preface
for Isabel as the sole or primary bearer of consciousness. But
in the passage above the same phrase refers ambiguously or
simultaneously to Merle standing before Isabel, in the person
of whom consciousness has been "offered" or fleshed out
for her. It also pertains to the Countess Gemini, on whom
Isabel's "revelation" first crucially depends. And the phrase
refers to Isabel's own consciousness, imaged above as an
embodied phenomenon, which pays an intrinsic price—the
loss of the intrinsic—for Isabel's knowledge of consciousness's reliance on both of these figures. Thus the integrity of
consciousness, its ethical wholeness or intactness, defined
by its containment in the metaphor of the "frailty of the vessel," is, in the chapter I have been examining and in the
novel as a whole, broken down or violated. What is disturbing about that is not its fact, deftly executed in the ways I
have been suggesting, but rather that its fact is contested
years later by James in the Preface. Why should this be so?
Why should consciousness have integrity only if it has autonomy? To put this question differently, as *What Maisie
Knew* does, What is the specific nature of the conflict when
consciousness is understood to be, as of course it is, intersubjective or relational?

IV

In the Preface to *What Maisie Knew* James singles out scenes
which are "to emerge and prevail—vivid, special, wrought
hard, to the hardness of the unforgettable" (xii) because they
register only by light of the child's consciousness to which
they matter:

> The infant mind would at the best leave great gaps and
> voids; so that with a systematic surface possibly be-
> yond reproach we should nevertheless fail of clearness
> of sense. I should have to stretch the matter to what
> my wondering witness materially and inevitably *saw*; a

> great deal of which quantity she either wouldn't under-
> stand at all or would quite misunderstand—and on
> those lines, only on those, my task would be prettily
> cut out. (ix–x)

By light of the passage cited above, the deficiency of
Maisie's consciousness is a consequence of her age. Hence
she is unable fully to comprehend the relations to which she
is subjected. But by light of other passages in the Preface,
the limitation of Maisie's consciousness is not a consequence
of James's subject, the depiction of a child's mind. It is
rather a consequence of his understanding that consciousness is a more complex, more restricted and contingent phenomenon than he has initially portrayed it. In line with this
second supposition, and from the vantage of other quotations in the Preface, the limitations of consciousness are intrinsic, with tension arising from the shifting barrier between consciousness and repression.* In the Preface, in the
context of this shiftiness, not knowing is a general case, only
epitomized by the child:

> The effort really to see and really to represent is no idle
> business in face of the *constant* force that makes for
> muddlement. The great thing is indeed that the mud-
> dled state too is one of the very sharpest of the reali-
> ties, that it also has colour and form and charac-
> ter. . . . For nobody to whom life at large is *easily*
> interesting do the finer, the shyer, the more anxious
> small vibrations, fine and shy and anxious with the
> passion that precedes knowledge, succeed in being
> negligible. . . . (xiii–xiv)

In the following pages I shall be examining different accounts of what produces the "muddled state." For if one

*James himself on the novel's third page uses the word "unconscious" to
mean "unwitting." Yet the child's blindness as it is described in the Preface
and represented in the novel often seems more adequately accommodated
by the explicitly Freudian notion of an unconscious, which designates content that is buried. Thus, although the adults think that "either from extreme cunning or from extreme stupidity, she appeared not to take things
in" (15), James, a few sentences later, corrects that idea ("She saw more and
more; she saw too much"), setting it immediately straight that for Maisie
not to take things in has nothing to do with the child's not *seeing* them. By
light of such passages tension exists between "those parts of her experience
that she understands" and those that "darken off into others that she rather
tormentedly misses" (x), as James officiates a connection between opacity
and pain.

way to construe James's assertion that Maisie's consciousness has limits is in terms of the child's sentimentalized
innocence (she lacks the experience to understand the immoral relations between her stepparents), another competing way to understand those limits is to see them in terms of
the dynamic relation between consciousness and unconsciousness. I shall suggest that these disparate accounts of
the deficiency of Maisie's consciousness—one externally
generated by what others conspire to keep from her or by
what she is unable to understand, the other contingent on
what she *will* know, in the sense of having volition to—depend on different spatializations of consciousness, different
pictures of where it is. Thus, although the Preface and the
novel, in distinction to those discussed earlier, are in accord
with each other (specifically, they agree about the *deficiency*
of consciousness, its inadequacy to apprehend the reality it
needs to), both also predicate different causes to account for
that insufficiency.

What is nerve-racking for the child, as also for the reader,
is the ultimate unclarity of whether Maisie knows too little
or too much about the sexual entanglements among her
stepparents. In this respect, although Mrs. Wix advances the
view that Maisie is "morally at home in atmospheres it
would be appalling to analyse" (205), it is more accurate to
say that she is *actually* at home there. Confusion is created
by others' attempts to manipulate what Maisie knows. Because consciousness and knowledge (traditionally associated
with awareness and with interpretation that is socially codified) are neither identical nor completely separable, the
space between the two is the ground of confusion. It is just
this space which, in opposite terms in the two scenes examined below, the mind would annihilate. Because the result-
ing two pictures—of how consciousness tries to enforce understandings and is itself governed by them—explain
James's conception of how consciousness negotiates with
what is external to it, the scenes are critical.

In the first of these, consciousness projects meanings, as
Maisie tries to coerce her mother's promiscuous relations
into a framework that sanctifies them. By chance meeting
the Captain, one of her mother's lovers, Maisie scripts for
him words that would explain her mother's relation to this

(yet another) strange man. She instructs him: "'Say you love her, Mr. Captain.'" But when he complies ("'Of *course* I love her, damn it, you know!'"), we see that Maisie's own feeling for her mother is suddenly made contingent upon the expression of affection which she has prescribed: "'So do *I* then. I do, I do, I do!'" (153). Maisie has to see the Captain's words as representing his feelings (with which she can then agree), as the reader has to see the same words as representing the child's feelings (which the Captain only uncomfortably parrots). For the vertigo of the passage, like the vertigo of the novel as a whole, depends upon the thin but requisite tissue between events supposed to be objectified and their impression on the child.

When, some time later, Mrs. Farange contemptuously dismisses Maisie's reference to the Captain (now a former lover), what Maisie sees as lost is not only her mother's relationship with the Captain but also *her* relationship with her mother and, as the protest in the following passage suggests, less specifically, herself. For what the Captain represents, and what he has ventriloquized, is *Maisie's* feeling for her mother.

> "He said things—they were beautiful, they were, they were!" She was almost capable of the violence of forcing this home, for even in the midst of her surge of passion—of which in fact it was a part—there rose in her a fear, a pain, a vision ominous, precocious, of what it might mean for her mother's fate to have forfeited such a loyalty as that. There was literally an instant in which Maisie fully saw—saw madness and desolation, saw ruin and darkness and death. "I've thought of him often since, and I hoped it was with him—with him—!" Here, in her emotion, it failed her, the breath of her filial hope. (224–25)

What happens in the conversation with Mrs. Farange is that Maisie embraces her own objectification only to discover its insubstantiality. Actually, in an attempt to tamper with cause and effect, she has tried to project the objectification, to make her feelings into his words and his words testimony to a reality to which she can consent. Mrs. Farange's disdain is powerful because it negates not simply the Captain but, more essentially, that impulse. The moral of the showdown Maisie has with her mother is that consciousness is a mere receptacle for impressions, and that it can itself do nothing but passively receive these. Consciousness cannot assert desires; it can only be impressed upon by them, for at those moments when it attempts otherwise—when, as with the Captain, it aggressively reifies what it feels—it is ultimately blocked and then brutalized.

In the scene between Maisie and the Captain there is initially no conflict because there is no appreciated difference between what is in the mind as desire and what is external to it as fact. Such a fantasized congruence, in which the idea of difference is close to unintelligible, is potentially fatal because the self is deprived of a sense of primary opposition from which it in fact needs protection, the kind of protection specifically facilitated by repression, where the mind forces out of consciousness what it nonetheless "knows" to be true. Hence Maisie's belief about the Captain is at the mercy of Mrs. Farange's contemptuous dismissal, which does to the child what in the second scene, to which I now turn, Maisie, by veiling her own thoughts, does to herself.

When toward the end of the novel Sir Claude, in France, returns home, flaunting a letter from Mrs. Beale, Maisie registers the event by fully repressing the image of her natural father, Mr. Farange (whom Sir Claude has now by his presence fully supplanted), and by suddenly liberating from repression the recollection of Mrs. Beale, her stepmother (of whom—now palpably attached to Sir Claude—she can therefore again afford to think):

> The mere present sight of Sir Claude's face caused her on the spot to drop straight through her last impression of Mr. Farange a plummet that reached still deeper down than the security of these days of flight. She had wrapped that impression in silence—a silence that had parted with half its veil to cover also, from the hour of Sir Claude's advent, the image of Mr. Farange's wife. But if the object in Sir Claude's hand revealed itself as a letter which he held up very high, so there was something in his mere motion that laid Mrs. Beale again bare. (252–53)

The passage is crucial because it exemplifies a paradigmatic action of the novel: wrapping impressions up and, conversely, laying them bare, with the inevitable second connotation of making them visible in the sense of sexually explicit, as in the lewd image of Mrs. Beale exposed or "laid bare." The exposure is of course double, pertaining to what happens to Maisie's mind, as Mrs. Beale is again revealed to it, and pertaining to what happens to Mrs. Beale's body, in Maisie's image of her stepmother. The passage is also crucial because it provides for the first time in James's fiction an overt understanding of the mind as dynamic—actively relating consciousness and unconsciousness, between which thoughts, in this case thoughts with sexual content, unmechanically have commerce. In this reformulation of the problem, what James represents is the hiddenness of charged material, the (to us) visible act of Maisie's submerging of it.

In the first of the scenes consciousness is limited by external constraints, by Maisie's failure to prescribe the nature of Mrs. Farange's relation to the Captain. In the second of the scenes impressions that are veiled and those that are laid bare are oppositely determined by a thought's penetration of the internal barrier between consciousness and repression. But the problem of so anatomizing what controls consciousness, and of specifying to what dichotomy its limitations owe reference, is that these spatializations are belied by the ultimate inseparability of the two contexts. In both of the scenes, the intrinsic and the extrinsic are distinct, to a point. We are meant to mark it.

In fact at many other points in the novel, as if to amend the notion that consciousness is located or delimited inside or outside, it is described as bipartite or double, although the terms of this doubleness do not remain stable. Thus, for example, Maisie's knowledge or consciousness is often accompanied by her inclination to simulate "extreme stupidity [in which] she appeared not to take things in." The concealment from others of what Maisie knows or is conscious of (pretending things are alien when they are actually internal) is explicitly associated with Maisie's discovery of "the idea of an inner self" (15). Still elsewhere, knowledge, referred to as "competence" (95), applies to the ability to understand what one shouldn't know. The questions of too much or too little knowledge or consciousness, of who has it and where it is, of only pretending to have it, or, oppositely, of pretending not to, are repeatedly spatialized in *What Maisie Knew*. Knowledge is out of reach, behind closed doors, in certain recesses, always, in any case, clearly compartmentalized— "Yes, there were matters one couldn't 'go into' with a pupil" (34), Maisie mimics to her French doll, Lisette—and such spatializations testify repeatedly to its double inaccessibility. Knowledge is what others withhold from you or you from others, and (as the ventriloquized conversation Maisie has with her doll suggests) knowledge is what you withhold— won't go into—with yourself. What is pertinent about these examples is not Maisie's knowledge, but rather her perception of its limitations.

Limitation, however generated, is in fact the most severe consequence of the separateness of one consciousness from another, of the mind from the relations it contemplates. By the time James writes *Maisie*, then, consciousness is at once disabled and made volatile with reference to that separateness. Since the domain, the authority, the potency of consciousness—what it can do, and with reference to which issues—is at the heart of the Prefaces' reconception of the early novels, *Maisie* potentially throws light on the problematic of revision I have been investigating. In *Maisie* thought takes place in a double arena, in that thoughts are shown to conflict with each other; in that obscuring a thought from oneself and obscuring it from another are separate cancellations; in that the attempt to control another's thought is complemented by the knowledge of the futility of the enterprise; in that consciousness for the self and consciousness for others are repeatedly differentiated. That the various states of knowing represented in the novel should be proximate, conjunctive, *and* not confused is the particular discovery James makes in *Maisie*. One last example, which takes place after Sir Claude receives a wire indicating that Mrs. Wix has been dispatched by Mrs. Farange to attend to her daughter, illustrates how consciousness in the self and consciousness for others, concurrent states, nonetheless escape the entanglement manifested in the earlier novels. As much to the point, however, the passage also insists that just the discriminations James makes on behalf of consciousness result in confusions about how the multiple contexts with which consciousness is associated are connected. In the conversation that follows between Maisie and Sir Claude, knowledge is what is "between" Maisie and her stepfather, not what she has *got:*

> "[Mrs. Wix] has seen your mother." . . .
>
> "Then she hasn't gone?"
>
> "Your mother?— to South Africa? I give it up, dear boy," Sir Claude said; and she seemed literally to see him give it up as he stood there and with a kind of absent gaze—absent, that is, from *her* affairs—followed the fine stride and shining limbs of a young fishwife who had just waded out of the sea with her basketful of shrimps. His thought came back to her sooner than his eyes. "But I dare say it's all right. She wouldn't come if it wasn't, poor old thing: she knows rather well what she's about."
>
> This was so reassuring that Maisie, after turning it over, could make it fit into her dream. "Well, what *is* she about?"
>
> He finally stopped looking at the fishwife—he met his companion's inquiry. "Oh you know!" There was something in the way he said it that made, between them, more of an equality than she had yet imagined; but it had also more the effect of raising her up than of letting him down, and what it did with her was shown by the sound of her assent.
>
> "Yes—I know!" What she knew, what she *could* know is by this time no secret to us: it grew and grew at any rate, the rest of that day, in the air of what he took for granted. It was better that he should do that than attempt to test her knowledge. . . . (235–36)

The passage records a series of discrepancies. They exist between the girl child and " 'dear boy,' " the stepfather's cool misdesignation for her. Between Sir Claude's idiom of exasperation, " 'I give it up,' " indicating the hopelessness of Ida's behavior or the hopelessness of Maisie's ignorance of it, and her interpretation of his words which visualizes, not inaccurately, an actual abandonment. Between the return of his thought and the delayed return of his eyes. Most dramatically, between Sir Claude's insistence that Maisie understand Mrs. Wix's reason for joining them in France (Mrs. Wix is infatuated with him) and Maisie's obliviousness to the sexual innuendo that would clarify such a motive. The discrepancies are important, for the passage variously, unmistakably, devastatingly anatomizes the conditions that secure the child's and the man's so-called equality. Maisie does not know what Sir Claude is talking about. Yet she rightly thinks that Sir Claude trusts her to understand him and that, moreover, he *supposes* she does so. Perfectly cognizant of the falseness of the supposition, she nonetheless relishes the privilege it affords her. She is therefore grateful to him for his selfish misassessment of her. In these distinct ways, the knowledge or consciousness Maisie has (in this passage the two words, though close, are not synonymous) and the knowledge that Maisie and Sir Claude share are not only disjunct; they are at odds with each other. For while Sir Claude knows what Mrs. Wix is "about," Maisie knows the categorical difference (between pretending to know and doing so) that he remains blind to.

In the previous passage, then, unlike those from *Maisie* I examined earlier, in which knowing is simply one-directional, or at best double, involving a bipartite operation, here consciousness and knowledge seem conceptually incoherent, unable to bear up under too much referentiality. This is just to say that the sweep of phenomena to which the idea of knowledge pertains is difficult to itemize. Knowledge is "in" the man, and it is differently "in" the child. But, as it also applies to what each supposes of the other and, still again, to the verbal equivocation through which such suppositions sound, it is, in yet further ways, also "between" them. It is just because of the discriminations on which James here insists that we are thwarted from understanding what the reiterated word "know" (and the idea of consciousness for which it sometimes doubles) means exactly. For "knowledge" as it refers to what Sir Claude has himself (or to what he expects of Maisie), "knowledge" as it connotes what Maisie desires to have for Sir Claude (but also what she actually possesses), and, finally, "knowledge" as it applies to the verbal negotiations which conciliate the above are categorically incommensurate. In this case the problem is not only too many permutations on related phenomena, but more the incomparability of their statuses. What is at stake in the passage's mazelike confusions, then, is not only Sir

Claude's presumption, or the child's acquiescence in it, but also our own bafflement about the relation among states that are not logically comparable.

The passage's proliferation of contexts for consciousness and knowledge is akin to that of the whole novel. While James frequently uses the word "knowledge" as a synonym for "consciousness," in fact, as I have noted, the conflict in the novel depends on understanding the difference between the state of consciousness (designating simple awareness in need of social tutelage) and the state of knowledge (designating understanding schooled by conventional agreement). Yet in particular instances the distinction is less rigid than this way of formulating it suggests. For at times consciousness is represented as a phenomenon in which the self comprehends the idea of knowledge in lieu of its fact (as when Maisie, talking to Sir Claude, "knows" she doesn't understand him), raising the question of whether, in such a state, she *has* knowledge or not.

In line with this unclarity, James's emphasis can be on what Maisie knows, however incompletely, as in the meeting with Sir Claude. At other times his emphasis can be on what she is conscious of, as in the unveiling of Mrs. Beale or in the exchange with the Captain. As these examples indicate, consciousness itself is defined volatilely. With respect to the Captain, it is defined in opposition to knowledge. With respect to Mrs. Beale, it is defined in opposition to unconsciousness. In either case, much like knowledge, consciousness is fetishized as comprehensible. It is portrayed as something the child could eventually gain access to, even as the idea of mastery, given the forces that oppose both knowledge and consciousness, is disputed categorically by the ontology portrayed by the novel. I am in fact struck by how the repetitions of the words "know" and "knowledge" in *Maisie* (repetitions whose meaning must survive shifting connotations) finally seem symptomatic of general incoherence, of the fact that James understands the conception of knowledge—that which is external to consciousness—as crucial without simultaneously seeing how to negotiate connections between knowledge and consciousness or, as I shall suggest, between knowledge and relations. Even, or especially, the last sentence of the novel ("[Mrs. Wix] still

had room for wonder at what Maisie knew") intones a form
of the word "knowledge" as it has been incanted many
times earlier, but now renders its meaning definitively eva-
sive. For in the novel's last sentence, as in its frequent itera-
tion throughout, emphasis and unclarity, corollaries of each
other, are the written equivalent of the process whereby
continued vocalization of a word obliterates its meaning.

In addition to being unclearly differentiated from knowledge, consciousness is opposed to the relations it contemplates. However simplistic, on the one hand, and cryptic, on
the other, this opposition as formulated, it is meant to
accommodate the fact that in *Maisie* we observe the child
witnessing what she is prevented from experiencing. Thus
consciousness and relations are, to the extent possible or
imaginable, dichotomized. This dichotomy is central to the
novel. In fact the novel ends when the sexual content of
Maisie's thoughts, however transgressive, is impossible to
repress. At that point Maisie comes to understand the exclu-
sions which define her dilemma: that consciousness is separate from relations (consciousness can take in or register
only what it is prevented from having) and that filial relations preclude sexual ones. In that moment Maisie, hounded
by her stepfather's, Sir Claude's, request that she abandon
her governess and come away to live with him and Mrs.
Beale (her presence would legitimize their immoral relations), invokes on her own behalf the principle at the heart
of his request: that relationship is a choice which ostracizes
others. She asks the same thing of him: whether he will
leave Mrs. Beale to come away and live alone with her:

> she had even a mental picture of the stepfather and
> the pupil established in a little place in the South while
> the governess and the stepmother, in a little place in
> the North, remained linked by a community of blank-
> ness. . . . (343)

To be refused by Sir Claude, as his silence assures her she
will be, is to be completely abandoned by him, since it is
only in terms of the exclusiveness he here denies her that
Maisie sees people "have" each other. What she "knows" at
the end is that filial and sexual relations are incompatible.
The always shifting line between consciousness and uncon-

sciousness marks the boundary between them. Another way to put this is to say that the commerce between the sexual and the filial can become conscious only when any actual connection between the two has been definitively ruled out—a recognition I take James to record on the novel's last page, where we are told of Maisie and Sir Claude, "their eyes met as the eyes of those who have done for each other what they can." What Maisie sees, looking at Sir Claude, is the limits of her relation with him, consequently its end.

In *Maisie*, then, James provides no single context for defining consciousness, a fact partly to be understood in terms of the representational complexity achieved in the later work. Yet these multiple contexts for consciousness are not, as I have argued, brought into coherent relation. In addition, as noted, in *Maisie* relation itself is made alternative to consciousness. In this respect the proposition implicitly advanced by the Prefaces to the early novels (that one consciousness is to be conceived as alternative to another) is supplanted in *Maisie* by the (also implicit) proposition that consciousness is to be conceived as alternative to relations. And the latter proposition (consciousness construed as alternative to relations), which could be said to lie at the heart of James's late novels, is itself unacceptable, or itself incomprehensible, albeit on different grounds.

In *Roderick Hudson* "relations stop nowhere," in the lack of differentiation among its characters' plights in the novel, as in speculation about them in one of the paragraphs of its Preface. In *Portrait* relations are said to stop absolutely because the outer scene is extinguished by the inner, though when Isabel and Merle meet toward the end of the novel (as in the other scenes examined), the separation is threatened. What is noteworthy about *Maisie* in light of the issues raised by the earlier works is not that it ultimately separates consciousness and knowledge or consciousness and relations (how could it do so?), but rather that it immediately, and temporarily, separates those phenomena. So doing, it exposes or lays bare what might be at stake in investigating the connection between consciousness and knowledge, between consciousness and unconsciousness, between consciousness and relations, and—this is crucial—it stops short of doing so. For what is important about the moments I have singled out for emphasis in *Maisie* is that they epitomize, and more to the point *recognize,* that as consciousness and relations are not in fact identical, something must be worked out specifically "between" persons, as Maisie does with the Captain, as Sir Claude does with Maisie, even while the confusions to which I have pointed prohibit our understanding of how this is to be accomplished. In a sense the novel's end is testimony to the prohibition, because when consciousness *does* comprehend relations, what it sees as a consequence of its difference from them is that the latter must be forfeited. Because of the categorical confusions in *Maisie* the novel stops short of investigating how what is "in" the self and what is "between" persons can find ground to negotiate meanings. In the context of the failure, utterances that enforce meaning through expressions of belief ("'Say you love her, Mr. Captain'") and utterances that discard meanings through expressions of incredulity ("'I give it up, dear boy'") are virtually identical. They are so because when the mind is only insisting on interpretations or when it is only dismissing them, what is demonstrated is despair at the separateness of other minds, which can only therefore be coerced or petitioned.

One way of interpreting the two Prefaces I have considered would be to see them as correcting not just the novels they introduce but also the confusions by which James is inundated in a novel like *Maisie,* which represents the complications of consciousness unharnessed by prescriptive declarations about it. Here I do not mean to argue that the Prefaces are explicitly a response to the particular novel *Maisie.* Rather that they might be regarded as a response to the confusions introduced in such a novel.[14] By the time James writes *Maisie,* he desires consciousness to have powers which he sees it does not have. One way of satisfying that desire is simply to reify it, to write it into being in the Prefaces to the earlier novels, for the subject of consciousness must be introduced, must first be present, before it can be addressed. That the Prefaces to *Roderick Hudson* (1907), *The American* (1907), *Portrait* (1908) should turn their backs on the complications acknowledged by *Maisie* (1897) and, even more ostentatiously, on those acknowledged in *The Golden Bowl* (1904)[15] is surprising only if one expects the consistency from fictional examinations of consciousness that is ostensibly achieved by an evolving scientific theory scrutinizing the "same" subject. Yet James himself cultivates this expectation. He does so in the dictate from "The Art of Fiction," "Try to be one of the people on whom nothing is lost,"[16] appealing for its supposition that consciousness is a phenomenon that could be *compiled*. He does so in the prescriptive, almost ritualistically insistent formulas invoked in each Preface, like that from *Portrait of a Lady*, "Tell me what the artist is, and I will tell you of what he has *been* conscious" (xi).* In the Prefaces, as in the declaration from *Portrait,* consciousness, for all the fanfare on its behalf, is subordinated and made secondary to James's rationalized propositions about it. The idea behind the implicit conditional in *Portrait* is that one could create, and not only in a sentence, just such a formula by which consciousness—circumscribed, represented as pure manifest content—could entirely, visibly, separately be delineated.

V

I have argued that the Prefaces and novels remain in contest with each other. Yet James's work continues to epitomize the idea of consciousness as a unified phenomenon. James himself, of course, recuperates such a notion of consciousness in the Prefaces, as I have been describing them, and the Prefaces become massively entrenched in the project of that reclamation.[17] But then, with exceptions, the interpretive community follows suit, as if what it were reading were the Prefaces not the novels. Thus James, himself one of his own first critics, tries to reconstruct and retain a totalized consciousness which the fictions themselves will not sustain. In

*What is noteworthy about that declaration is the counterintuitive order of its clauses. Everything preceding the paragraph, and any logical assumption about the kind of hypothesis postulated, suggests that the two-part conditional should be specified conversely: If you tell me of what the artist has been conscious, I will tell you who or what he is. Yet however perplexing the disorder I am describing, it is exactly consonant with the wilfulness of the Prefaces, taking in hand as they do, rectifying as they can, the kind of confusion manifested in a novel like *Maisie*.

conclusion, I want to extrapolate from my discussion of particular novels reasons why the consciousnesses represented there are, even for Henry James, so difficult to conventionalize.

James's Prefaces psychologize the idea of consciousness by imagining it as centered, subjective, internal, and unitary. They stabilize a connection between consciousness and the self by asserting that the self is where consciousness resides. The representations of consciousness in the novels contradict that placement. What they critique, however, is not the idea of consciousness, but rather the idea of consciousness that has been psychologized. In the novels I have described, consciousness is not stable, not subjective, not interior, not unitary, as James's Prefaces claim. But it is also, as a consequence, not dismissed or deconstructed. Rather it is disseminated. In the novels consciousness is not in persons; it is rather between them, whether this manifests itself between Rowland and Roderick, or Isabel and Pansy, or Isabel and Merle, or between Maisie and Sir Claude. Thus, although the Prefaces attempt to revise or redetermine our conception of consciousness, the more radical revision is advanced by the novels themselves, in James's structural reconceptions of consciousness. For in the novels consciousness is disengaged from the self. It is reconceived as extrinsic, made to take shape—indeed, to become social—as an *inter*subjective phenomenon.[18] What is radical about this reconception is that it dispenses with the idea of a psychology while preserving the idea of a consciousness.[19] In fact, it valorizes consciousness just to the extent that consciousness can be separated from the confines of a self.

To italicize the extraordinariness of Henry James's position—consciousness is not defined in terms of subjectivity, but it is therefore as a consequence also not dismissed—I want to contrast it with one held by William James in a piece first published in 1904, and reprinted posthumously in *Essays in Radical Empiricism* (1912), "Does 'Consciousness' Exist?"[20] In that essay, William James argues that consciousness is not to be defined in relation to a center for which self is the name. Rather, " 'consciousness' . . . is an affair of relations, it falls outside not inside the single experience" (7). Henry James would agree. But William James's conclusion from that assumption is more predictable or conventional.[21] If consciousness can be proved not to be subjective, it can also be proved not to be at all. William James therefore answers the question in his own title explicitly in the negative. There is no such thing as consciousness because there are no properties specifically intrinsic to it. There is, he says, "no aboriginal stuff . . . of which material objects are made, out of which our thoughts of them are made" (4). And there is no "one element, moment, factor—call it what you like—of an experience of essentially dualistic inner constitution, from which, if you abstract the content, the consciousness will remain revealed to its own eye" (6). If this sounds extreme, William James is quick to clarify. He is denying neither the existence of thought nor the function of knowing; he is, however, insisting that both thought and knowing *are* what he calls "functions," not entities in or of themselves. Thus, for example, as the passage cited above suggests, it is impossible to subtract "content" from "consciousness" and to be left with anything. In fact, knowing is a matter of addition, or intersection, not of subtraction. It is so because a single experience, in one context, may be a state of mind (subjective), whereas, in another context, it may be a thing known (objective). Paint serves to exemplify the general proposition. In a shop, paint seems a commodity, an object or a thing. On a canvas, it seems expressive; it signifies as a thought. For William James the point about the paint is that it is material, and that it is the *same* material, though differently apprehended on the shelf of the shop (as a thing) than on the picture of a canvas (as a thought) (7). Proposing that such unitariness also holds true at a single moment of perception (for, although contexts can "double up," any actual experience is always itself indivisible), William James asks the reader to visualize a room. As a subjective phenomenon, the room will disappear if you close your eyes. As an objective one, a gang of men or an earthquake is required to demolish it. Yet the point about the room is that, although the physical and mental associations that accrue to it are incompatible ("in the real world, fire will consume it. In your mind, you can let fire play over it without effect" [9]), still, the perceptual object (the room) is not a thing "within" but rather must be understood to have its single reality outside the self. There is no separate object hidden inside the thinking subject. Even a *remembered* room (a room from the past) is no less external than the one viewed in the present, for the origin of the memory is also "outside." Hallucinations, of course, have no actuality, but if they did, William James contends, the golden mountains and centaurs would exist "'off there' in fairy land, and not 'inside' of ourselves" (11).

In each of these examples there is no separation of experience into consciousness and content. Subjective and objective are functional attributes only; knowing connotes a relation to experience, not a second or separate experience. Indeed, for William James, the significant difference between percepts and concepts, on the one hand, and objects, on the other, is that the former have no consequences, hence, he concludes, no reality:

> Mental fire is what won't burn real sticks; mental water is what won't necessarily (though of course it may) put out even a mental fire. Mental knives may be sharp, but they won't cut real wood. Mental triangles are pointed, but their points won't wound. With "real" objects, on the contrary, consequences always accrue. (17)

"Does 'Consciousness' Exist?" concludes with one definitive assertion: "the stream of thinking . . . is only a careless name for what, when scrutinized, reveals itself to consist chiefly of the stream of my breathing" (19). Breath is William James's triumphant example because, in a reduction conceived as a transcendence, it hierarchically reverses the priority and the derivation of the spiritual and the material. It insists that matter precedes spirit, or that spirit *is* matter:

> breath, which was ever the original of "spirit," breath moving outwards, between the glottis and the nostrils, is, I am persuaded, the essence out of which philosophers have constructed the entity known to them as consciousness. *That entity is fictitious, while thoughts in the concrete are fully real. But thoughts in the concrete are made of the same stuff as things are.* (19)

The passage is extraordinary on a number of counts. First, it is produced as a final retort to the imagined cry of disbelief from imagined, obstreperous readers, who say that they know consciousness exists because they *feel* it within them.

The answer that introduces the passage above is "I, too, have my intuitions" (19)—intuition now being called upon as the very authority that seems to have been dismissed, or in any case discounted, in the scientific debate about the oneness of thought and thing. Here it is as if, since demonstrations are to be supplanted by intuitions, on those grounds, too, William James's contention holds. Second, the intuition depends upon the predication of a first entity or thing: of breath extricated from spirit, and made to be prior to it, or of breath exemplifying spirit and made to be inseparable from it. For "breath . . . was ever the original of spirit" is deliberately ambiguous, implying both "comes before" and "is one with." But, although William James wants the ambiguity so that if there is a priority, it is clear which comes first, he also wants the ambiguity resolved. For, if breath, which is material, is a first entity, indivisible from spirit, then consciousness has been falsely abstracted from *it*. Consciousness has been gratuitously introduced as an unreal, second entity which divides and interiorizes what is essentially concrete, external, and *whole*. There would be more to say about this passage in its own right, but for the purposes of comparison, the point to be made is that for William James, once consciousness can be shown to be something "out" there, dissociated from subjectivity (the room is in the house not in the mind; the stream is of breath rather than of consciousness; both are material and both are external), it can conclusively be demonstrated not to exist as an entity at all.

In arguing that consciousness does not exist because the stuff of which it is made is outside the self, William James wants to preserve a psychology of experience dissociated from the idea of consciousness. He is scientifically attacking the conditions of a psychology that isolates consciousness, allies it with a self, and falsely conceives it as anterior and interior. In arguing that consciousness *does* exist, and commands attention, because the stuff of which it is made is outside the self, Henry James wants to preserve the idea of consciousness salvaged from a psychology. For the Henry James of the novels, if consciousness is not semioticized, not associated with subjectivity or interiority, it is not, as a consequence, made to disappear. Rather it is freed up. What is dizzying about the two notions, viewed in proximity, is not simply that the same premise, that consciousness is outside the self, leads to opposite conclusions (for William James it is done away with by the materialism that consumes it; for Henry James consciousness exists in a realm that cannot be touched by a materialist account) but, as much to the point, that each James is intent on rendering the mind—and in William James's case the body—that enclosure from which consciousness is liberated, even in fact purged. For whether the conclusion is materialism or its antithesis, exhilaration attends the extrication of consciousness from the self, in general, and from the body, in particular.

The question of where consciousness is placed, not generally in relation to the self but specifically in relation to the body, returns me, in closing, to the issue of dictation raised at the beginning of my chapter. Perhaps the reason that for Henry James there is so little difference between the writing of his novels and the dictation of them ("only the difference . . . that I walk up and down," only a difference that is "material and illusory") is that consciousness—at least the representation of consciousness in the novels—is not associated with interiority. It is not, as it is for Eugene O'Neill, intrinsically and inevitably associated with the self. To recall the passage in which Gelb and Gelb report that after O'Neill developed Parkinson's disease he could not make the transition from the writing of his novels to the dictation of them:

> O'Neill attempted to dictate his thoughts to Carlotta [his wife] but found it impossible. Thinking that perhaps the mere presence of another person . . . was the stumbling block, Carlotta bought him a recording machine. They experimented . . . O'Neill reading passages . . . into the machine from different distances and playing back the results; but, though he mastered the technique of the machine, his mind could not function creatively when he was left alone with it. An electric typewriter was tried but that, too, proved useless. His thoughts, he told Carlotta, flowed from his brain, through his arm and into his pencil; there was no other process by which he could write.

It is interesting to contemplate O'Neill's implicit assumption that different distances from the recording machine will affect what he is able to think, whether he is able to think,

or if the thoughts that he has can be picked up or transmit-
ted. Being in right relation to the recording machine implies
a kind of reverse psychokinesis, in that it is O'Neill's self or
his thought (rather than the machine) that he needs to get
operating. Whether he can do so depends on his discovering
the specific position or angle from which he can transmit
thoughts and, prior to that process, from which he can *have*
them. Thoughts, in this context, are like electronic signals in
relation to an aerial. Or to alter the analogy, one more time,
for none of these is quite right—and none as bizarre as the
conception I am analogizing—thoughts are like uranium in
relation to a Geiger counter, not simply palpable but also
only perceptible, only even present, if the machine is in the
right proximity to the self from which they originate.
O'Neill, as described above, epitomizes the extreme plight
of a self victimized by the belief that thoughts are at once
material *and* internal, since the end of the thought seems literally equivalent to the end of its contact with the body in
which it originates. For O'Neill, who stopped being able to
write his plays when he stopped being able to write them
down, consciousness flows from the brain, through the arm,
into the pencil, and onto the paper, where it ends. For the
Henry James of the novels, as for his characters, that is
where it starts: at the limits of the self, it is ultimately defined by its sweep or its range. Outside and between persons, therefore undemarcated, consciousness may be said to
be or begin.

THREE

Thinking Speaking: *The Golden Bowl* and the Production of Meaning

As Amerigo watches Maggie Verver place on the chimney-piece the fragments of the smashed crystal, "dashed boldly to the ground" moments earlier by Fanny Assingham, prose in *The Golden Bowl* suffers recognizable convolutions:

> "Yes, look, look," she seemed to see him hear her say even while her sounded words were other—"look, look, both at the truth that still survives in that smashed evidence and at the even more remarkable appearance that I'm not such a fool as you supposed me. Look at the possibility that since I *am* different there may still be something in it for you—if you're capable of working with me to get that out. Consider of course as you must the question of what you may have to surrender on your side, what price you may have to pay, whom you may have to pay *with*, to set this advantage free; but take in at any rate that there *is* something for you if you don't too blindly spoil your chance for it."
> . . . And her uttered words meanwhile were different enough from those he might have inserted between the lines of her already-spoken. "It's the golden bowl, you know, that you saw at the little antiquario's in Bloomsbury. . . ." (2.187–88)

When critics of Henry James's novel have discussed utterances like "'Yes, look, look,'" where inferences enclosed in quotation marks bear all the signs of quotation except that they are never spoken, they have blurred the categorical distinction between thinking and speaking by suggesting that there is no difference between the two (because talking becomes a way of thinking out loud). Or by suggesting that there is no difference between thinking and overhearing another's thinking (because the unspoken utterances are indeterminately attributable to the character who imagines them and to the one to whom they are assigned). Or by suggesting that thinking replaces speaking (because it is by thinking rather than by speaking that Maggie can secure the neutral space in which to rearrange relationships).[1] Most of the characterizations I have summarily depicted arrive at their descriptions of the unspoken utterances without specifically examining them. Indeed critics have license for this omission because the object of their attention is not the unspoken utterances but rather the moral, epistemological, and realistic implications of the plot in whose service the utterances are being interpreted. Thus in a moral context it is argued that "If Maggie is finally to have the golden bowl 'as it was to have been' . . . she must defeat Charlotte without disturbing the peace." In an epistemological context: that since speaking is a measure of knowing, which characters resist, "the full truth . . . is never spoken." In the determination of realism (not, in fact, a separate context, but rather the site of assessments about morality and epistemology): that such utterances demonstrate an aggressive preemption of consciousness over social reality.[2] But while considerations like these are invited by the novel, they are also problematized by it. To accept the story as a story (moral or not) is to accept the conditions which make it work out as it does, and these, I shall explain, are unintelligible. Moreover, it is difficult to protest the terms of this unintelligibility (the subversion of realism) before examining the circumstances which precipitate the unspoken utterances where that subversion is most ostentatiously acted out. And although there is much talk among characters and critics about what is known and by whom—Does Adam Verver know of the adultery? Does Charlotte Stant know of Maggie's discovery of it?—these questions, posed with obsessive frequency, deflect attention from the fact that characters in *The Golden Bowl* are not concerned with what can be known but rather with what can be done. In the realm of knowledge operative notions are those of epistemology or truth. In the realm of meaning the operative notion is that of politics. Truth is how knowledge is measured. Effectiveness is how rhetorical manipulations of meaning are measured. I shall argue that in *The Golden Bowl* the primary concern is not with knowledge but rather with meaning. Thus in examining the novel's unspoken utterances in the pages that follow, I want to ask questions about the politics of interpretation raised by the unspoken utterances which are preliminary to the critical conclusions summarized above.

What compels the radical revision by which the presumed functions of speech and thought appear inverted, so that speech is emptied of significant implication and thought is laden with significance by being imagined as overheard? Why do thought and speech need to exchange properties? And how is it possible to suppose they could do so? In *The Golden Bowl* it often seems as if the measure of a successful thought were its psychic communicability. Yet the novel is charged with a tension between an empowering of consciousness and a contesting of that power. For the issuing of a promissory note on magical access to other minds (akin, say, to the ability to "read" another's mind) is simultaneously called into question by the fact that what is visible, or audible, when a character engages in such scrutiny looks, or sounds, like thought's impenetrability.

In the pages that follow I explore these questions and propositions, suggesting that the relation between thinking and speaking is not static but develops. In section I, I focus on the first half of the novel and primarily on utterances that are spoken. I examine the belief, reiterated in several passages, that one person could speak "for" another in the sense of taking charge of, or dictating, his meanings. In section II, I consider the way in which the novel's second half attempts to correct this mistake by substituting utterances that are thought for those that are spoken. Acknowledging the transgression of speaking "for" another, the novel retreats from the possibility of speaking "meaningfully" at all, and attention shifts from speech to thought. Thus, as in the passage with which I began, characters suppose they have access to each others' minds without reference to their speech. Section III examines the failure of the correction, arguing that the novel's second half elucidates the logical impossibility of escaping the predicament it attempts to correct. These unspoken utterances demonstrate not the audibility of others' thoughts—not magical access to others' minds—but, instead, the ventriloquism of thinking. Here I

take up James's ambivalent responses to the torture of thinking. For at times he appears to predicate as inevitable the
mind's enforcements of its meanings on others, while at
other times he recoils from endorsing that inevitability by
explicitly censuring characters who victimize what they see
by inflicting interpretations on it. I conclude by examining
the novel's title for the way in which, with respect to the
central symbol of the bowl, the reader, like the characters, is
disallowed a neutral relation to the production of meaning.

Throughout these pages I mean to insist on the agency
that my diction will imply. Characters do not only use
speech. To the extent that some communications are kept
out of speech and others thrust into speech, characters can
be said to *assign* a use for speech, and alternately for
thought. Thus characters are operators not actors. In the
first half of the novel Charlotte in particular tries to control
what kinds of things are said and by whom they are said. In
the second half of the novel Maggie in particular tries to control what kinds of things are thought and by whom they are
thought. To ask from what vantage characters suppose they
have the power to dictate these determinations is to point to
a privileged position that is virtually unimaginable, even unintelligible. But it is also to point to the situation which
James coerces us into imagining. Because of this predicament, necessarily consequential, in which characters attempt
to exert power over meanings (over what these meanings
are, over who is to govern them, over whether they are to
be located in speech or in thought), topics customarily addressed in discussions of this novel—knowledge of unlaw-
ful relations, the morality of Maggie's redetermination of
those relations—must be understood as subordinated to a
prior problematic: the (impossible) procedures by which
meanings are assumed by the self and legislated for others.
In examining the novel, I want, then, to consider the conditions of impossibility to which critics who discuss the novel's plot have been made to submit. One way to describe my
own discussion of these characters' attempts to manipulate
communications is as a narrative of the narrative of *The
Golden Bowl,* rather than, for example, as a series of illustrations of attempts to control meaning. But that is not quite
right. For how meaning is determined in the narrative of *The*

Golden Bowl and the narrative of *The Golden Bowl* are, I shall argue, disarticulated from each other.

I

At the beginning of the novel, on the eve of the Prince's wedding, Amerigo and Charlotte embark on the expedition that culminates in the discovery of the golden bowl. They do so, Charlotte tells her former lover, the Prince, so she may search for a wedding present for Maggie, her friend: " 'some little thing . . . absolutely *right*, in its comparative cheapness' " (1.92). At first it appears that the present is a pretext. " 'To have one hour alone with you' " is what Charlotte says she also wants (1.89), an hour, moreover, in which "the absolute secrecy of their little excursion" is "of the essence" (1.94). It makes no sense to distinguish between an actual and an ostensible motive for the outing, however, since the ostensible motive never conceals the actual one or even calls it into question.

But if indeterminacy about motive is only superficial, there is real indeterminacy about a related series of questions: (1) Whom is the present for? While initially Charlotte and Amerigo set about to find something for Maggie, the Prince soon asks Charlotte whether she would receive a present from him. She counters the request by inquiring whether he will allow her to give him a gift. (2) Are giving and receiving necessarily inseparable, so that the recipient of the gift cannot have a passive relation to it? Or can Charlotte, as she claims in the following passage, absolve Amerigo from participating in the illicitness of their time spent together?:

> "I wanted you to understand. I wanted you, that is, to hear. I don't care, I think, whether you understand or not. If I ask nothing of you I don't—I mayn't—ask even so much as that. What you may think of me— that doesn't in the least matter. What I want is that it shall always be with you—so that you'll never be able quite to get rid of it—that I *did*. I won't say that *you* did—you may make as little of that as you like. But that I was here with you where we are and *as* we are— I just saying this. Giving myself, in other words,

away—and perfectly willing to do it for nothing."
(1.97–98)

(3) In the sentence "'What I want is that it shall always be
with you,'" the pronoun designates the time now spent together but already projected into a memory, the passion of
the past, and the gift that will presumably make the two indistinguishable. What remains less clear, remains even questionable, is whether the significance of a shared experience
can be assumed by one person for another and so, as Charlotte implies, be made unreciprocal. Significance and reci-
procity—what something means and whether that meaning
is necessarily mutual—are two subjects that are again
brought together in a conversation between Charlotte and
Amerigo which begins in the Bloomsbury shop when Charlotte chastises the Prince for his proposal that he buy her
something she could wear:

> "Would it be," Charlotte asked, "your idea to offer
> me something?'
> "Well, why not—as a small ricordo?"
> "But a ricordo of what?"
> "Why of 'this'—as you yourself say. Of this little
> hunt."
> "Oh I say it—but hasn't my whole point been that I
> don't ask you to. Therefore," she demanded—but
> smiling at him now—"where's the logic?"
> "Oh the logic—!" he laughed.
> "But logic's everything. That at least is how I feel it.
> A ricordo from you—from you to me—is a ricordo of
> nothing. It has no reference."
> "Ah my dear!" he vaguely protested. Their enter-
> tainer meanwhile stood there with his eyes on them,
> and the girl, though at this minute more interested in
> her passage with her friend than in anything else,
> again met his gaze. It was a comfort to her that their
> foreign tongue covered what they said—and they
> might have appeared of course, as the Prince now had
> one of the snuff-boxes in his hand, to be discussing a
> purchase.
> "You don't refer," she went on to her companion. "*I*
> refer."
> He had lifted the lid of his little box and he looked

into it hard. "Do you mean by that then that you would
be free—?"

"'Free'—?"

"To offer me something?"

This gave her a longer pause. . . . "Would you allow me—?"

"No," said the Prince into his little box. (1.108–9)

The passage is difficult because it is not obvious how the
word "reference" is being used: what it would mean for one
person to "refer" for another, and why Amerigo interprets
Charlotte's claim to "refer" for him as associated with a gift
("'Do you mean by that then that you would be free . . . to
offer me something?'"), for James introduces the abstract
idea of reference in the concrete discussion of the bequeathal
of gifts. In the semantic context implied by Charlotte's insistence that the "logic's everything," referents are terms
which name, denote, or identify objects and events. Reference pertains to laws of application over those things, the
rule for inclusion or exclusion, for distinguishing members
of a class from nonmembers. "Reference" in this context
suggests something close to "meaning," but more restricted,
because applying only to denotable phenomena: for example, to a moment, event, or feeling to which a ricordo would
refer. Reference is a relation between proper names and
what they name; complex singular terms and what they denote; predicates and the entities of which they are true.
When Charlotte declines a ricordo (a remembrance or souve-
nir) from Amerigo because, she says, "'a ricordo . . . from
you to me . . . is a ricordo of nothing. It has no reference,'"
she means quite simply that it doesn't stand for anything. It
doesn't stand for anything because the fiction of the outing
is that nothing is between them which a ricordo could denote. At least there is nothing that is legitimately between
them. And, as I shall suggest, nothing is between them that
is mutual or shared. Therefore nothing is between them that
can be commemorated.

But when Charlotte adds, "'You don't refer, I refer,'"
the semantic problem of whether there is something a ricordo
could identify shifts to a larger, and looser, concern with the
assignation of meaning itself, and with who controls it.
Charlotte's claim that "'a ricordo . . . from you to me . . .

is a ricordo of nothing'" does not, in fact, abolish the idea of
reference. That claim only excuses the Prince from any com-
plicity in its determination. Because Amerigo understands
the shift from the idea of no reference (no denotable meaning) to the more liberating idea of no reference or significance *he* is obliged to designate, he agrees to the excursion.
What allows him to suppose he could, with impunity, accompany his former lover on the eve of his marriage is her
assurance that his doing so has no implications for him.
This, he in fact considers, is

> *his*, the man's, any man's, position and strength—that
> he had necessarily the advantage, that he only had to
> wait with a decent patience to be placed, in spite of
> himself, it might really be said, in the right. (1.49–50)

According to such logic (different from the semantic one)
Charlotte would be free to offer *him* a gift, for giving gifts to
Amerigo, like giving meaning to the time they spend to-
gether, is just what she has proposed to take upon herself.

In the end, of course, no gift is purchased. Nothing is
bought for Maggie, for whom nothing ever seems to have
been intended. Nothing is bought for Charlotte because,
contradicting her promise to "'ask nothing of you,'" she
wants nothing short of the exquisite but invisibly cracked
golden bowl, the purchase of which Amerigo—being, in
Charlotte's word, "superstitious"—believes would threaten
his marriage. Nothing is bought for Amerigo because, he
tells Charlotte, he will not accept a gift to which an impossible condition is attached: "'I mean, of my keeping your gift
so to myself'" (1.120). A gift Amerigo has to keep to himself
is one that he cannot show to Maggie. But it is also one that
he cannot reciprocate with Charlotte. Charlotte has insisted
she will accept nothing from him. More to the point, however, given the discrepancy in their plights, there is no gift
he could offer her that would comparably compromise her.
An exchange of gifts can be considered, then, only on the
day that *she* marries. "'You *must*,'" therefore, he tells her,
"'—seriously—marry'" (1.121). For only when she does so
will there be symmetry between them. Only then will two
marriages rather than one equally be jeopardized by the exchange now merely contemplated.

The conversation between Charlotte and Amerigo which I have been examining involves no exchange. In the literal sense, no transaction takes place. But the conversation also involves no exchange because of the lack of linguistic parity in the two situations. From the vantage of Charlotte's presentation of their predicament, she assumes the risk of referring (placing Amerigo in the right by herself assigning significance to the meeting) so that he will not need to. From the vantage of Amerigo's reconsidered perspective, Charlotte cannot impute significance to the meeting (or her doing so fails to count) because, with no marriage of her own at stake, she has nothing yet to risk. Charlotte's assertion "'You don't refer, I refer'" points to an asymmetry with which, for different reasons, then, Amerigo concurs. The consequence of that asymmetry is that reference is not shared. Reference is rather projected by one person *onto* another; bequeathed, like the unpurchased gift, by one person *to* the other; determined and assumed respectively by one person *for* the other. For the particular passage I have been considering, like the novel as a whole, departs from the semantic or logical connotations of "reference" initially predicated. It does so in two ways. First, the sense of "reference" is implicitly extended so that the word applies not only to the rules governing the denoting of objects and entities but also to the rules governing all meaning. Second, the peculiarity of those rules is just that they are *not* agreed upon. Hence one person can assume responsibility for determining meaning while another repudiates it. Thus the semantic connotations of the word give way, leaving "reference" to be understood as a nominalization of the verb "referring": the act of assigning or attributing significance. In the case of the pronoun voiced by Charlotte's hope, "'that it shall always be with you,'" reference involves the ability to govern the antecedent: to make "it" ambiguously include the present meeting, the past affair, and the emotion that will continue to draw the two together. In the case of the proclamation "'You don't refer, I refer'" what is implied by reference is something like agency, specifically, the power to exert control over meanings.

Although in one passage Charlotte implicates the Prince ("'that it shall always be with you'") and in the other she

suggests that it is possible to extricate him from implication
or to render his engagement with it passive ("'You don't refer, *I* refer'"), reference—what it is, who determines it,
whether one person can refer for another—is a topic generally central to the novel. And the conversation points to the
novel's paradigmatic action: one character's attempt to prescribe meanings for another, to assume responsibility for reference so that he doesn't need to or so that he isn't able to.
The notion that reference can be obscured as well as assumed or assigned is underlined in Charlotte's thought as
they speak Italian before the English shopman: "It was a
comfort to her that their foreign tongue covered what they
said." The assumption—false, as it turns out—that the intimacy will go undetected because they have changed the language in which it is made intelligible suggests the degree to
which James means us to take the idea of controlling reference, here generalized as meaning, literally.

Charlotte's assumption that one person's assignment of
meanings would be acceded to by another is shared by the
Assinghams, whose marriage consists of Fanny's delivery of
stories and explications of other people's lives to the man
whose only function in the novel seems to be to receive
them. Bob Assingham is the passive container of meanings
twice removed, of references (in the sense of interpretations)
that are made about others as well as by an other. But all relationships established by the novel's beginning are similarly
characterized by the shifting positions occupied by those
who determine meanings and those who accede to them.
Thus, when Charlotte and Amerigo justify the eventual re-
sumption of their affair, they do so with reference to (now in
the colloquial sense of "with an eye on") the behavior of the
Ververs: "'We must act in concert. Heaven knows . . . *they*
do!'" (1.308–9), as if their transgression has been defined as
well as dictated by the example of father and daughter:
"'What else can we do, what in all the world else?'" (1.303).
Thus Amerigo, after his marriage, in Fanny Assingham's
words, "knew what he was about" (1.163). Knowing what
he is about (what he will be moved to do) means, with his
"appetite . . . for the explanatory," collecting evidence that
will testify to what Maggie, his wife, is about, specifically
with respect to her feelings for her father:

the Prince was saving up, for some very mysterious but
very fine eventual purpose, all the wisdom, all the answers to his questions, all the impressions and general-
isations he gathered; putting them away and packing
them down because he wanted his great gun to be
loaded to the brim on the day he should decide to fire it
off. He wanted first to make sure of the *whole* of the
subject that was unrolling itself before him. . . .
(1.163)

Amerigo's "putting away" of observations about his wife's
relation to her father so that "his great gun [will] be loaded
to the brim on the day he decide[s] to fire it off" is intended
to justify his own violation of the codes of his marriage by
referring or alluding to Maggie's prior violation of it, when
she subordinates her feelings for her husband to her feelings
for her father.

Although the connotations of reference are diverse, they
have in common the notion that one person's often verbal
dictation of significance will determine what another should
think and even how he should act. " 'You regularly make me
wish I *had* shipped back to American City. When you go on
as you do—' " (2.271), Adam Verver tells his daughter, correctly ascribing causality for that "wish" to her implicit but
clearly reiterated desire to have him go away. And as if par-
odying the state in which others' determination of significance legislates the meaning of one's own actions, Charlotte,
before marrying Maggie's father, ostensibly requires his
daughter's consent. What does it mean to act as if the self
had no agency, or as if two selves had one agency? Perhaps
what causes the desire not to have agency or, alternatively,
to assert sole agency (" 'You don't refer, *I* refer' "), to be referred for by others or to refer for others, is the realization,
repetitively acted out in this novel, that more often than not
reference is unshared. Reference—again in the sense of the
nominalization of the word "referring"—is unshared because situations are asymmetrical, and so, therefore, are
thoughts, or understandings of meaning. Or because the
thought in the mind and the reality outside of it fail to cor-
respond.

It is Maggie's inaccurate assumption at the novel's beginning that thoughts (about facts, about relations) have con-

gruity with each other. "'They thought of everything but
that I might think'" (2.332), Maggie tells Fanny Assingham,
implicitly suggesting that, as she now understands it,
"thought" involves acknowledging the difference between
one mind and another. In light of that recognition, as
Amerigo, confronting the bowl, neatly shattered into three
pieces at his feet, tries to cajole his wife into the conceptual
dependence that previously made her manageable, she corrects the impression that his understanding of what he sees
is requisite for hers:

> "But what would you have done," he was by this
> time asking, "if I *hadn't* come in?"
> "I don't know." She had cast about. "What would
> you?"
> "Oh, *io*—that isn't the question. I depend on you. I
> go on. You'd have spoken to-morrow?"
> "I think I'd have waited."
> "And for what?" he asked.
> "To see what difference it would make for myself.
> My possession at last, I mean, of real knowledge."
> (2.201)

In the context of Amerigo's behavior, his words "I depend
on you" really have an opposite meaning, which could be
paraphrased as follows: "I suppose you to depend upon me
to dictate a meaning we fictionalize by calling mutual." This
is how I understand the idiomatic interrogative which functions as a declarative: "'You'd have spoken to-morrow?'"
For Amerigo presumes his wife's ability to understand
meaning only by referring it away, by letting someone else,
her father or her husband, determine it for her. Maggie's de-
murral contradicts that expectation: "'I think I'd have waited
. . . to see what difference it would make for myself.'"
Moreover, as she has acceded to the separateness of her
knowledge, which no longer requires Amerigo for its valida-
tion, so she will insist on the isolation of his. She will em-
phasize the fact that knowledge counts differently for him
than for herself.

> "My only point now, at any rate," she went on, "is
> the difference, as I say, that it may make for *you*. Your
> knowing was—from the moment you did come in—all

I had in view." And she sounded it again—he should
have it once more. "Your knowing that I've ceased—
. . . . Why to be as I was. *Not* to know." (2.201–2)

There are several ways to understand the numerous times
the passage touches on the word "know." For example,
"Your knowing [that you know]" (one possible way of interpreting Maggie's words) is not identical to "that you know I
know." Yet disparities like this obscure a more pertinent
one. Amerigo's knowledge is to be viewed, not to be had,
for his knowledge and hers are not the same thing. They are
first to be distinguished. They may, second, be brought together in the reflexivity of Maggie's telling Amerigo that she
wishes him to "know that I know." But they are never again
to be falsely equated. For the mistake or the fiction of shared
reference—a fiction comprising the idea that reference and
explanation are externally generated by one person for another, whether by Charlotte for Amerigo, by Fanny for Bob,
by Maggie for her father, or by Amerigo for Maggie—is one
the novel's second half exists to contest.

II

In part 1 of *The Golden Bowl* the mistake seemed to arise from
the assumption that one person could speak for others in
the colloquial sense of voicing their thoughts or determining
meanings for them. (The idea of voicing another's thoughts
is connected to that of determining his meanings, because
"referring" for another is undertaken for the purpose of dictating how something is understood by him, as well as for
the purpose of designating meaning so that he will not need
to. To voice another's thoughts, therefore, is not sympathet-
ically to understand those thoughts but rather preemptively
to produce them.) Part 2 of the novel diagnoses such a mistake in terms curiously literal. It comprehends being unable
to speak "for" another as "being unable to speak on his
behalf." But it also identifies the problem as "being unable
to speak *to* him," hence as being unable to speak (meaningfully) at all. It is not clear why the colloquial and the literal
should be equated or confused, not clear why the false belief
that one's "thoughts could be voiced by another" should
make the idea that "thoughts could be voiced at all" also

seem false. Yet the two ideas seem associated, if for no
other reason than that part 2 corrects both assumptions. It
does so through a logic whereby thoughts become the
medium in which meaning is made audible, and speech the
medium in which it is blocked. This inversion suggests that
what is deemed transgressive between characters who are
illegitimately paired is meaning that is *spoken*. Since speech
is the medium through which one person exerts improper
authority over another's understanding, then it follows that
while speech cannot really or wholly be emptied of significance, it can be depleted of significance by being assigned
the task of designations that are either trivial or misleading.
The consequence in part 2, in a way arguably different from
that in the novel's first half, is a form of communication
that looks curiously like mind reading. Because speech
is made incommunicative, what characters think can only
be intuited, as in the following passage in which Maggie
greets Amerigo upon his return from the country with
Charlotte:

> "You've seemed these last days—I don't know what:
> more absent than ever before, too absent for us merely
> to go on so. It's all very well, and I perfectly see how
> beautiful it is, all round; but there comes a day when
> something snaps, when the full cup, filled to the very
> brim, begins to flow over. That's what has happened to
> my need of you—the cup, all day, has been too full to
> carry. So here I am with it, spilling it over you—and
> just for the reason that's the reason of my life. . . .
> I'm as much in love with you now as the first hour; ex-
> cept that there are some hours—which I know when
> they come, because they almost frighten me—that
> show me I'm even more so. They come of them-
> selves—and ah they've been coming! After all, after
> all—!" Some such words as those were what *didn't*
> ring out, yet it was as if even the unuttered
> sound had been quenched here in its own quaver.
> It was where utterance would have broken down by
> its very weight if he had let it get so far. Without
> that extremity, at the end of a moment, he had taken
> in what he needed to take—that his wife was *testify-
> ing*, that she adored and missed and desired him.
> (2.18–19)

Despite the fact that Maggie's words "didn't ring out," Amerigo hears her as "testifying." Her unspoken words are so well perceived—I am pressed to say "heard"—that Amerigo breaks them off because he can no longer endure them. How thoroughly consciousness is experienced by Maggie herself as a phenomenon that is communicative is reiterated in the passage, touched on earlier, in which she sees Amerigo's eyes drawn to the ground where the pieces of the golden bowl lie, shattered by Fanny Assingham:

> "Yes, look, look," she seemed to see him hear her say even while her sounded words were other. . . . "Look at the possibility that since I *am* different there may still be something in it for you. . . ."

Maggie registers her own words not, as she has a moment earlier, from the vantage of wishing to speak them ("She wanted to say to him 'Take it, take it . . .'" [2.184]) but more complexly from the vantage of (virtually) hearing them understood. In passages like these, crucial exchanges are carried on in spite of the spoken, or in the midst of the spoken, or explicitly as a counter to it. For what characters refuse to talk about they do not also refuse to think. Such a choice has consequences, for the novel consistently demonstrates that the unsaid is not commensurate with the unheard.

The substitution which turns communications that are unuttered into those definitively heard is dramatically illustrated at that moment when Charlotte, leading visitors through the gallery at Fawns to show them Adam Verver's treasures, is apprehended by the consciousnesses of the novel's other characters. In this scene, in which Charlotte Stant is excruciatingly understood, comprehension is like cruelty—at least it is like violation—because it bores through words to the pain they attempt to obstruct. As Charlotte is elaborating impersonally on the history of the possessions to spectators, who are strangers absorbed by her words,

> Maggie meanwhile at the window knew the strangest thing to be happening: she had turned suddenly to crying, or was at least on the point of it—the lighted square before her all blurred and dim. The high voice went on; its quaver was doubtless for conscious ears

only, but there were verily thirty seconds during which
it sounded, for our young woman, like the shriek of a
soul in pain. Kept up a minute longer it would break
and collapse—so that Maggie felt herself the next thing
turn with a start to her father. "Can't she be stopped?
Hasn't she done it *enough?*"—some such question as
that she let herself ask him to suppose in her. (2.292)

Maggie's desire that Charlotte somehow be stopped is
only barely separable from her request to Adam Verver that
he hear his daughter give voice to that desire. The counter-
dialogue of Charlotte's pain to Charlotte's words, of what is
understood to what is said, is immediately made subordinate to subsequent unspoken communications between
Maggie and Amerigo and between Maggie and Adam
Verver, predicated on the initial one, whose audibility is, as
a consequence, implicitly taken for granted. For the unuttered shriek is heard not only by Maggie but also by her
husband and her father. (Although Adam Verver's and
Amerigo's responses to the sound are filtered through Maggie's consciousness, that fact does not call their autonomy
into question. It rather demonstrates the particular power
which consciousness has to observe distinctions among
points of view, to hold them in mind, while simultaneously
differentiating them from that of the perceiving consciousness. Or, power is a consequence of the mind's belief in its
ability to make such a distinction. The point is in fact crucial,
for, as I shall explain, the problem of other minds is explicitly cast in terms of whether one character is *permitted*, or
willing, to understand another's thoughts rather than of
whether he is *able* to do so.)

Maggie, who causes the suffering, experiences it as intolerable. Adam Verver, who bears a passive relation to it, sees
his wife's suffering more neutrally as piteous: "he struck
[Maggie] as confessing, with strange tears in his own eyes,
to sharp identity of emotion. 'Poor thing, poor thing'"
(2.292). Amerigo, person become instrument by which Maggie inflicts pain, tries to extricate himself from the suffering,
physically to retreat to the solitude of Portland Place: "he got
off to escape from a sound. The sound was in her own ears
still . . . the wonder for her became really his not feeling
the need of wider intervals and thicker walls" (2.294–95).

Maggie intuits her father's apprehension of his wife's pain in a "snatched communion" with him, understanding his compassion as something she shouldn't see him feel (2.292). She quite differently construes Amerigo's vision of Charlotte's suffering as momentarily so identified with her own as to render gratuitous even an unspoken exchange with him. In fact Maggie's feeling that Charlotte's pain is unbearable becomes Amerigo's inability to bear it, as he literalizes her recoil by leaving the house:

> She made [Amerigo] out as liking better than anything in the world just now to be alone with his thoughts. Being herself connected with his thoughts, she continued to believe, more than she had ever been, it was thereby a good deal as if he were alone with *her*. (2.293–94)

The strange state of Amerigo's sanctuary, in which being alone with his thoughts and being alone with his wife have become indistinguishable, is seen through Maggie's eyes. But it is also specifically dissociated from the idea of her projection of it by a second picture of the husband and wife's actual proximity that validates as an objective correlative the intimacy that Maggie feels:

> his idea could only be to wait, whatever might come, at her side. It was to her buried face that she thus for a long time felt him draw nearest; though after a while, when the strange wail of the gallery began to repeat its inevitable echo, she was conscious of how that brought out his pale hard grimace. (2.295)

It is not of course true that Amerigo is alone with his wife any more than it is true that he is alone with his thoughts. Charlotte Stant's "shriek" or "wail"—I shall call it her cry— is the content of those thoughts, as, in some sense, her misery is the object of the contemplation that unites husband and wife. Since Charlotte Stant's cry is no kind of language—not that of speech nor that of thought—it is fit text for the explication offered it by the novel's other characters, who are intent on reading not the meaning of the cry of pain but rather their relation to *each other* as a consequence of its expression. The point Charlotte's suffering is made to have is to show the ranges of its register in the other characters.

The cry is what allows them to think to each other. "The strange wail of the gallery," detached from Charlotte, obliterates the person of Charlotte, as Maggie acknowledges when at the novel's end she asks Amerigo, "'How can we not always think of her? It's as if her unhappiness had been necessary to us—as if we had needed her, at her own cost . . .'" (2.346). Charlotte is sacrificed by the making of her suffering meaningless—by the making of her suffering not in fact hers, since her being understood depends on the others' not wanting, as well as not having, access to her thoughts. She is the text rendered inscrutable so that other characters can "interpret" her in the absence, specifically the annihilation, of any meaning she might herself specify for it.

But a similar sacrifice is also exacted of the novel's other characters. In part 2 of *The Golden Bowl* relation repeatedly defines itself at the moment when characters are blocked in their attempts to understand each other or to be understood. While it may initially have seemed that access to another's mind is being purchased by the unspoken communications I have been examining, it is more frequently being obstructed. Thus, once Amerigo takes in that his wife is "testifying" that she misses him, he cuts into her thought so as to cut it off. Similarly, the point of hearing Charlotte Stant's cry is not to acknowledge her pain but rather to refuse to do so. In both cases a negation of another's thought is predicated on an unwillingness to understand rather than on an inability to do so. More is in fact at stake, for if exchanges of speech are preempted (especially in part 2 of *The Golden Bowl*) by exchanges of thought, then exchanges of thought are themselves displaced by moments when verbal meaning of any form is explicitly rebuked. The claim may seem abstract. Particular instances illustrate that James is nowhere more concrete than in his description of characters in the act of legislating, which here means limiting, what can or may be said and thought.

When, for example, Maggie, talking to her father, differentiates among kinds of love—that in which "'when you only love a little you're naturally not jealous'"; that in which "'when you love in a deeper and intenser way . . . your jealousy has intensity and . . . ferocity'"; that in which "'When . . . you love in the most abysmal and unutterable

way of all—why then you're beyond everything'" (2.262)—
she establishes a comparative and a superlative in the context of which her father is asked to measure his daughter's
love for Amerigo. But Adam Verver misunderstands. He interprets the comparative not as a measure of his daughter's
feeling for her husband but rather as a measure of his
daughter's feeling versus his own. He supposes Maggie to
say that she can love as he has never been able to. (It is true
that Adam Verver knows Amerigo is the object of Maggie's
love, but Amerigo is absent from the picture in which Adam
Verver fantasizes the intensity of his daughter's feeling, because of how minimally thus far Amerigo figures between
them.) He, moreover, dismisses the comparison of his
daughter's feeling and his own because of his assumption
that nothing *is* between father and daughter, nothing differentiates or separates them. He therefore concludes that
Maggie's "bliss" *is* his "in a communicated irresistible way"
(2.263).

Out of a comprehension of Maggie's pleasure that is, in
fact, an appropriation of it, Adam Verver initiates the following exchange:

> "I guess I've never been jealous," he finally remarked.
> And it said more to her, he had occasion next to per-
> ceive, than he was intending; for it made her, as by the
> pressure of a spring, give him a look that seemed to tell
> of things she couldn't speak. (2.264)

Maggie understands from his words something different
from them, something more or beyond them, not their conscious implications. Her propensity to see something he
doesn't mean, or mean to say, belies the coincidence of
point of view on which his "'I've never been jealous'" is
predicated. Adam Verver sees that his daughter makes of
his words something he did not intend by them. Something
different is said, then, from the words that are said. Or
something different is heard from the words that are said.
And what is said back, or what Adam Verver sees in his
daughter's face, is that what there would be to say in retort
to the thing heard cannot be said. This series of exchanges
implies a linguistic situation antithetical to that of the fiction
of shared reference at the novel's beginning. For if the nov-

el's beginning suggests that one person's meaning could suffice for another ("'You don't refer, I refer'"), the novel's conclusion suggests rather that the closest one can get to another is the distance requisite to see that meanings are not mutual.

The point or the effect of overhearing another's thoughts is repeatedly to illustrate that when you see into another's mind, what you see is its difference from yours. This idea— that meanings are not mutual, that reference is unshared— is, I take it, what lies behind the multiple instances in which characters mistake references, imagining, in repeated conversations, that a parent or a lover rather than a spouse is meant. ("'I should feel, you see,' [Maggie] continued, 'that the two of us were showing the same sort of kindness.' / Amerigo thought. 'The two of us? Charlotte and I?' / Maggie again took a moment. 'You and I, darling'" [2.63]). Such mistakes are instrumental because what must be corrected is the arrangement of the quartet so that the lovers and the Ververs are separated from each other. But the mistakes are also axiomatic. They exist in part to prove that since reference *is* unshared, it is easy to mistake it, that one is liable as well as able to do so. For Maggie there is value in such a distinction since she wants her father not to understand what she says but rather to do what she wants. Specifically, Maggie wants her father to take his wife back to American City. She also wants him to suggest the idea as if it were his own. What Maggie hears in Adam Verver's "'I've never been jealous'" is something the rest of the chapter exists to refute.

If my paraphrase of what passes between father and daughter is accurate, then in what sense can the Ververs be said to misunderstand each other? Underlining this question: Maggie's demand that her father suggest his return to American City as if it were his own idea, when in fact it is hers, seems to subvert the separate points of view on which the rest of the chapter insists. One way of accommodating these apparent contradictions in which the denial of shared reference is gainsaid by the imposition of reference (as in Adam Verver's entirely adequate understanding that his daughter wants him to go away) is to note that perfect misunderstanding, much like perfect understanding, is a fiction. When Bob Assingham says to Fanny, "'There's nothing in life, my dear, that I *can* make out' " (1.73), this is not a literal statement about what he comprehends. It is rather a statement about what he will admit of what he understands. It is a statement about the fact that he will subordinate his comprehension to his wife's interpretive governance of it. What Maggie denies Adam Verver and what she teaches him to deny her, then, is not comprehension but rather its presumption. For to the extent that shared reference is not an illusion, it is a transgression. Accordingly, in an earlier chapter we are told of Maggie that "she might yet, as at some hard game over a table for money, have been defying him to fasten on her the least little complication of consciousness" (2.84–85). Maggie must dissuade Adam Verver from the idea he specifies in the chapter which I have been considering that "her father could from experience fancy what she meant" (2.262).

Maggie is herself subjected to the idea of understanding conceived as trespass when Charlotte and Amerigo return from their day spent at Matcham, Maggie contriving to meet her husband at home rather than at her father's house:

> It was such a trifle, her small breach with custom, or at any rate with his natural presumption, that all magnitude of wonder had already had, before one could deprecate the shadow of it, the effect of a complication. It had made for him some difference that she couldn't measure, this meeting him at home and alone instead of elsewhere and with others, and back and back it kept coming to her that the blankness he showed her before he was able to *see* might, should she choose to insist on it, have a meaning—have, as who should say, an historic value—beyond the importance of momentary expressions in general. (2.16)

As "all magnitude of wonder" shades into "a complication," that complication into "some difference that she couldn't measure," and the last into a "blankness" which Maggie tries unsuccessfully to penetrate, we are shown what it looks like to prevent an understanding (from Amerigo's perspective) and to be kept from an understanding (from Maggie's). What is notable about the progressions in the passage is their facility for registering not the nuances of incomprehension, understood as a static state, but rather its successive stages. Blankness is a confusion through which Amerigo passes before he sees what to do to remedy the fact that his wife has understood something may be amiss between them.

Amerigo's suppression of surprise at his wife's presence at home resonates against another picture of suppression, which occurs in *Maggie's* mind less than a page earlier. Maggie has been thinking about the confusions of her marriage as "accumulations of the unanswered," which she has hidden in a room on which she has momentarily "pushed the door open" to see thoughts "never as yet 'sorted,' which for some time now she had been passing and re-passing, along the corridor of her life." Her glimpse of "unanswered things" is immediately recoiled from and then disrupted:

> It made her in fact, with a vague gasp, turn away, and what had further determined this was the final sharp extinction of the inward scene by the outward. The quite different door had opened and her husband was there. (2.14–15)

The two scenes of the extinction of meaning—that of Maggie's vision by her aversion, and that of her husband's expression of wonder by the blankness with which he replaces it—are temporally related by Amerigo's arrival. But Maggie's comprehension that her own mind conceals things, from herself as well as from others, that minds *can* conceal things, seems requisite for the understanding that his mind can conceal them, too.

Part 2 of *The Golden Bowl* dramatizes an extensive repertoire of such concealments of meaning. In this context Charlotte Stant, who is consigned to a fate of "having gropingly to go on, always not knowing and not knowing" (2.202), suffers a fate differentiated from that of the other characters not by its extremity but rather by the fact that *we* are denied access to her perception of it. In the latter half of the novel each of the characters is subjected, as Charlotte is, to the repeated comprehension that something which must be understood cannot be understood. This prohibition against meaning—the proposition of meaning rather than the experience of it, seeing that meaning exists as if from outside of it—is repeated, with variations. Meaning is evaded because the self is afraid of it, as in the room filled with "accumulations of the unanswered" which Maggie "passed . . . when she could without opening the door" (2.14). Or meaning is inaccessible because others withhold it. "'Oh I can't tell you that!'" (2.336), Maggie says dismissively to Fanny Assingham when the latter asks, in a conversation which Maggie has initiated, how Amerigo survives the uncertainty of what will happen to his marriage. Or meaning is denied because characters speak in contradictions. When Charlotte asks whether Maggie thinks her stepmother has wronged her, the former must listen to an answer that negates what Maggie will leave in words without negating what she has put in words: "'I accuse you—I accuse you of nothing'" (2.250). Or meaning is impenetrable because it cannot *appear* to be understood. "'I know nothing,'" Maggie says to Fanny Assingham, "'If I did. . . . I should die'" (2.305).

(In these instances it may look as if I am using "meaning" as a synonym for "knowledge." Yet with respect to the unspoken utterances, the two are not equivalent. "Knowledge" implies the clear internality of the thing which is known with the possibility of also expressing it. To examine questions of meaning in *The Golden Bowl* is to see that expression and thought are made alternative to each other, that significance resides in speech *or* in thought. Thus, when meaning is shifted from speech to thought, speech is emptied of significance, or that is the fiction endorsed by the novel. Yet to provide an account of how meaning is manipulated is also to challenge the conventional account of how knowledge functions in the novel, for I want to argue that to invoke formulaically the question of inert knowledge—as first characters, and then critics, do—is, in the case of the characters, a rhetorical means of deflecting attention from a more subversive question about the unstable placement of meaning: Who obfuscates or enforces it, and where? In the quotations above, for example, what is desired is not knowledge but rather verbalization, the moving of meaning from thought to speech.)

For Adam Verver, who blithely announces, "'I guess I've never been jealous,'" the prohibition against meaning is a consequence of his false equation of his daughter's experience with his own. For Maggie, who watches the surprise of

Amerigo's expression turn to blankness, the prohibition against meaning requires learning that surfaces can be seen past without necessarily being seen into. For Amerigo, listening to Maggie tell him she knows of his affair with Charlotte, the prohibition against meaning involves knowing Maggie could answer the question she implicitly precludes him from asking: whether his father-in-law, like his wife, knows of his adultery:

> his eyes might have been trying to hypnotise her into giving him the answer without his asking the question. "Had *he* his idea, and has he now, with you, anything more?"—those were the words he had to hold himself from not speaking and that she would as yet certainly do nothing to make easy. (2.192)

According to the conventional explanation, Amerigo "has to keep his hands off" the question he is considering because to ask whether Adam Verver knows is, definitively, to implicate Charlotte, and thus to lend credence to his wife's description that " 'so much [was] between you before—before *I* came between you at all' " (2.199). Such an explanation is contingent on the assumption that if something cannot be said, it cannot be said to have happened. This way of putting it ignores the fact that what is contested in the novel is not the events themselves but rather the language that would describe them. What is contested is the proposition that language *should* describe them. But if words are made empty of significance, this emptiness is not only in service of denial or dismissal (the traditional understanding of it). It is also oppositely in service of the preservation of the thing unsaid. For in the Jamesian logic, designation (the "precisely nameable") and dismissal are related to each other. If something can be put into words, it can simultaneously be put away. Such a notion literalizes the idea of the expressing of something as a getting rid of it. By virtue of this logic, for Maggie, who wishes to conserve what is between herself and Amerigo, in the novel's second half thoughts are preferable to words, and evasion is preferable to thoughts. Thus the moments in the novel most charged with import are those shaped by a tension between a character's perception of significance and his commensurate understanding of his unwillingness to penetrate it. The unsaid and the unthought are consistently made superior to anything that could be designated either by utterance or by thinking. They are, in the colloquial expression, "full of meaning." And they are allowed to remain so because in a quite literal sense they are not depleted of it.

Amerigo is made to appreciate this fact when, after his exchange with his wife over the pieces of the broken bowl, we are told, "by their having, in their acceptance of the unsaid, or at least their reference to it, practically given up pretending—it was as if they were 'in' for it . . . but the dread . . . was . . . a seduction, just as any confession of the dread was . . . an allusion" (2.265). As in the following unspoken words of Amerigo's, which succeed, by a few days, his wife's informing him that she knows of his affair, silence provides the grounds for the intimacy it appears to contest:

> "Leave me my reserve; don't question it—it's all I have just now, don't you see? so that, if you'll make me the concession of letting me alone with it for as long a time as I require I promise you something or other, grown under cover of it, even though I don't yet quite make out what, as a return for your patience." She had turned away from him with some such unspoken words as that in her ear, and indeed she *had* to represent to herself that she had spiritually heard them, had to listen to them still again, to explain her particular patience in face of his particular failure. (2.221)

The content of the passage negates the idea of shared reference dominant in part 1 of the novel. It does so because Maggie and Amerigo do not think they speak of the same thing. They do not speak at all. The subject of the unspoken words is itself "reserve," the disinclination to disclose what is on one's mind. Something is known that is not acknowledged. Something is kept, or, in the archaic sense of "reserve," kept secret, from another. The sense of secrecy here also pertains to the self who would conceal his thoughts from others and who has concealed from himself the consequences of so doing. Hence the promise Maggie imagines Amerigo will produce ("'something or other . . . even though I don't yet quite make out what, as a return for

your patience'") is characterized by indeterminacy. What
Amerigo can't "quite make out" for himself is not an understanding, and what he won't deliver to Maggie is not an explanation, for both understandings and explanations are
what husband and wife have ceased providing for each
other. When Fanny Assingham asks Maggie, "'he didn't explain—?'" Maggie replies, "'Explain? Thank God, no! . . .
And I didn't either'" (2.215). Because what is kept from
Maggie by Amerigo is the same thing Amerigo keeps from
himself, it does not stand between husband and wife as separation would. Or rather separation is the state that they are
represented as sharing. Nothing brings them closer than this
moment, when the content of that closeness, envisioned
through Maggie's eyes, is the prohibition against it. What
brings them together is not a state of shared reference. That
is what separates them. What is between them is the implicitly agreed upon terms of their isolation.

III

I have described a series of equivocations in part 2 of *The
Golden Bowl*, which could be summarized as follows. Because speech is often empty, characters must intuit each other's thoughts, but to look into another's mind is to be
blocked by its impenetrability; this prohibited access leads to
an isolation that characters are represented as sharing. In
lieu of any certainty, moreover, their impressions become
intimations, taking on the status of propositions just to the
degree that a supposition about another's thought cannot be
externally corroborated. If this is the case, then do the novels' complicated exchanges, which negotiate the turns I am
describing, illustrate *how* meaning is shareable, even provide
the contractual terms by which significance is first posited
and then, albeit suppositionally, assumed to be mutual? In
other words: Is the denial of shared meaning undertaken by
part 2 itself denied? I think, finally, not, for in the novel's
second half, in a way parallel to that in the novel's first half,
meanings are not being understood; they are rather being
imposed. When characters appear to read each other's
thoughts rather than to listen to each other's words, they
create those thoughts.

Thus part 2 seems initially to correct the belief that characters could assign meanings for each other. Ultimately, though, the novel's second half illustrates the logical, or ontological, impossibility of escaping the predicament it attempts to correct. But the predicament itself has been re-defined. It is not one caused by illegitimate relations. Rather, the predicament pertains to meanings and relations that have been painstakingly sanctioned. In fact, the way in which relations have come to be sanctioned is by Maggie's discovery of how to discern (that is, dictate) meanings. For if speech must be seen through, it is not only unreliable to suppose that one's intuition could ascertain what is in an-other's mind. It is also unavoidable. Then the denial of shared meaning stands. Meaning is not shared in part 1 be-cause it is projected *for* another. Meaning is not shared in part 2 because it is projected *onto* another.

Here one could object: for practical purposes characters understand each other perfectly. Solipsism is *not* what is be-ing represented. Characters understand each other perfectly in the sense that Maggie makes the others, as she tells Fanny Assingham, " 'do what I like' " (2.115). Yet action and comprehension are not equivalent. Moreover, because char-acters do not understand each other primarily through speech, because there are numerous conversations in which what is said is opposite to what is meant, or in which what is meant cannot be said, or in which what is meant is thought rather than said, meaning as a phenomenon con-ventionally shareable is *variously* as well as repeatedly dis-puted.

Meaning is unshareable, then, not because it is unknow-able but rather because it is unacknowledged and, more to the point, asymmetrical. Solipsism is not involved because what is typically at stake is not a failure of understanding but rather a failure of symmetry. Therefore meaning is sub-ject to manipulation. (To return to an earlier distinction be-tween knowledge and meaning: you cannot manipulate an-other's knowledge, in the sense that he has it or he doesn't. But you can manipulate another's experience of meaning; you can determine it for him.) For characters in *The Golden Bowl* the most successful way in which to manipulate mean-ing is not to withhold it but rather to move it around from speech to thought, to subject another by thinking. Because meaning is positional—produced by some characters and acceded to by others—it exists in a realm that makes the politics of interpretation possible. The world of *The Golden Bowl* could be described as one of pure politics, because the point of the manipulations is the governance of another's meanings as if for its own sake.

The implication of the belief that reference is not shared is a fascism of interpretation. "'They thought of everything but that I might think,'" Maggie has declared to Fanny Assingham. The import of Maggie's learning to think, however, is not primarily her ability to conceptualize the discrepancy between her own thoughts and the others', although I have touched on this in the previous section. It more dynamically amounts to exploiting that discrepancy by dictating others' understandings of what they must do. Such legislation amounts to lawlessness, which may be surmised but may not be interfered with because there is no arena—no common space of meaningful articulation—in which it can be challenged. In *The Golden Bowl* any transgression can be committed if it is kept out of speech. In part 1 the transgression amounts to one person's, Charlotte's, speaking or "referring" so Amerigo does not need to. In part 2, contingent on substitution instead of delegation, the transgression is more extreme, for it involves thinking *rather than* speaking. In this context we are told that Maggie assumes the burden of omission and evasion, that she presides over the "unuttered and unutterable," which is simultaneously "the constantly and unmistakeably implied." For she can control what is understood, and what is *done* about what is understood, by censoring what is said. Thus her need to be "impenetrable to others" (2.240) depends on her treating meaning as if it were a surface, visible but impervious, not to be gone into.

One might say, not to be read. Yet while the idea of "going into" could be viewed as a denial of reading (which is of surface marks), and so seem to invite a larger discussion of that subject, it is just this discussion which I intend to avoid. For the problematic in the novel is not to decipher meaning but rather to project it, as I have been elaborating. Moreover, the substitution of thinking for speaking derides the stable relation of inner and outer, hence of depths and surfaces, on which any consideration of determinate reading depends. Because what is being "read" cedes as an issue to what is being "referred," and because referring itself is shifted from speech to thought, general questions about reading are subordinated to specific questions about reference, which is positional rather than semantic ("'You don't refer, *I* refer'"), having to do with one person's relation to another, or of thought's relation to speech.

The problematic of referring—rather than of reading—can be understood in the context of the externalization of thought taken up throughout these chapters. If *The American Scene* exercises extravagant projections of thought, and is licensed to do so in the arranged absence of others, and if the early novels externalize thought by situating it between persons, in *The Golden Bowl* consciousness is externalized in the different sense of made positional—much as meaning is—defined alternately with respect to speech and other minds. The making of consciousness positional does not blur identities as in James's early works. One could even argue that *The Golden Bowl* prohibits the confusions of consciousness discounted in the Prefaces and enacted by the early novels. It does this by legislating the impossibility of confusing consciousnesses: consciousnesses cannot be confused because they are defined asymmetrically. But as a result of the specific procedures for communication negotiated by the novel, that separation then itself becomes the object of confusion. For in what sense are we to understand that although persons are permitted to think, they are not, in most cases, permitted to do so simultaneously, or that meaning is assigned exclusively either to speech or to thought? The Prefaces are characterized by those prescriptions about consciousness which are then challenged by the novels. In *The Golden Bowl* thinking is prescriptive in a more radical sense, being associated not with the dictate of consciousness's interiority but rather with the dictation of what is in another's mind. Thus the idea of separate minds is insisted on by the novel, but with subversive consequences. For, notwithstanding the conventional characterization of Maggie as learning to think for herself, it is more strikingly the case that for Maggie (as for the other characters) thinking for oneself—the customarily assumed person whom thinking is "for"—is not the primary function of thinking in the novel. Thinking for oneself is rather preempted by others' thinking for one or by one's thinking for others. In part 1 Maggie is thought for; in part 2 she thinks for Amerigo. (This prescriptiveness of thought—which also delegates it—in James's late novels is italicized in *The Wings of the Dove* and taken up in the next chapter.)

In the last paragraph of *The Golden Bowl* James turns away from consciousness (or has Maggie do so by burying her eyes in Amerigo's breast), a consciousness whose meaning-making faculties he so consistently exalted in the five hundred pages preceding it. The novel ends because what has kept it going is Maggie's productions of meanings *for* Amerigo, which are here understood as fatal.* If there *were*

---

*At the novel's end Maggie covers her eyes because she understands that if Amerigo sees nothing but her (sees nothing, in other words, but what she has made him see), she has nothing at all. Therefore she sees, or hides her face so as not to continue to see, the destruction she has wrought. One can examine the vision from which Maggie recoils by looking past the novel's end to *The American Scene,* which illustrates inadvertently what she will no longer regard. In *The American Scene,* much as in *The Golden Bowl,* but now purified of any plot that could distract from consciousness's operations, the mind subjects by thinking. Thus James, riding on a Pullman train, hears "the great monotonous rumble . . . which seems forever to say to you: 'See what I'm making of all this—see what I'm making, what I'm making!' " (463). The moment is vertiginous because the train is no sooner given a voice than its claim is disputed, as James retorts contemptuously: " 'I see what you are *not* making [of it].'" The colloquy is notable, then, in that it isn't one. What is being exposed is the trickery behind the ventriloquism. In fact, because the passage concludes a book in which the reader is overwhelmed by James's "senses" and "impressions" (" 'more impressions than you know what to do with'" [108]), the train's counterclaim, " 'See what I'm making of this,' " seems to issue not simply from the Pullman but from *The American Scene* itself, as if the book being written, or the land being burdened with significances, enjoyed a momentary liberation from the interpretations it is made to labor under. For the boast of the Pullman, " 'See what I'm making of all this'" (making out of the land in the sense of forging or creating from it), with its pun just barely separable from the "making of it" that is interpreting (the act which has characterized James's cogitations), posits the Pullman's "utterance" as an ostensibly competitive one. As I have noted, the point of the ventriloquism is to contest it, to reestablish the self as the single author of impressions. For impressions are the only alternative to the blank idiocy of being both thoughtless and speechless, a condition grotesquely described in *The American Scene* as "irreflectively gap[ing]" (463). This, Maggie surmises, is Amerigo's condition, when he is reduced to specularity.

an alternative to thinking as projection and an alternative, as well, to not thinking at all (in *The American Scene* called "irreflectively gaping"), it would be in the portrayal of the mind's relation to meaning as a question. Yet to regard meaning as not only open to question, but also fundamentally as questionable, is insupportable. It is so in the passage below, in which Maggie is made to query Amerigo's relation to Charlotte, and—to introduce a final subject—it is so for us, the novel's readers, who, contemplating the novel's title, are first subjected to confusions and then implicated in procedures, shared by the novel's characters, for laying these confusions to rest. I shall arrive at the second point by way of the first. For I wish here to argue that we are made to regard (to see) the imposition of meaning in which, albeit in another context, we are also made to engage. In the picture in Maggie's mind, "Back to back," together only by virtue of their connection to her, is how Maggie supposes Amerigo and Charlotte should be. Yet she sees them forever as face to face, asking questions of each other about *her* suddenly contingent relation to them:

> she had affected them, or at any rate the sensibility each of them so admirably covered, in the same way. To make the comparison at all was, for Maggie, to return to it often, to brood upon it, to extract from it the last dregs of its interest—to play with it in short nervously, vaguely, incessantly, as she might have played with a medallion containing on either side a cherished little portrait and suspended round her neck by a gold chain of a firm fineness that no effort would ever snap. The miniatures were back to back, but she saw them for ever face to face, and when she looked from one to the other she found in Charlotte's eyes the gleam of the momentary "What does she really want?" that had come and gone for her in the Prince's. (2.35–36)

The inevitability of Maggie's connection to her husband and stepmother does not specify the terms of it. These can be altered, and in the miniatures at which Maggie gazes—the images in the mind suddenly turning themselves around to be consonant with the images outside of it—she sees that they have been altered. Reacting to that reversal, Maggie ostensibly wants no greater harm to Charlotte than "that she meant to go out with her" (2.36). Yet the innocence of the description is derided. We are told of the spectacle in Maggie's mind that "She had been present [to it] as personally as she might have been present at some other domestic incident—the hanging of a new picture say, or the fitting of the Principino with his first little trousers" (2.36). Because the "hanging of a new picture say" is in this precise context not a random or neutral example, is even a retort to the pictures in the mind, Maggie is already treating the latter as if they were to be assaulted, to be replaced, not attended to. It is an indeterminacy like that recorded in the paragraph I have been examining to which the drone of referring would administer coherence, because its unclarity is intolerable. Yet, prior to Maggie's thought of "the hanging of a new picture," we are shown what it looks (feels) like to contemplate meaning indirectly, suppositionally, inferentially, incompletely. We see meaning framed as an image *of* uncertainty.

Like the miniatures, but on a larger scale, the golden bowl in the novel's title is full of meaning by virtue of containing questions about meaning. The bowl's meaning is indeterminate because different characteristics are attributed to it. It is precious, according to the shopman, but worthless, according to Amerigo. Indeterminacy about how the bowl is to be valued is reiterated by the question of what the bowl costs (which fluctuates) and by the question of who is to receive it (which shifts). The question of the bowl's worth, as determined by its intrinsic properties (whether its crystal has a flaw) and the question of the bowl's worth as determined by the person who is to receive it are brought together by Amerigo on the evening of his marriage when he associates *his* worth with *its* intrinsic characteristics. He remarks to Maggie's father: " 'Oh if I'm a crystal I'm delighted that I'm a perfect one, for I believe they sometimes have cracks and flaws—in which case they're to be had very cheap' " (1.139). The point about the connection between its worth and his person, or about the worth of his person figured as a crystal, is that it is made without being made sense of—like some joke without the punch line, or like an explanation without the conclusion. For the effect, if not the point, of bringing together the two contexts (of its value and his person) is precisely to show that they have nothing substantive to do with each other.

The gesture toward a connection only reinforces the relentless indeterminacy which governs the question of how
the bowl is to be valued *and* in relation to what context its
value, and hence meaning, is to be ascertained. Or to put
this in different terms: To what does the bowl, as symbol,
refer? It seems able to contain any connotation and, as eas-
ily, to be emptied of it. It is her belief that the bowl's meanings can be disposed of which leads Fanny Assingham to
dash it to the marble floor, explicitly associating the breaking
of the bowl with the dispelling of its meanings. "'Whatever
you meant by it,'" she says to Maggie, "'has ceased to exist'" (2.179). It is Maggie's corollary belief that meanings can
be recovered that leads her to hold the shivered pieces together with her hands and to suppose she can transfer the
flaw from the bowl to "the dire deformity of her attitude"
(2.240) about it.

But if in the novel the bowl's meanings are fluid and re-
versible, the novel's title, alluding both to Ecclesiastes and
Blake's *Book of Thel*, fixes the symbol at two determinate
points. These referents are "outside," not subjective, and,
made prominent by the title, they seem to have the last say.
Moreover, the content of the two passages, I shall suggest,
implies that what they have a say about is whether meaning
can be manipulated in the ways I have been describing. The
biblical reference is introduced when Charlotte presses the
shopman on his claim that Amerigo will not discover the
bowl's crack. "'Not even,'" Charlotte asks, "'if the thing
should come to pieces?'" "'Not even,'" she reiterates, "'if
he should have to say to me "The Golden Bowl is broken"?'" (1.116). I cite the passage from Ecclesiastes 12:1–8 to
which she here refers:

> Remember now thy Creator in the days of thy youth,
> while the evil days come not, nor the years draw nigh,
> when thou shalt say, I have no pleasure in them. While
> the sun, or the light, or the moon, or the stars, be not
> darkened, nor the clouds return after the rain: In the
> day when the keepers of the house shall tremble, and
> the strong men shall bow themselves, and the grinders
> cease because they are few, and those that look out of
> the windows be darkened, And the doors shall be shut
> in the streets, when the sound of the grinding is low,

and he shall rise up at the voice of the bird, and all the
daughters of musick shall be brought low; Also when
they shall be afraid of that which is high, and fears
shall be in the way, and the almond tree shall flourish,
and the grasshopper shall be a burden, and desire shall
fail: because man goeth to his long home, and the
mourners go about the streets: Or ever the silver cord
be loosed, or the golden bowl be broken, or the pitcher
be broken at the fountain, or the wheel broken at the
cistern. Then shall the dust return to the earth as it
was: and the spirit shall return unto God who gave it.
Vanity of vanities, saith the preacher; all is vanity.

The biblical passage suggests that, as all earthly forms are
flawed, nothing is suitable for a present if the criterion for
being suitable is that the object endure. My point here is not
that there exists a necessary contradiction between "everything is impermanent and hence ultimately flawed" and
"*this* thing is immediately flawed, therefore is especially in-
appropriate to commemorate a marriage, which is meant to
testify to the earthly lasting of things." My point is rather
that the two meanings are set against each other because ev-
eryone's erroneous idea seems to be that something—the
right thing—could *in fact* be ensured. Maggie and Charlotte
think that the bowl is perfect; Amerigo thinks some *other*
bowl would be. It amounts to the same thing. Each has an
idea of perfection that could survive devastation, which experience contradicts.

While the passage from Ecclesiastes figures the perfection
it negates in terms of permanence (and so is pertinent to the
wedding), the motto from *The Book of Thel* ("Can Wisdom be
put in a silver rod? / Or Love in a golden bowl?")[3] figures
the perfection it negates in terms of things that remain intact
because unviolated by experience (and so is pertinent to
Maggie's attempt to salvage her marriage). Thel will not en-
ter a world in which desire is inseparable from violation.
(Hence her questions repel experience by refusing to understand it: "Why cannot the Ear be closed to its own destruction? / Or the glistning Eye to the poison of a smile! / Why
are Eyelids stord with arrows ready drawn . . . ?" [*Thel*,
4.11–13].) Like Thel, Maggie, at the novel's end, reaffirms
her innocence rather than relinquishing it. She wants " 'The

golden bowl—as it *was* to have been. . . . The bowl with all our happiness in it. The bowl without the crack'" (2.216–17). And she supposes that if love is kept in "the steel hoop of an intimacy," formally held in check, it will repel "artless passion" (2.141). When Maggie averts her gaze from Amerigo's face, she recoils from an image of violation in which there is, in Thel's words of domesticated horror, "a little curtain of flesh on the bed of our desire" (*Thel*, 4.20).

The two passages thus offer a judgment on the meaning-making procedures inside the novel. Because the passage from Blake answers the biblical one by insisting there is no alternative to it, Maggie's attempt to make things mean according to a design that would rescue what she loves from destruction is doubly incriminated. The passage from the Bible condemns Maggie's attempt to hold the bowl intact from the vantage of the end of experience (which no meaning-making facilities can forestall). The passage from Blake suggests that it is possible to keep the object of desire intact only from the vantage of innocence, only from a vantage uncontaminated by experience because outside of, or prior to, it. The two passages therefore stress the falseness of Charlotte's initial assurance to Amerigo that the ricordo (which, as it happens, *is* the golden bowl) has no reference, or that its reference is arbitrary in the sense that it can be assumed by Charlotte at the novel's beginning, or assigned by Maggie at the novel's end. For the novel's title alludes to two passages which enforce the idea of determinate meaning not subject to regulation.

Yet in interpreting the novel's title and its central symbol, with reference to the biblical and the Blakean quotations, I have arranged to suggest a determinacy outside the novel governing the significance of its meanings that I have in fact imposed. There is no evidence that James read Blake in general or *Thel* in particular, although critics from F. O. Matthiessen on have assumed the connection. They have done so for a reason. There are suggestive external indications that James could have read *Thel*.[4] There are suggestive internal reasons to indicate he is likely to have done so, for Thel's plight seems specifically to address Maggie's relentless innocence, by way of an unequivocal comment on it, as the passage from Ecclesiastes does not. Yet because there is no evi-

dence that James read Blake, this reference cannot be inferred. It rather has to be assumed or assigned. A more trou-
bling imposition is operative with respect to the biblical
passage to which James's title certainly alludes. For when
the shopman confesses to Charlotte that the bowl *could* be
broken " 'by dashing it with violence—say upon a marble
floor' " (1.116), he refers to something that has not yet happened, though to something that *will* happen just as he has
worded it. At a moment like this one, James seems to want
to remove his tale from any meaning we can make of it that
is not connected to the imposition first of reference and then
of occurrence. To clarify this observation one could here
point to the retrospective confirmation of proleptic reference
by event. Yet it is more than that, or there is another point
to be made about it. For it is not accidental that in two of the
novel's central passages—that of "the hanging of a new picture say" and that of the dashing of the golden bowl " 'with
violence—say upon a marble floor' "—"saying" and violation are made linguistically inseparable.

Because of the insistent indeterminacy about what references are implied and what are imposed, and because of the
suspicion, as in the shopman's prediction (or predication,
" 'with violence—say upon a marble floor' ") that there is no
distinction between meaning that is implied and that which
is vehemently imposed, it is unclear how we are to understand reference in the novel.* This is particularly the case
with respect to whether we are to understand the assigning

---

*The novel's most prolific referrers are the Assinghams, whose name
puns on (spoken) assignments/assignations of meaning. Thus within the
space of a few pages:

> "Do you remember what I said to you long ago—that
> evening, just before their marriage . . . ?" / "What haven't
> you, love, said in your time?" . . . / "I never spoke [the truth]
> more, at all events, than when I declared . . . that Maggie
> was the creature in the world to whom a wrong thing could
> least be communicated . . ." (1.384). "Say he had married a
> woman who would have made a hash of [the forms]." / . . .
> "Ah my dear, I wouldn't say it for the world!" / "Say," she
> none the less pursued, "he had married a woman the Prince
> would *really* have cared for." / "You mean then he doesn't care
> for Charlotte—?" / . . . she simply said: "No!" (1.390–91).
> "We're as innocent," she went on in the same way, "as
> babes." / "Why not rather say," he asked, "as innocent as they
> themselves are?" (1.400).

of meaning as inevitable or as intolerable. And it is the case with respect to the bowl in the novel's title, which, initially seeming to answer the question, in fact only reiterates it. In the novel itself the bowl's connotations are deliberately made disjunctive, or when they coincide in the person of Amerigo figured as a crystal, the coincidence produces a presumption of coherence that is instead a parody of it. Thus we, like the novel's characters, remain in the position of "always not knowing" to what the bowl as symbol refers. In addition, the very question of reference—raised by Charlotte's initial conversation with Amerigo, recapitulated on a larger scale in Charlotte's assumption of meanings in part 1 and Maggie's assignment of meanings in part 2, reiterated in the substitution of thinking for speaking which most outrageously underscores these manipulations—asserts reference to be a topic central to the novel. But that topic remains dissociated from the ostensible or officially sanctioned thematic of the daughter's too close connection to the father, and from the rectification of this wrong by the aggression of another one. Thus the novel's problematic, which I have been developing, and the novel's subject have curiously little to do with each other. One could argue that the problematic of referring is the means through which the plot is solved. And on a mechanistic level this is so. Maggie's thinking "for" others is what makes the story come to an end. But, as the problematic itself remains unintelligible (one person cannot refer for another) and even in fact unsanctioned (this fiction set in motion by James is only ambiguously endorsed by him), its status as a solution remains enigmatic.

This is more the case since *The Golden Bowl* sets forth successive, competing models for communication, as if it were deliberating in a rigorous way how communication should

---

What is to be remarked upon about this outbreak of emphasized saying, is that it precedes part 2, in which, if the Assinghams are not effectively silenced, they are engaged in conversations to prove that speaking has no effect because meaning has been transferred from speaking to thinking.

This transfer notwithstanding, James continues to equivocate about whether referring for others *can* be negated, for in Fanny's conversation with Bob at the end of part 1, she predicates part 2. Of Maggie, "again she projected her vision. 'The way it comes to me . . . is that she'll triumph'" (1.383).

work. Meaning placed in speech cedes to meaning placed in thought. But these models, once specified, have an equivocal relation. For having established representations that pose ostensible alternatives to each other—alternatives that question rather than endorse the meaning-making procedures required by the acknowledgment of other minds—James eschews specifying in any definitive way how referring in speech and in thought might legitimately be related. He eschews this even as the relentless interrogations on behalf of the disparate ways of predicating meaning would seem to demand a conclusive way of relating them. Or, as the dumbness and the unconsciousness of the novel's last paragraph implies, he imagines the solution to lie, after all, outside of speaking *and* outside of thinking—hence, after all, outside of representation.

It is a not entirely sanguine fact about our implication in the issues about which I have been speaking that we can understand the novel's plot without understanding the novel's problematic of how reference is to be determined. For when, like Maggie, we are unable to sustain the idea of meaning as a question, we moralize about the novel, see its thematic as one of morality, which is an ultimate act of codifying the arbitrariness of our interpretation by making a special case for its inevitability. As a consequence, the intrigue of the plot replaces interest in the problematic. What makes this usurpation dismaying is how little the dissociation affects a traditional understanding of James's project. What makes the fact stranger still is that the same dissociation—of the problematic from the plot, of what is to be understood from what is to be done—characterizes, with its attendant imposition or its attendant predication, what James represents as *thinking*.

In one crucial instance—I conclude with it—a similar dissociation characterizes what James represents as *speaking*. When, at the end of the novel, the Ververs part, we are told that the two cannot acknowledge the leave-taking because "such a passage . . . would have torn them to pieces, if they had so much as suffered its suppressed relations to peep out of their eyes" (2.362). Yet when Maggie (reiterating the words with which she introduced to her father the idea of marrying Charlotte because " 'she's so great' " [1.180]) says to Mr. Verver, " 'Father, father—Charlotte's great!' "

and he replies, "'Charlotte's great'" (2.364), what is being circumvented is not a transgressive intimacy between father and daughter but rather the particular words of parting that would express it. This would seem parallel to the fiction entertained by Charlotte for Amerigo at the novel's beginning: intimacy—unattested to in language and dissociated from any object, like a ricordo, that can be said to denote it—can be denied to exist. But the situations are not parallel. In the initial exchange Charlotte refers for Amerigo. In the final exchange between father and daughter reference is agreed upon, even in fact echoed. "'Charlotte's great' . . . 'Charlotte's great.'" But, as the words have been divorced from what they claim to designate (they here have little to do with Charlotte and less to do with an appreciation of her), there is nothing about which the two logically "can" agree:

> "Charlotte's great" . . . . he looked at her. "Charlotte's great. . . . She's beautiful, beautiful!" . . . It was all she might have wished, for it was, with a kind of speaking competence, the note of possession and control; and yet it conveyed to her as nothing till now had done the reality of their parting. They were parting, in the light of it, absolutely on Charlotte's *value*. . . . (2.364–65)

"'Charlotte's great'" does not "signify" the parting—not denotatively and not connotatively. Parting is what the Ververs are doing. It is not what they are talking about. Moreover, their relation to the same words is not symmetrical. And, unlike many verbal exchanges in the novel, this one is made sufficient in that no "unuttered" other words are thrust behind or beyond, effectively preempting it. In this state of "speaking competence"—this triumph over reference, or devastation of it—speech, opaque as thought, comes to mean nothing penetrable; almost, it seems, like the cry at the novel's center, to mean nothing at all.

FOUR

Thinking It Out in
The Wings of the Dove

At the beginning of *The Wings of the Dove* it is arranged—by Susan Stringham and Aunt Maud, on the one hand, and by Kate and Densher, on the other—for Milly to suppose (or think) that although Densher is in love with Kate, Kate, not reciprocating the feeling, "could only be sorry and kind" (1.298). This is untrue. At the novel's end, after Lord Mark informs Milly that Kate and Densher have all along been engaged, Susan Stringham asks Densher, "'will you deny to Milly . . . what she has been made so dreadfully to believe?'" When Densher requests to know what *Mrs. Stringham* believes (or thinks), he is apprised that this is contingent: "'What I believe will inevitably depend more or less on your action. . . . I promise to believe you down to the ground if, to save her life, you consent to a denial'" (2.292). Yet, though Mrs. Stringham notifies Densher that what she will "believe" about the truth of Lord Mark's claim depends on what Densher does, his action cannot influence what Mrs. Stringham thinks. It can only determine what she agrees to say she thinks. Finally, after Milly's death, when Aunt Maud attributes Densher's ineptness to his grief rather than to his guilt, this interpretation of his feelings replaces his own understanding of them:

> She thus presented him to himself, as it were, in the guise in which she had now adopted him, and it was the element of truth in the character that he found himself, for his own part, adopting. (2.336)

We see here an extreme instance of one character's governance of thought for another character. The instance is extreme because the passage I have pointed to does not only substitute a supposition that is false for one that is true, as in the initial lie about Kate's relation to Densher. Nor does it more complexly suggest that whether a claim is thought false or true is explicitly conditional—to be negotiated or bargained over—as in Mrs. Stringham's attempt to make Densher falsely deny his guilt to Milly. It more transgressively reveals one consciousness dictating to another how the latter thinks of itself. In the first case the problem is what to think of someone else (what conception Milly should entertain that will accurately identify Kate's relation to Densher). In the second case the problem is how someone else thinks of you (how Mrs. Stringham will imagine Densher's relation to Kate). In the third case the problem is how you can be made to think of yourself. How does "thinking" work here? What is being exemplified?

The answer is not obvious in part because the examples are not immediately comparable. For instance, Milly *believes* what she is told (that Kate and Densher are not engaged) at the beginning of the novel, though at the end of the novel she only behaves as if she believed it. Thus by the end of the novel Milly is in the position of most of the novel's other characters for whom what is believed and what is attested are opposite to each other. Yet even when the examples are made comparable, what is being exemplified is still difficult to identify since, when characters "think," or deny what they "think," or attempt to influence what others "think," these operations or procedures are, as I shall elaborate, not easy to associate with consciousness or with thinking, as we customarily understand it.[1] This novel, like all of James's, purports to show the workings of a character's mind, to exemplify the mental processes of conceiving, considering, exercising the mind, and to represent the stream of associations we identify with these activities. (Here the active nature of idioms like "think through," "think out," "think over" is illustrative.) Yet, as I shall suggest, James calls into question the no longer implicitly understood internal ground of this activity. I want immediately to acknowledge the problem inherent in attempting discriminations like the ones I have anticipated or like those which are to follow. As the *OED* states, " 'think' is the most general verb to express internal mental activity excluding mere perception of external things or passive reception of ideas." Moreover, in the

dictionary, as in common usage, and no less so in the novel,
ostensibly discrete connotations of thinking shade into each
other. In the examples I have introduced so far, distinctions
could be predicated. What Milly is "to think" implies what
she is "to suppose." What Mrs. Stringham is to think implies what she will claim to "believe." What Densher is to
think implies how he is "to regard" himself. These differences notwithstanding, "to think," as "to picture," the
OED's fourth definition—"to form or have an idea of, to
imagine, to fancy, conceive, picture"—is not simply the
loosest but also the most accurate way to delineate what is
implied by thinking in all three contexts.

Yet even when we suppose that we know how thinking is
being represented by James, there are problems with our
understanding. The idiom which specifically associates
"thinking" and "picturing" (being able to "picture" something) is one which implies being able to imagine something
not in fact there. It therefore connotes a mental activity or a
mental operation. But in James's work, as I have argued
throughout, thinking is often represented as if its inception
occurred outside the mind, which only subsequently takes it
in, as in Mrs. Lowder's thinking of Densher in terms then
appropriated as his own. Or thinking is represented not
simply as relational but as that specific interaction characterized by coercion, as in Mrs. Stringham's notification to Densher of the conditions that regulate her understanding of
him. Milly, in her correct assumption that she can will what
she thinks, can make Densher the beneficiary of her will
(which in this context means she can bequeath to Densher
not simply her riches but also her image of him as it dictates
what he is, as if involuntarily, to do), performs the novel's
ultimate manipulation. She refuses to countenance the evil
of the world. She will not say she believes in it. So the character who is supposed to be exempt from thinking as manipulating is most successfully engaged in it.[2]

In the pages that follow I examine in detail four examples
of thinking in *The Wings of the Dove*. The framework for my
consideration, however, is not a reading of that novel.
Rather, in looking at these examples, I mean to investigate
the characteristics of thinking instantiated in this work but

no less typical of James's representations generally. In the first example, I shall argue, "thinking" is confused with looking. In the second, thinking is revealed in one character's looking at another character's thinking. In both cases, the location of thinking is displaced by being represented as projected and externalized. Thus, in a complex transference of impressions between characters before a portrait, thinking is confused with regarding a picture, in one instance, and with regarding what another mind is picturing, in the second. In the third example, thinking is explicitly connected to a fantasized conception of how one will oneself be pictured, thought of, or regarded. In the fourth example, the *function* of thinking is to invert or turn inside out the *content* of what is thought, as in the apparently formulaic, and therefore trivial, statement of Milly's, " 'Since I've lived all these years as if I were dead, I shall die, no doubt, as if I were alive . . .' " (1.199). The previous sentence, I shall argue, is not in fact a random illustration, for although in *The Wings of the Dove* many formulations are made chiastic (characters predicate a thought only to turn it around syntactically and semantically), the thought most frequently tampered with in this way is the thought of death.

To see how thinking works in these examples—to see that thinking is confused with manipulating another's thinking; that looking is confused with thinking; that the point of one character's thinking is to observe another character's thinking; that the content of a thought (specifically the thought of death) is itself manipulated by being rhetorically pictured as turned around—is to arrive inevitably at a critique and a question, stated preliminarily as follows. In reading James's novels, we want characters to think less, and for good reason. Thinking is treacherous in these representations. On occasion, in *The Wings of the Dove*, it also appears lethal. To take in more broadly the sweep of James's work is to see that James could not stop thinking of consciousness and that he could not represent it except in ways that contradict its defining limitations. To put this in different terms: if the examples I shall examine are typical—and I wish to claim they are—consciousness is not being represented in these works; it is rather being repudiated. But if

this is the case, why do we associate James's work with—
even imagine it to epitomize—a subject which, in terms I
now investigate, it rather makes unrecognizable?

I

Twice in the chapter in which Lord Mark leads Milly to see
the Bronzino we are told "things melted together—" (1.219,
220). This phrase first refers to Milly's general impression of
the benevolence of the glances sent in her direction as she
follows Lord Mark through his house. The second time it refers to the particular fusion of the past and the present (of
"the beauty and the history and the facility and the splendid
midsummer glow . . ." [1.220]). Other blurrings in these
pages are not explicitly signaled. In the chapter I am considering Lord Mark asks Milly:

> "Have you seen the picture in the house, the beautiful
> one that's so like you?" . . .
>   "I've been through rooms and I've seen pictures. But
> if I'm 'like' anything so beautiful as most of them
> seemed to me—!" It needed in short for Milly some ev-
> idence which he only wanted to supply. She was the
> image of the wonderful Bronzino, which she must have
> a look at on every ground. (1.217)

When Milly, implicitly in her broken sentence, asks to see
the picture that looks "like" her, what does she want to look
at? Why, at the moment that she asks to see what the
Bronzino "looks like," does she find herself "looked at" or,
in James's words, "looked over" by "kind lingering eyes"
(1.218) as Lord Mark leads her through his house of guests?
These repeated locutions—"looked like," "looked over,"
"must have a look at"—insist first on the multiplicity of contexts for looking and, as a consequence, on the uncertainty
of where the looking is directed and where it is coming
from. The confusion is underscored by the narrator's explanation that "the Bronzino was, it appeared, deep within"
(1.219). The description specifies the painting's location in
the house. But given Lord Mark's insistence that the picture
in the house is "'so like you,'" a comparison ratified by Milly's immediate identification with it, the remark alludes,
obliquely, to a different location for the picture. Or it alludes

to a different picture, which will be drawn out from Milly's mind.

"Looked like" designates the result of an act of perception, initially Lord Mark's. "Looked over," in this context, indicates an act of being inspected and perceived, of being penetrated rather than penetrating. Because the looking seems to come from so many places, it is not clear what the looking is about. The unclarity is underscored because looking and the object of looking are fused in these crossings. Also fused, in the novel as a whole, and in the following passage in particular, are looking and thinking. Thus, when Milly sees the Bronzino,

> she found herself, for the first moment, looking at the mysterious portrait through tears. Perhaps it was her tears that made it just then so strange and fair—as wonderful as he had said: the face of a young woman, all splendidly drawn . . . a face . . . that must, before fading with time, have had a family resemblance to her own. The lady in question . . . was a very great personage—only unaccompanied by a joy. And she was dead, dead, dead. Milly recognised her exactly in words that had nothing to do with her. "I shall never be better than this." (1.220–21)

It is difficult to understand the process represented in the passage, even at the grammatical level. The "this" in "'I shall never be better than this'" seems as if it would signify either "better than I am now" or "better than this lady in the portrait." In fact neither is implied. For Milly looks at the portrait and has thoughts not of her present self, and not of the woman as painted, but rather of the representation of the woman epitomized by its lifelessness, of an image of death, which Milly analogizes to her own image and which she sees in the woman's place. Moreover, what Milly does is not purely like "looking," because she apprehends the portrait through tears that (virtually) precede her vision of it; hence they appear not quite to be generated by it. In fact, they are themselves looked at by Milly (who is shown throughout the passage to think introspectively about what she sees) as a vision in their own right: "Perhaps it was her tears that made it just then so strange and fair." And it is not like "seeing" in the sense of perceiving the meaning only of what is in front of her, because she "recognised her exactly in words that had nothing to do with her." What Milly does is rather like "thinking." Or it is like what thinking is for James, which means that thought is as if beheld, is held up before the eyes.*

But what, again, does Milly see? Milly, looking at the portrait, rather thinks of the woman out of the portrait, not existing in a frame, but existing in time. We are told the face "must, before fading with time, have had a family resemblance to her own." What has faded, of course, is not the painting but the face after it was painted, since the face in the painting is that of a young woman. Thus "the lady in question" at whom Milly looks is not the one in the painting, but the original of that lady, the one presumed to have sat for her portrait—extrapolated, projected forward, and conceptually located between her youth and her fading. Milly projects the image of the lady forward from the moment of the painting and projects the image of herself backward; in the intersection of those moments resemblance is located: she sees the woman as she sees herself, another woman who is dying. But ultimately there is a difference between the woman and herself, for the image that Milly also sees is not only that of youth (not the image in the painting) nor only that of projected identification (the image drawn up between the lady's youth and her fading) but in addition a different projection that has reached fulfillment in the realization of the woman's dying: "she was dead, dead, dead."

What is being recognized—in the specific sense of realized—is Milly's thought of "her" death. Milly is made to see her thought—to picture the thought of death—and then she is given words for it: "'I shall never be better than this.'" Thus, while Lord Mark and the others see Milly's likeness to the Bronzino, she sees that she is only the image

*From the vantage of another vocabulary, thinking that is beheld is thinking that is involuntary, connected with associative sequences that register on the mind, as opposed to thinking in which ideas are arranged, directed toward a goal, and thus explicitly willed. This distinction is important, for it is as *willed*, I shall argue, that the end of the novel differently represents thinking. Moreover, as the tears are also involuntary, and as they are emblematic of the blurring of looking and thinking (as well as of Milly's ocular perception), insofar as will is presumed to be part of the mind, they too suggest that looking and thinking are here imposed from outside the mind.

of the dead girl, sees precisely the fact that she does not *yet* look like her. They see a physical likeness. She intuits the difference between herself and the figure in the painting, which inspires, or could itself be identified as, the thought of death. They see a connection between Milly and the Bronzino through which her thinking drives a wedge. Yet even while we are made to appreciate the difference between what they see and what she thinks, there is no less a sense in which the thought of death appears external to the mind that is then made to entertain it. This is the case because Milly's thought is literally pictured (held up for her to see) and because Milly's thought of her likeness to the (dead) girl in the picture does not arise in her mind, but rather in Lord Mark's. Thus the thought (of likeness) is two steps removed: it is not initially in Milly's mind, and it is not in the picture of which she is "the image." It is in, or originates from, Lord Mark's suggestion that "'the picture in the house'" is "'so like you.'"

Another way to put this is to say there is a sense in which looking at the painting and thinking about it are not clearly in the mind and not entirely elicited by the painting, since Milly is not exactly looking at what is in the painting, and since she is not exactly thinking, when she looks at the painting, only of her own death. She is doing something that blurs the distinction between thinking and looking, and that something, or that blurring, is reiterated when it is not just she who looks at the painting but also the others, who note her resemblance to the woman in the painting and who look at Milly as she walks through the house to observe what they see. For, as I have indicated, the initial thought of Milly's likeness to the painting is not hers but theirs. This blurring of looking and thinking, or this confusion about its agency, raises the question of where looking and thinking are coming from, making it almost appear—although of course this is impossible—as if the looking and thinking, as well as the painting, were outside Milly's mind.[3]

What Milly thinks she will have in common with the image in the painting is the death of the woman. What is *Milly* dying of? Kate formulates the question, "'What in the world is the matter with you?'" (1.227). That question is continually repeated in the novel, and as continually thwarted. After Mrs. Stringham's conference with the physician, Sir Luke

Strett, she reports: "'He says it *isn't* a case. . . . It isn't, at least . . . the case she believed it to be. . . . she hasn't what she thought'" (2.109). As Mrs. Stringham fails to ask Sir Luke Strett what disease Milly thought she had, we also are not allowed to countenance it. Characters' speculations are similarly discredited. When Densher asks if Milly has consumption, the expression on Kate's face prompts his own retraction of the idea: "'Do you mean she has something that's past patching?'" (2.53). Any diagnoses, any guesses about "cause," are axiomatically trivialized. So when Densher expresses horror at making up to a dying girl, Kate reassures him: "'She won't die, she won't live, by inches. She won't smell, as it were, of drugs. She won't taste, as it were, of medicine. No one will know'" (2.53).

Yet despite the various dismissals of the question "What is Milly dying of?" it is made inevitable at just the point in the novel I have been examining. For Milly's illness is introduced here as if it were a consequence of—at any rate it directly follows from—her having been shown the Bronzino. (Her illness, though alluded to earlier, is earlier dismissed by being treated as trivial, or nonconsequential.) It is as if, after Milly has looked at the Bronzino and thought of the girl as dead, her own life is put in jeopardy. As if, to put it glibly, the thought of death could kill. This is all the more strange when we recall that the thought of Milly's likeness to the Bronzino was first Lord Mark's. The point to be made, then, is that thought is inflicted, and then registers fatally. It is not irrelevant that later in the novel Lord Mark reveals a connection between Densher and Kate that could actually be said to kill Milly. Causality between thinking about death and being afflicted by the thought is differently demonstrated by Kate's looking at Milly as they stand before the Bronzino and "hop[ing] she wasn't ill" (1.225). Why, *then*, does she look so? And by Milly's request, following this, that Kate accompany her to the doctor because "the matter with her was what exactly as yet she wanted knowledge about" (1.227). We are subsequently told that Milly has requested a consultation with Sir Luke Strett. But this information is withheld until, or so that, Milly's thoughts about the painting and her thoughts about the visit to the doctor are shown to be sequential, even, say, causal.

It may still not be clear why "thinking" is the word that describes what happens in the particular scene I have been discussing. And other examples of thinking in the novel make the phenomenon less recognizable. The subsequent three scenes to which I turn exemplify, respectively, thinking as looking at another character's thinking, thinking as picturing how other characters (will) think of one, thinking as reversing. I shall suggest they are related.

II

In the first of the scenes, narrated through the eyes of Milly's traveling companion, Mrs. Stringham, we are twice told indirectly that the older woman is Milly's confidante. What is to be remarked about this characterization is that Milly has nothing to confide. Milly doesn't tell Susan Stringham anything, and Milly doesn't need to. Thus one afternoon in Switzerland, where the two are staying for a while, Milly, for her "preferred detachment," takes a walk alone. She is trailed by Susan Stringham, who, inconspicuously, wishes to check on the girl. As she catches sight of Milly (this is also the first time *we* see her) sitting on "a slab of rock at the end of a short promontory . . . that merely pointed off to the right at gulfs of air[,] . . . Mrs. Stringham stifled a cry" (1.122–23). We are told, "A thousand thoughts, for the minute, roared in the poor lady's ears, but without reaching, as it happened, Milly's" (1.123–24). Whose thoughts are these? And what is there to be alarmed at?

Mrs. Stringham is thinking apocalyptically of Milly thinking. Specifically, she supposes—and then thinks better of it—that Milly is "deeply and recklessly . . . meditating a jump" (1.124). Milly, on second thought, is not thinking of renouncing things but rather of having them: "She was looking down on the kingdoms of the earth. . . . Was she choosing among them or did she want them all?" According to Mrs. Stringham, Milly is thinking of

> taking full in the face the whole assault of life. . . .
> She wouldn't have committed suicide; she knew herself
> unmistakeably reserved for some more complicated
> passage; this was the very vision in which she had,
> with no little awe, been discovered. The image that

> thus remained with the elder lady kept the character of
> a revelation. (1.125)

Revelation of what? This question is instigated by the fact
that an iconographic impulse is allowing Mrs. Stringham to
read Milly's position in that landscape with reference to two
other pictures, those of Christ's temptations on the temple
and the mountaintop (Matt. 4:5–10). Thus it looks as if Mrs.
Stringham's entry into Milly's mind does not involve depth
but rather involves treating Milly as a surface whose meaning is predetermined. Because Milly does not seem scrutinized, but only superficially glossed, it has to be asked
whether the thoughts recorded here reveal something about
Milly. Are these thoughts "of" her also her thoughts?

Such questions are illuminated by an apparently irrelevant
coda to the episode I am describing. Mrs. Stringham, who
initially wished to see the girl without being observed, now
decides to leave Milly a note conceding her presence. But
the *"à bientôt!"* (see you soon) which she pencils on the
cover of a book Milly has placed nearby (on the book rather
than in it, since its pages are uncut) is left behind. Thus the
book's writing remains unread on both the outside and the
inside. Milly, not seeing the *"à bientôt!"*, never supposes herself to have been discovered. *Has* she been? In the first instance Mrs. Stringham imagines her thoughts about Milly to
have the character of a revelation, to reveal something *about*
Milly. In the second instance she wishes to notify Milly of
her presence, to reveal something *to* Milly. Initially, Mrs.
Stringham's thoughts do not, in James's words, "reach"
Milly because Milly does not hear them. Mrs. Stringham
does not intrude on the girl's illusion of solitude. But the *"à
bientôt!"* also does not reach Milly, in that the girl is oblivious of it. Yet if "not reaching" Milly as "not communicating"
something to her and "not reaching" Milly as "not accurately representing" something *of* her are related—as the
otherwise gratuitous book incident suggests—it is in no obvious way. "Not communicating something to" Milly (not
writing something that will be read *by* her) is not an indication of whether Mrs. Stringham is communicating about
Milly, of whether she is, as she thinks, accurately reading
the girl. Indeed communication about Milly is functionally a
substitute for communication to her. This is so because all

we hear of Milly's thinking passes through Mrs. Stringham's mind. No other account of Milly's thoughts at this moment is given us. It is so because thought which exists between two characters without being communicated from one to the other makes Mrs. Stringham's thinking about Milly seem continuous with Milly's thinking about herself. Nothing mediates this thought, demonstrates it to be the property of one mind rather than of another—not speech, which would be either attributed or owned, and not the unread *"à bientôt!"* which, differentially designating one of the characters as writer and the other as reader, would attest to the separateness of the two minds. Finally it is so because the narrator suggests Mrs. Stringham's characterization of Milly is of a piece with Milly's self-characterization, preparatory to what "will more distinctly [more directly?] appear for us" (1.126). (In the Preface to the novel, less obliquely in his own voice, James acknowledges with respect to this scene: "I allot to Mrs. Stringham the responsibility of the direct appeal to us . . . on the alpine height. . . . Mrs. Stringham has to register the transaction" [xxi].) Thus (contrary to the expectations created by Mrs. Stringham's initial, inaccurate reading of Milly) we are meant to see Milly's vision, as discovered by Mrs. Stringham, to be not for that reason ultimately any less Milly's. How insistently Mrs. Stringham thinks *for* Milly (in that she thinks what Milly thinks) is emphasized a page later, when, on Milly's return, Mrs. Stringham interrupts Milly's speech because it is gratuitous:

> "Should you think me quite abominable if I were to say that after all—?"
>   Mrs. Stringham had already thought, with the first sound of the question, everything she was capable of thinking, and had immediately made such a sign that Milly's words gave place to visible relief at her assent. (1.127)

But it is not only that Mrs. Stringham is repeatedly confirmed as thinking thoughts for Milly, or as thinking Milly's thoughts so that Milly is relieved of the burden of thinking or speaking them. It is also that, when speech is allowed to represent thought, what is being represented is deliberately made ambiguous. Thus in the exchange following the Alpine climb:

". . . But I sometimes wonder—!"

"Yes"—[Mrs. Stringham] pressed: "wonder what?"

"Well, if I shall have much of it."

Mrs. Stringham stared. "Much of what? Not of pain?"

"Of everything. Of everything I have."

Anxiously again, tenderly, our friend cast about. "You 'have' everything; so that when you say 'much' of it—"

"I only mean," the girl broke in, "shall I have it for long? That is if I *have* got it." . . .

"If you've got an ailment?"

"If I've got everything," Milly laughed.

"Ah *that*—like almost nobody else."

"Then for how long?"

Mrs. Stringham's eyes entreated her. . . . "Do you want to see some one? . . . We'll go straight to the best near doctor." . . .

"I don't think I've really *everything*," Milly said as if to explain—and as if also to put it pleasantly. . . .

"But what is it you think you haven't got?"

Milly waited another moment; then she found it, and found for it a dim show of joy. "The power to resist the bliss of what I *have!*" (1.130–31)

What is being talked about?* Milly's pain or the fact that Milly doesn't feel pain? Milly's wealth or Milly's illness? What Milly has or what Milly lacks? Is the peculiarity of the conversation, half tautological, half contradictory, a consequence of Milly's despair at not having "everything"? Or is it symptom-

---

*To look exclusively at the last two paragraphs of the passage cited above is to answer the question "What is being talked about?" at a different, comprehensive level whose scope is the whole novel. For when Mrs. Stringham asks Milly, " 'What is it you think you haven't got?' " Milly looks for a thought; then she finds it; then she finds *for* it its manifestational correlative (the "dim show of joy"); then she expresses her thought aphoristically: " 'The power to resist the bliss of what I *have!*' " The expression encrypts one way of specifying the novel's theme: the relentlessness of joy. Here Milly has the "joy" without the "power" to regulate it. At the novel's end, she is made equivalent to the joy, at which point it kills her. For when the joy becomes boundless, she becomes unrepresentable. But at that same point— when the joy overwhelms its possessor—it also becomes a legacy. The novel unfolds the implications of that enigma, even as Milly finds in the periodic sentence not her thought but the means to encrypt it. Thus what we see her making is a stylistic discovery. From still another perspective, the dialectic of the book requires the extraneousness of pain. This conversation marks one of the few moments in the text when we see pain being elided. For the novel's reiterated paired terms are not pain and joy, but rather power and joy.

atic of pleasure at having more than most? Such questions recall Mrs. Stringham's surmise of Milly's thoughts as she looks
down earlier from her rock: "Was she choosing among them
or did she want them all?" For, as Milly's words here reverber-
ate against Mrs. Stringham's reflections on Milly's thoughts,
this conversation echoes the questions Mrs. Stringham was
thinking Milly was thinking,—was thinking on Milly's behalf.

Mrs. Stringham's thoughts do not of course echo Milly's.
As they precede Milly's, one could say Milly's thoughts echo
Mrs. Stringham's. Whose thoughts these are then remains
ambiguous, not because characters' thoughts seem undiscriminated (although the question of a thought's autonomy
is not here incidental) but rather because the source of
thought remains unclear. What is confusing is whose
thought is being represented: Milly's or Mrs. Stringham's.
And what is also confusing is the content of thought. The
confusion is a specific one. It is not clear whether one thing
is meant or whether its antithesis is meant. Is Milly contemplating suicide or does she mean to have it all? Just this sus-
ceptibility to reversal typifies *thinking* in *The Wings of the
Dove*. Thinking is inverted by being externalized because it is
instigated by a source outside the self, as in Lord Mark's
suggestion of Milly's likeness to the painting. Thinking is inverted or externalized by being confused with looking, as in
Milly's viewing the Bronzino and thinking of death or as in
Mrs. Stringham's looking at Milly and thinking of Milly
thinking. Thus thoughts have a life outside the mind to
which they occur.* Yet if the scene with Susan Stringham

---

*" 'Every one asks me what I "think" of everything,' " Spencer Brydon
scoffs, at the beginning of "The Jolly Corner," " '. . . even were it possible
to meet in that stand-and-deliver way so silly a demand on so big a subject,
my "thoughts" would still be almost altogether about something that concerns only myself' " (435). The metaphor of being asked to respond to the
question "What do you think?" is one of highway robbery—of thought expressed under compulsion—here barely masked by the sense of rhetorical
delivery. In the story, however, Brydon *is* delivered of his thought, not because he voices it, involuntarily or otherwise, but rather because he sees it.
Specifically, Brydon first stalks, and is then menaced by, "the bared identity
. . . [that] was too hideous as *his*" (476), by the reification of the thought of
what he might have been, made—in the looking at—external and other.
So the entirely private thought is embodied, after all, in the visage of a
ghost, the self turned inside out. And this thought made incarnate is visible
not only to Brydon but also to his friend, who, as if to confirm the externality of the image, recognizes the ghost even before he does.

illustrates one way of imagining thought to be out of Milly's mind (it is out of Milly's mind and in Susan Stringham's, or it is in Milly's mind and also in Susan Stringham's), a second way of imagining thought to be out of one's mind is not then to see it as in someone else's, but rather less explicably, to see it as in no one's mind—as out of the mind and in the world. (The intersubjective or political sense of "out of one's mind" and "in" someone else's is elaborated in my discussion of *The Golden Bowl*.) As a consequence of this externalization, as even perhaps its point, we see a second way in which thinking is connected with inversion: the mind reverses or turns around the content of a particular thought. We see this anticipated in the equivocation of Milly's thinking of suicide or wanting "everything" and again in the ambiguity about whether what Milly "has much of" is pain or joy. But thinking as reversing is not only formulated by near oppositions. It is also governed by logical strictness, as we see when Milly's thought "She could live if she would" takes the form of a chiasmus, "She would live if she could." These apparently antithetical ways of understanding are then made to be compatible.[4] I shall return to this particular example in which the thought of death is turned around, but I want, in the third scene, to which I now proceed, to touch on the ways in which turning the thought of death around initially involves staging one's understanding of it.

III

Preliminary to turning the thought of death around is manipulating how—arranging the circumstances in which—one is to learn of it. Milly will not knowingly think of her dying in the presence of another. It is false to do so, since, as she tells Sir Luke Strett, others don't make any difference, "'I mean when one *is*—really alone'" (1.239). Thus, although Milly brings Kate along for her first meeting with Sir Luke Strett, that visit, cut short, is structurally made perfunctory. As Milly will not think of her dying in the presence of another, so she will not be present when another is made to think of it. She will not relinquish a primary relation to her thought of death, hence will not be a mere witness to another's learning of it. When Sir Luke Strett arrives to tell Susan Stringham of the severity of Milly's illness, the girl leaves the house. Then, framed between the averted danger of thinking of her death in another's company and the averted danger of being company to another who is alerted to think of her death, Milly is seen as being alone with the thought of her dying.

Or we see her almost so. Milly, alone with Sir Luke Strett, sees she has been "found out" (1.236). But this is not because she has spoken to him and not because he has asked about her. It is also not because he has spoken *to* her. Like a prototype of the analyst, Strett puts before her the "so crystal-clean . . . great empty cup of attention" (1.230). And what she sees in that emptiness—the picture with which she fills it up—is a split image, which, though she cannot comprehend it, she thinks of as saving her: "he looked, in the oddest manner, to her fancy, half like a general and half like a bishop, and she was soon sure that, within some such handsome range, what it would show her would be what was good, what was best for her" (1.231). Yet, though Strett's visage (mystifying, inscrutable) solicits her attention, seems to promise her salvation, what it in fact gives or shows her is death. What Milly sees as she sits across from him, before any words have passed between them, is that she is to die. That this should be her perception is noteworthy in light of what Sir Luke Strett eventually *says*, what he reiterates—that she is to live:

> "Well, see all you can. That's what it comes to. Worry about nothing. You *have* at least no worries. It's a great rare chance." . . .
> "Shall I at any rate suffer?"
> "Not a bit."
> "And yet then live?"
> "My dear young lady," said her distinguished friend, "isn't 'to live' exactly what I am trying to persuade you to take the trouble to do?" (1.245–46)

One way to interpret Milly's comprehension by inversion is to see that she simply does not believe him. This is the case because, as she figures later, "she either mattered, and then she was ill; or she didn't matter, and then she was well enough. Now he was 'acting,' as they said at home, as if she did matter" (1.253). It is the case because, although he tells her she will live, "one wasn't treated so—was one?—unless it had come up, quite as much, that one might die" (1.248). And it is the case because she attributes Strett's desire to know more about her to something like pity: "and when pity held up its telltale face like a head on a pike, in a French revolution, bobbing before a window, what was the inference but that the patient was bad? He might say what he would now—she would always have seen the head at the window . . ." (1.240). This picture—with the head on the pike framed by the window—summons up a brutal image. For pity ought to be the *response* to the head on the pike, as opposed to *being* the head on the pike. Understanding the unconventionality of the image means seeing that Milly interprets pity not only as the death sentence but also as the emblem of death. Pity, so construed, is what produces heads on pikes. Through pity Milly gleans what Strett is not going to tell her.

Yet the inversion of the words that Strett says with the words Milly intuits is not to be attributed only to her failure to believe him. For before he speaks at all, although Milly thinks "he might say what he would," he hasn't said a word. (Later, as she walks through Regent's Park, she thinks, "What indeed she was really confronted with was the consciousness that he hadn't after all pronounced her anything . . ." [1.251].) Like the Bronzino, then, Strett externalizes and mirrors Milly's thought of her dying. But although it is one thing to see death in a picture, as Milly Theale does when she looks at the Bronzino and thinks that the girl is "dead," it is another to picture one's own death (the "head on a pike") in the verdict of a silent visage. Still another to think of one's death as if it could be an actual picture for others to look at. This Milly Theale does as she scans the examining room and imagines death as converted into the state of the photographic portraits on the wall, which will posthumously be displayed for others to look at:

> she should be as one of the circle of eminent contemporaries, photographed, engraved, signatured, and in particular framed and glazed, who made up the rest of the decoration, and made up as well so much of the human comfort. . . . she also wondered what *she* would eventually decide upon to present in gratitude.

> She would give something better at least than the
> brawny Victorian bronzes. (1.237)

Why, when Sir Luke Strett says she is to live, is death pictured? And why in the picture, by the idea of an actual picture, is the thought of death negated or reversed? For in the
scene I am considering Milly thinks of her death as inevitable. But, in seeming opposition, death is something that Milly's thinking can mitigate. Death, first thought of, is then
thought better of.

This doubling of thought back on itself is further complicated by the fact that Milly's image of death raises rather
than settles the question of what is being contemplated.
Specifically, in that same passage, sitting in Sir Luke Strett's
chambers, Milly attempts to imagine her death, but this is
confused with her simultaneous imagining of the place
where she is now recognizing it:

> She had come forth to see the world, and this then was
> to be the world's light, the rich dusk of a London
> "back," these the world's walls, those the world's cur-
> tains and carpet. (1.237)

To try to gloss the image is to see how it resists the attempt
to separate the trappings of the vision from the trappings of
the room. This is not simply because the room is where the
vision occurs. It is also because the vision is *of* the room, or
of the light in the room, and of the room's furnishings and
boundaries, with tenor and vehicle seemingly indistinguishable. Or distinguishable as follows. The dwindling of the
world's light (life would be an acceptable paraphrase) to the
size of Milly's comprehension of it in "the rich dusk of a
London 'back'" signals Milly's understanding of its finitude.
Yet the vision of finitude is recorded in her consciousness as
a finitude of vision. The image operates as a chiasmus,
though it is not verbalized as one. To shift my terms slightly:
what Milly sees is as much the picture of a room expressing
boundedness as the picture of a doom expressing boundedness. The several conflations have consequences. They dis-
place the image of death with the very picture of the self
("photographed . . . signatured . . . framed . . . glazed")
whose identifiable features would be presumed obliterated

by it. Moreover, to aestheticize the thought of death, to imagine it as literally commemorated by a picture hung in the same room which—with whatever referential ambiguity—also metaphorizes that death, a room which marks as well the place of Milly's perception of it, is seriously to question whether death is being recognized or whether the recognition is being sabotaged. To aestheticize death is to treat the thought of death formally. And what is formally conceived can be formally rearranged. Milly's thought of death is designed to negate itself.

I take this to be the thrust of the narrator's observation that "she was secretly romancing . . . in the midst of so much else that was more urgent, all over the place" (1.237). "All over the place" is the right idiom, since, for Milly, countenancing death involves not only a distraction from the present recognition, but as the verbs of the following indicate, its explicit subversion. The retrospective "She had come forth to see . . ." becomes the prospective "She should be intimate with the great bronze clock. . . . she should be as one of the circle of eminent contemporaries. . . . "Should," in its auxiliary function of expressing futurity from what appears a perspective that is past, denies the present except as that place where being can be imagined as a keepsake for other people: "she also wondered what *she* would eventually decide upon to present in gratitude." In these various ways Milly does not imagine the passing of life except into an image memorialized for others to gaze at. (Densher, and James too—I shall return to this point— imagines Milly's death likewise.)[5] Milly's thought of what she should give, how she should take her place among the "framed and glazed," points not to the question of what she is to leave behind her, what she is to give up or lose. It points rather to the question what she is to leave *of* herself, as she proleptically imagines the terms on which she is to remain and be viewed. Left out—explicitly missing from Milly's thought of extinction—is the extinction being contemplated.

As if to reiterate the connection between picturing death and averting it, when Sir Luke Strett visits Mrs. Stringham to tell her Milly is dying, Milly does not aimlessly leave the house; she goes to the National Gallery to look at "'pictures and things.'" James makes the connection explicit: "the quiet chambers . . . made her presently say 'If I could lose myself *here!*' There were people, people in plenty, but, admirably, no personal question. It was immense, outside, the personal question; but she had blissfully left it outside . . ." (1.287–88).*

In the scene in which Milly regards the Bronzino, she projects the idea of death. She reads the picture as a gloss on her own death. In the scene with Sir Luke Strett, Milly glosses her death as if it were a picture. The relation of these two scenes, then—like the relation between tenor and vehicle in the scene in Sir Luke Strett's examining room—is chiastic. Also chiastic, as I elaborate in a moment, is the way, leaving Sir Luke Strett's office, Milly formulates her understanding of the diagnosis he has delivered to her.

Although Sir Luke Strett tells Milly she is going to live, she sees she is going to die. Yet, as Milly leaves Sir Luke Strett's office, she is vitalized by the thought of death, which is explicitly construed as "something firm to stand on" (1.236). There is a proper way to understand this—one consonant with Sir Luke Strett's explanation "'You *have* at least no worries. It's a great rare chance.'" I take this to mean, "Since you know what the outcome is, you are free to live. In the most trivial sense, if you did not know what the outcome was, you would worry about it. But as you are—certainly—going to die, that certainty, or your knowledge of

*James anticipates what I shall argue is the realization of this idea. For, as Milly stands in the National Gallery to look at "'pictures and things,'" she is also looked past, while a picture is looked at, as if she were herself a thing. Or as if she were herself an as yet unlooked-at picture. For when one of the beholders comments, "'Handsome? . . . In the English style'" (1.291), we are told that "Milly took the reference as to a picture." The unexpected ambiguity, the option of taking the remark in more ways than one, and the "as" in that construction which invites us to reflect on it, suggest that Milly thinks the remark *could* pertain to herself. The passage continues to engage this option, as when we are told that "she saw . . . that she was in fact among small Dutch pictures," a phrase which, by virtue of its placement, insinuates a second, if subordinate, meaning. In fact, sentences like these suggest that, making good on the desire formulated in Strett's chambers ("she should be . . . signatured . . . framed . . . glazed"), Milly goes to the National Gallery as much to see herself as a picture (and to imagine *that* others might picture her) as to look at "'pictures and things.'"

that certainty, suggests you therefore have a chance to live. But you have this chance because you realize that, however paradoxical such a formulation, both parts of it are true, and cannot be mitigated." Milly, however, tries to mitigate the verdict in the fourth of the scenes to which I now turn, and in the following formulation, "One could live if one would." A moment later she inverts this to "one would live if one could" (1.254). Both propositions, however they contradict each other, more seriously contradict the inevitability put to Milly by Sir Luke Strett. They make the absolute contingent by introducing the idea of desire and the idea of thinking as phenomena which can regulate life and death, states no longer conceived as absolute.

IV

To think of death in Sir Luke Strett's chambers, as Milly does, is to make of death a picture, looked at by others, into which the self will be transmuted. It is not to think of death at all. Walking through Regent's Park, after leaving the physician's chambers, Milly is likewise still distracted from the thought of death. She is still, now in another context, imagining others' views of it:

> Here were benches and smutty sheep; here were idle lads at games of ball, with their cries mild in the thick air; here were wanderers anxious and tired like herself; here doubtless were hundreds of others just in the same box. Their box, their great common anxiety, what was it, in this grim breathing-space, but the practical question of life? They could live if they would; that is, like herself, they had been told so: she saw them all about her, on seats, digesting the information, recognising it again as something in a slightly different shape familiar enough, the blessed old truth that they would live if they could. All she thus shared with them made her wish to sit in their company; which she so far did that she looked for a bench that was empty, eschewing a still emptier chair that she saw hard by and for which she would have paid, with superiority, a fee. (1.250)

Although Milly's supposition is that "here doubtless were hundreds of others just in the same box," the verb that designates their contemplation of that state ("she saw them all

about her . . . digesting the information"), like the subsequent deprecation ("She looked . . . at her scattered melancholy comrades—some of them so melancholy as to be
down on their stomachs in the grass, turned away, ignoring,
burrowing . . ." [1.254]), derides the idea that their perception is like hers—that it exists at all. It is not just that the
others are depicted as mired in the plight which Milly stands
above but that as a consequence, Milly recognizes a possibility which those around her see denied them. For the
"blessed old truth that they would live if they could" is the
perceptual, as well as syntactic, antithesis to the one Milly at
first fathoms. Milly could live if she would; by "her option,
her volition" (1.249), she retains the hope they see willed
away from them.

Yet if these opposite stances are not initially made commensurate, they are eventually made so. For as Milly sits beside those others, connection to whom she inaccurately first
fantasized, her vision changes to *become* theirs. "The last
scrap of superiority" leaves her when, calculating how she
should gauge Sir Luke's assessment of her illness, she feels
herself "subtle exactly in the manner of the suspected, the
suspicious, the condemned" (1.253). From that reduced vantage, she sees that she is a "poor girl—with her rent to pay
. . . for her future; everything else but how to meet it fell
away from her in pieces, in tatters" (1.253–54). Then Milly
has what those around her have, which is to say, nothing:

> Well, she must go home, like the poor girl, and see.
> There might after all be ways; the poor girl too would
> be thinking. It came back for that matter perhaps to
> views already presented. She looked about her again,
> on her feet, at her scattered melancholy comrades—
> some of them so melancholy as to be down on their
> stomachs in the grass, turned away, ignoring, burrow-
> ing; she saw once more, with them, those two faces of
> the question between which there was so little to
> choose for inspiration. It was perhaps superficially
> more striking that one could live if one would; but it
> was more appealing, insinuating, irresistible in short,
> that one would live if one could. (1.254)

In the movement from one passage to another the ambi-
tion implicit in thinking (in thinking as willing to avoid one's

death) becomes the acknowledged inefficacy of such conceptual machinations. In fact the chiasmus which purports to
transform the thought of death, to turn the thought of death
around, fails on two counts. First, although Milly would like
to feel the kinship of her view of death with that of others,
the chiasmus, on strictly logical grounds, calls the analogy
into question, for it exposes an opposition in points of view
supposed to be proximate. But second, the opposition of the
chiasmus is then itself called into question, for if, rhetoric
aside, there is "so little to choose for inspiration," the chiasmus expresses two ways of viewing death whose ostensible
antithesis is only a formal one. If death is inevitable, there
are not two views of death, or these are only views. It does
not matter how one thinks of death, for thinking cannot alter it. Or if a way of thinking is, in fact, superior, that way
(contrary to Milly's initial supposition) is one which acknowledges the insufficiency of "viewing" and the insufficiency of "willing" to do anything but express desire, which
is certain to be negated: "It was perhaps superficially more
striking that one could live if one would; but it was more appealing, insinuating, irresistible in short, that one would live
if one could." The adjectives are shocking. Why should the
power of willing be ceded with such fervor? If in the identification of a necessity—a necessity not a choice—the elation
of the adjectives seems even hysterically generated, this is
because elation erupts from the violence of rejecting the first
view, the superficially more striking one which Milly stood
so much to gain by.

There would be another way to explain the hysteria of this
formulation. For the incessant reversing of "would live/
could live," which makes the position being advocated almost unidentifiable, also seems impersonal. (Here it is as if
the words from the National Gallery were both anticipated
and actualized: "There were people, people in plenty, but,
admirably, no personal question. It was immense, outside,
the personal question; but she had blissfully left it outside.")
Although Milly is said to look at other persons' thoughts as
well as her own as she walks through Regent's Park, her
looking at thoughts—with this idea psychologized—is repeatedly problematized by James's description. In fact, as if

to parody thought associated with persons, his figure of speech, "the two faces of the question," displaces visage, as revealing mental bearing, from persons to questions. In addition, the proposition "would live/could live" is entertained not by actual persons but rather by hypothetical ones ("here doubtless were hundreds of others"), making the idea of persons as thinkers itself hypothetical. Thought in this scene is not in Milly's mind; she sees it as something exterior to her mind—as something outside, not a personal question—which she has been sent out to regard. But because persons are shown as down on their stomachs, "turned away, ignoring, burrowing," thought is not exactly shown as in someone else's mind. Thought is as if pictured in the world, as a thing would be. So understood, Regent's Park becomes the site of thinking, and other people personifications of the site of thinking. To be in the park is to see the externalization. For thought in the park is not like a mental activity. It is rather associated with benches and sheep.

What are the relations among the scenes I have been examining? The point of conflating thinking and looking (and of treating a thought as if it were a picture) is to introduce confusions that will ultimately be enabling. In the scene with the Bronzino the novel illustrates the idea that thinking has consequences, for looking at the picture, Milly sees/thinks she is dying. The scene in which Mrs. Stringham views Milly alone with her thoughts further erodes the distinction between picturing and thinking and between one character's thinking and that of another in that Mrs. Stringham correctly pictures *what* Milly is thinking. (In this instance, picturing another's thoughts is represented as accurate; put in other terms, the insight is passive. Later, also by virtue of access to others' minds, different insights—Milly's about Densher, Densher's about Milly—will appear respectively dictatorial and clairvoyant. For since thinking of another's thought is treated as picturing it, thinking *composes* the vision ostensibly only being registered, as a picture, also ostensibly, would do.) This scene—in which Mrs. Stringham is not sure whether Milly is thinking of giving it up or of having it all—also introduces "reversing" as the central activity in which thinking is engaged. Thus if the scene with the Bronzino suggests that thinking has consequences, the scene with Mrs. Stringham clarifies further what they are: to cancel a thought or call it into question by imagining its antithesis. The scene with Sir Luke Strett, when Milly, told she can live, rather thinks she will die—and then thinks dying into picturing—functions as a mimetic exercise in the mastery of such inversions. For the vision in Strett's chambers stands in purely formal antagonism to the vision entertained before the Bronzino: death thought of in a picture becomes a picture thought of in contemplating death. In the scene which introduces the novel's actual chiasmus, the point of these obsessive reversals, the point of the antagonism, is suddenly clarified, for what is specifically being reversed as Milly walks through Regent's Park, and in the novel as a whole, is the thought of death.

In fact it will have become apparent that in the examples I have examined—of looking and thinking (as Milly regards the Bronzino); of looking at thinking (as Mrs. Stringham regards the thoughts presumed to pass through Milly's mind); of thinking and picturing (as Milly in Sir Luke Strett's office sees prospectively her portrait on the wall); of thinking and reversing (as Milly contemplates the power of willing and then the impotence of it)—thinking does not have a neutral content but is repeatedly thinking of death. Moreover, the consistent point of thinking in these scenes, or at any rate its effect, is to manipulate death so that it is "reversed" or turned around. If one way in which thinking is associated with reversal is by its occurring outside the mind presumed to generate it, and if a second way in which thinking is associated with reversal is by its actively negating the thought of death, a third way in which thinking is associated with reversal is that the particular thought of death is repeatedly treated as indeterminate. In the novel, in fact, it appears that the way in which death would ultimately be canceled or reversed is by immediately, and continuously, making one's relation to it active. Death is therefore represented in one scene as thought to be inevitable, *and* death is represented in another as thought to be avoidable. The alternation of these attitudes reveals the assumption that the condition contemplated can be made pliable by thinking: that the reversal of one's attitude toward death can itself be transferred to the *object* of the thought here being contemplated. The thought of death is turned around from one scene to another in the sense that while one scene appears to embrace death as inevitable, a subsequent scene appears, as if a corrective, to reject death as inconceivable. In the scene with the Bronzino, death is looked at and identified with. In the scene in which Mrs. Stringham looks at Milly thinking, death is looked at and repudiated ("She wasn't meditating a jump. . . . She was looking down on the kingdoms of the earth . . ."). In the scene in Sir Luke Strett's office, death is countenanced and then displaced—countenanced so as to be displaced, even dismissed—by the picture of the self that survives it. For in Sir Luke Strett's office her mind is not engaged in contemplating a picture. It is rather engaged in projecting a picture which will epitomize the self to be left as its memorial for others to contemplate. Yet the shift in perspectives is not only between scenes; it is also in scenes, especially in the one last considered, that in Regent's Park, where opposed "views" are first weighted one way and a moment later weighted another way. Moreover, in Regent's Park (which incorporates aspects of looking as thinking, of looking at others' thinking, of thinking as picturing), the self is liberated from any fixed mental state by the novel's treating that state as if it could be understood by analogy to frames of mind dissociated first from one's own person and then, further, from actual persons. This is not a case of prescribing a picture for others to regard but, conversely, of construing the park as a receptacle for pictures one wants one's own mind free of.

Even to conventionalize the terms of this externalization reiterates its peculiarity: Milly in Regent's Park, looking at others' thinking and looking at her own thinking, sees two pictures (or "views") of death. And it remains indeterminate how the two views of death are to be regarded. In the space of the two passages in question the reversals are vertiginous: Milly's "view" is like that of the others because she wishes it to be ("here doubtless were . . . others just in the same box"); Milly's view is not like that of the others because, as the chiasmus demonstrates, "would" and "could" occupy reversed positions in their separate formulations of it; Milly's view is like that of the others because Milly reverses her view. This shifting of the propositions calls into question, radically destabilizes, any conviction that there could be a settled conclusion about how death is to be conceived, and, in this scene, about *whose* death is being conceived. If death is a picture the mind can reverse—if the work of the novel is to engage in such reversals, to do so relentlessly, automatically (these are related)—the subsequent lack of finality inevitably attaches not simply to the idea of pictures, but also the idea of death.* This the conclusion of the novel ostentatiously demonstrates.

I do not wish to rehearse here the ways in which the novel's end underscores Milly's death as generative rather than annihilative, for this is tangential to the question of thinking about death as I have throughout been concerned with it. Except in this respect: when Densher, before reading it, allows Kate to burn Milly's letter to him—the one that, presumably, informs him not simply of the fortune she willed him, but also of her motives for doing so—he permits the letter's destruction in order to *think* of, rather than to know, what she has written. The thought is like a relic:

> The thought was all his own. . . . He kept it back like a favourite pang; left it behind him, so to say, when he went out, but came home again the sooner for the certainty of finding it there. Then he took it out of its

---

*There would be a more than passing connection between Milly's picturing death in a way that negates or turns it around and the notebook passage from *The American Scene* discussed in my chapter 1, where James, recalling Alice's death, instructs himself to "do that (the picture)," only in the published book to reverse the picture initially being contemplated. For in *The American Scene,* as in *The Wings of the Dove,* James does away with the picture of death ostensibly being done. I therefore take the echo of "picturing," as associated with death, and the idea of picturing death by turning it around not to be accidentally repeated from one text to the other. To elaborate picturing death in the context of the novel: Milly's turning her face to the wall has traditionally been taken to mean that she turned away from life, turned toward death. Yet in the context of the novel's insistent reversals it also, oppositely, means that she negated the death ostensibly being turned to. Or, in different terms still, that in agreeing to die, she both cancels her existence and transfers it from the life to the picture: first to the one on Strett's wall, "signatured . . . framed and glazed," then to those in the National Gallery and in Regent's Park, then, finally—reclaimed from these too public places—to the devotional inward mental picture of Densher's.

sacred corner and its soft wrappings; he undid them
one by one, handling them, handling *it*, as a father,
baffled and tender, might handle a maimed child. But
so it was before him—in his dread of who else might
see it. Then he took to himself at such hours, in other
words, that he should never, never know what had
been in Milly's letter. . . . The part of it missed for
ever was the turn she would have given her act. This
turn had possibilities that, somehow, by wondering
about them, his imagination had extraordinarily filled
out and refined. It had made of them a revelation the
loss of which was like the sight of a priceless pearl cast
before his eyes—his pledge given not to save it—into
the fathomless sea, or rather even it was like the sacrifice of something sentient and throbbing, something
that, for the spiritual ear, might have been audible as a
faint far wail. (2.395–96)

What is curious about this sacrifice is that nothing seems
lost. Milly's relinquishing of her life, or Densher's relinquishing of her letter, does not extinguish sentience but
rather arouses it. This offers a gloss on Milly's decision to
die, disabling the numerous sentimental interpretations
which might otherwise explicate it. For the meaning of Milly's death lies in its power to awaken Densher's feelings for
her; to instruct him, albeit brutally, that he think correctly of
(worship) her; to redeem how he acts in his desire to be
worthy of her; or, as Kate succinctly summarizes it, "'she
died for you then that you might understand her'" (2.403).
Milly's death inspires, empowers, enriches, saves—like its
Christian analogue. Thus the novel, in which thinking about
death ends characteristically in attempts to reverse it, concludes with an actual death that reverses Densher's thinking
so that as a consequence of Milly's death, now choosing between the available alternatives—call them good and evil,
though here they are personified—Densher comes to love
Milly, to love Milly not Kate.

Yet the terms of Milly's sacrifice, as presented, are outrageous. For the sentence incantatorily repeated about Milly's
death, "'She has turned her face to the wall'" (2.274) (Milly
choosing to die because of Densher and Kate's betrayal of
her), must be construed less as a reaction to her discovery of

their treachery than as a defiant illustration of her refusal to tolerate it. In fact her decision to die can be understood not only in terms of the pain Milly experiences but also in terms of that which she inflicts. She denies that she believes a wrong has been done her, leaving Densher with only his self-recrimination. She seals that denial by willing him her fortune, as if irrevocably to insist that she will not think ill of him. And in these two actions—her refusal to countenance his treachery, and her refusal to live in a world where it is impossible not to countenance it—turning her face to the wall must ultimately be associated with the earlier act of willing, "She could live if she would," here imperiously negated but not for that reason any less (to be conceived as) willed. So the emphasis of the chiasmus is reversed one last time. But with the exercising of Milly's negative power, it asks to be construed in the single way we had been unprepared to understand it.

V

In a moment I shall move away from these examples to inquire, in concluding, how they might be pertinent to James's work generally. Before doing so, however, I summarize the curiosities introduced specifically by the material discussed thus far. First, one of the reasons that thinking seems unrecognizable in the examples I have considered is that, with the notable exception of Densher's picture of Milly, thinking is not private and it is not internal. As I have indicated, it appears to emanate from others, as in Mrs. Stringham's thinking of what Milly is thinking, or as in Milly's thinking of what the people in Regent's Park are thinking. Moreover, in Regent's Park, as I have argued, the question "Whose thought is this?" gives way to the more disturbing question "Is this thought?" Another way to put this is to say that thinking exists in the public domain, where it can be viewed. This disables our comprehension of thinking as a mental activity, rather locating it in some amorphous space where changes can be wrought on it and where thinking is itself free to have effects that transcend the subjective, free to work changes. I take this to be the point of the externalization being manifested. For if the purpose of thinking seems inseparable from manipulation, then a prerequisite for this task is that thought be exteriorized so that it can be gotten at. Thinking about death exists to reverse what it contemplates, and, to enable this transformation, the representation of thinking is itself reversed from our ordinary ways of understanding it.

Second, in the scenes I have examined, how death (a particular thought) is to be viewed or pictured, with the interrogative an open question, contests the idea of death's inevitability. Milly, dying, does not smell of medicine. And Milly, dead, only seems vibrant. She is so rich with life as to loosen Densher's hold over the woman he loved and the riches he desired so that he can embrace instead thoughts about the dead girl. To repeat James's words, which indicate what Densher is allowed to possess in exchange for what he is required to renounce, "The thought was all his own." It hardly needs comment that thinking should suffice for the loss here incurred, that the loss, so trivialized, is not even experienced just to the extent that thinking or consciousness is itself conceived as recompense. (In fact Milly's picture of herself after her death—the image she fantasizes will exist for futurity on Sir Luke Strett's wall—is triumphantly realized in Densher's fetishized conception of Milly.)

But why should Densher's image of Milly at the novel's end be at once treated as a picture (something he is shown as looking at) and also be as if intentionally veiled from our view? We hear much about Densher's reverence of Milly, not much about what the reverence is for. Densher's thought of Milly is specifically made secret as if to prohibit our seeing her as *he* does. Preserving the image of Milly means ensuring its concealment. The attempt to cherish the thought of Milly exempt from others' scrutiny signals that Densher wishes sole possession of her. In this novel, that means having exclusive rights to think of her. Why should this be so? Say Densher wants to treat the thought of Milly as if it were an actual picture rather than to allow Milly to continue to be pictured—to be the object of others' thought, with the manipulation that thinking of her entails. For in the park, as I have noted, thought is explicitly not private. But because it has there been displayed, has therefore been externalized, even assumed to be visible, it can then be appropriated or "willed." In fact the thought of Milly is not "in"

Densher until after her death it is assumed to be owned by him. For Densher to have Milly as a picture—"engraved, signatured . . . framed and glazed"—is for him to reclaim her from the park as a visible thing. And it is specifically as a visible thing (hence as a thing needing protection from visibility) that Densher construes the thought of Milly: "The thought was all his own. . . . [He] left it behind him . . . when he went out, but came home again the sooner for the certainty of finding it there. Then he took it out of its sacred corner and its soft wrappings; he undid them one by one, handling them. . . ."* Thus what Densher learns at the end of the novel, sacramentalized readings to the contrary, is not how to relinquish things (not about sacrifice) but rather how to preserve them: how to keep his thoughts to himself. Thinking thus of Milly, the one-directional movement, from life to death, the movement with no backward turn, is as if definitively reversed, as Densher substitutes thinking of Milly for having her.

Third, thinking, conceived as James portrays it, solicits our credence precisely because it *continues* to be associated with reversal. The verbal chiasmus, which tirelessly reverses the emphasis of "would live/could live," along with scenes in the novel that function chiastically in relation to each other (death seen in the picture becomes the picture seen in-

---

*In *The Sense of the Past*, begun in 1900 and left unfinished at James's death, there is a phantasmagoric literalization of this reversing of death by picturing it. The narrator claims, "It was when life was framed in death that the picture was really hung up" (48). This is not a static metaphor, for when Ralph Pendrel, living in 1910, enters a London house and looks at a portrait of a man alive in 1820, he finds the man returning the stare and then stepping down from the portrait so that the two can swap identities. James writes in his *Notebooks*, "My fantastic idea deals then with the phenomenon of the conscious and understood fusion, or exchange, that takes place between them . . ." (504). James analogizes the planned novel to both "The Jolly Corner" (in which thinking is externalized) and *The Turn of the Screw* (in which thinking which cannot be externalized, cannot be verified). But in *The Sense of the Past*, where reversing death (turning it into life) and externalizing this phenomenon (by getting the man out of the painting) are conjoined, the result is a rupture: James's abandoning the story. This seems to testify to the fact that the minute you allegorize the picture of death, or animate its reversal—the one on the wall, the one in the mind—you also betray it, as if there were no place for life "framed in death" but the one that is thought, or the picture that is "hung up."

stead of death), is repeatedly presented as something whose emphasis will change. The emphasis of the chiasmus cannot ever ultimately be determined because there is no fixed place where the formulation is safe from further being contemplated, and hence from further being reversed. From James's vantage *perpetuating* these reversals is strategically crucial. For though it would be preposterous to credit the belief (it appears to be Densher's) that one could reverse death, it is hardly impossible to discredit the desire to continue trying to do so. Even the conclusion of the novel resists the interpretation of finality. It does so because, while on the one hand, Milly's death has few of death's properties (so that Densher does get Milly, or Milly does get Densher), despite Densher's understanding of this as plenitude, Milly, on the other hand, really is dead. And even this is not the end of it. For *The Wings of the Dove*, though published before *The Ambassadors*, was in fact written after it. Seen in its chronological context, Milly's death—her "willing" to die, however beatifically—is superseded in *The Golden Bowl*, the last of the three novels, by Maggie Verver's refusal to do so.

And even that is not the end of it, for two years before his own death in 1916, in the autobiographical *Notes of a Son and Brother*, James retells the story of the prototype for Milly: his cousin Minny Temple, who died at twenty-four of tuberculosis. Several facts are pertinent to James's recounting of this story. James's narrative of Minny's death incorporates—distinctively, remarkably, as nowhere else in the autobiography—extensive, sustained portions of Minny Temple's letters. How do we understand James's narrative stepping-aside, so that his own thoughts are preempted by letters put forth as primary documents, except as the impulse to allow Minny Temple, long dead, nonetheless to continue to tell her story?

"What follows here," James says, in the forty-some pages devoted to writing about her, and to quoting her letters,

> has, in its order, I think, that it still so testifies to life— if one doesn't see in it indeed rather perhaps the instinct on the writer's part, though a scarce conscious one, to wind up the affairs of her spirit, as it were, and be able to turn over with a sigh of supreme relief for an end intimately felt as at hand.[6]

It may be pressing too hard, on associations too amorphous, to hear the equivocation of "would live/could live" as background to these words. But James's expressed interest in the life of his cousin is his wondering whether, if given the chance to live, Minny Temple would have continued to have desired to do so: "In none other have I so felt the naturalness of our asking ourselves what such spirits would have done with their extension and what would have satisfied them; since dire as their defeat may have been we don't see them, in the ambiguous light of some of their possibilities, at peace with victory" (*Notes*, 528).

The sentence that ends the story of Minny Temple, and ends as well *Notes of a Son and Brother*, refuses the consolation of James's own artistic memorializations of her: "Much as this cherished companion's presence among us had represented for William and myself—and it is on *his* behalf I especially speak—her death made a mark that must stand here for a too waiting conclusion. We felt it together as the end of our youth" (544). Yet the hyperbole notwithstanding, what is striking here is the way in which the thought of Minny Temple's death for James, like the thought of Milly Theale's death for Densher, lies in its power to vitalize. What James values is Minny Temple's consciousness. When that is extinct, what he values is his consciousness *of* her; this, in the autobiography, through the reproduction of her letters, is almost equivalent to *being* her consciousness.*

*In this context it is worth querying the resemblance between the ends of the first two volumes of the autobiography. *A Small Boy and Others* concludes with what James calls "a lapse of consciousness that I shall conveniently here treat as a considerable gap" (236). What precedes the eclipse of consciousness is the intuition "that something had begun that would make more difference to me . . . than anything had ever yet made." But the intimation remains elliptical. And the vision, first opaque, is then blacked out. There are additional questions about why a blackout of consciousness should be seen as fit end to a book which celebrates consciousness as the only gift that James claims he, as a child, possessed. *Notes of a Son and Brother* concludes by recording not a gap in consciousness but its explicit extinction in Minny Temple's death. Yet the end of the first book could be said to preempt, as well as to prefigure, the end of the second. This is the case because the *lapse* of consciousness experienced by James as a child— portentous, mysterious, ultimately self-dramatizing—is depicted more catastrophically than the *loss* of consciousness in Minny Temple's death. Perhaps this is because James presumes that when his consciousness is re-

Five years earlier, for a symposium on immortality, James delivered a talk later published under the title "Is There a Life after Death?" There he argued for a doctrine of the elect based on degrees of felt consciousness. The more conscious one was in life, the more likely one's consciousness would sustain the assault of death. What is this theory if not the specific explication of the equation between thinking, thinking about death, and mentally negotiating the reversal of that death which I have been considering? The specific theory of "Is There a Life after Death?" is that if you aren't conscious in life, you won't care—because you won't know—whether you are conscious after death. ("How *can* there be a personal and differentiated life 'after' . . . for those for whom there has been so little of one before?" [*JF*, 602–3].) But if you are conscious in life—and indeed the more conscious you are—the more you can will or desire to be conscious after death. Such desire has consequences, amazingly stated as follows:

> I "like" to think . . . that this, that, and the other appearances are favorable to the idea of the independence [that is, endurance] of my individual soul; I "like" to think even at the risk of lumping myself with those shallow minds who are happily and foolishly able to believe what they would prefer. It isn't really a question of belief . . . it is on the other hand a question of desire, but of desire so confirmed, so thoroughly established and nourished, as to leave belief a comparatively irrelevant affair. . . . If one acts from desire quite as one would from belief, it signifies little what name one

stored, it will repair the loss of hers. Such reparation is suggested when, in 1870 after Minny Temple's death, Henry James writes to William: "The more I think of her the more perfectly satisfied I am to have her translated from this changing realm of fact to the steady realm of thought. . . . She lives as a steady unfaltering luminary in the mind rather than as a flickering wasting earth-stifled lamp." Still in the letter to William, but now *addressing* Minny: "In exchange, for you, dearest Minny, we'll all keep your future. Don't fancy that your task is done. Twenty years hence we shall be living with your love and longing with your eagerness and suffering with your patience" (*The James Family*, ed. F.O. Matthiessen [New York: Knopf, 1947; reprint, Vintage Books, 1974], 61–63; cited hereafter as *JF*). More than forty years later, momentarily in collaboration with her—as James voices Minny Temple's thoughts through the reproduction of her letters—*Notes of a Son and Brother* is written.

gives to one's motive. By which term action I mean action of the mind, mean that I can encourage my consciousness to acquire that interest, to live in that elasticity and that affluence, which affect me as symptomatic and auspicious [of immortality]. I can't do less if I desire, but I shouldn't be able to do more if I believed. (JF, 614)

"One could live if one would" reverberates through these words, becoming, without contest, their most extreme manifestation.

VI

The link between *The Wings of the Dove* and "Is There a Life after Death?" has been remarked upon frequently, although without elaboration. To press on the relation of the two, as I now do, is to interrogate the connection in James's work between thinking about death and thinking more generally. At least superficially both essay and novel seem to illustrate that James keeps telling the same story, and the story he keeps telling is that of the attempt to reverse death. If you believe that enough thinking (a sufficient amount of consciousness) can ensure what James calls "posthumous renovation" (JF, 606), then consciousness of death is the ultimate manipulation, for it is the ultimate attempt to defy or reverse the strictures of reality. Yet, differently understood, thinking about death is the ultimate *redundancy*. It is so since, from the essay's special vantage, you do not need to think about death in order to reverse it. To ensure survival all you need is to think: to have, in reserve, a plenitude of consciousness. Consciousness in quantity, regardless of its content, allows for "the improved discussability of a life hereafter" (JF, 610).

Then one way to understand the relation between "Is There a Life after Death?" and *The Wings of the Dove* is to see the works as contradictory. *The Wings of the Dove* implies that you have to think about death in order to reverse it, dictating the understanding as follows: if you want to survive your death, make sure you manipulate others so they will continue to think of you, and you will continue to live in their thinking of you. "Is There a Life after Death?" takes exception to this, implying, conversely, only self-reliance: as long as you are thinking, the content of the thought is inconsequential. "Inward reactions . . . awareness of things" (even "of the very stuff of the abject actual") sufficiently establish the ground, accumulate the store, initiate the connection, prepare the way, for "renewed being" in a life hereafter (*JF*, 612, 104, 605).

Or maybe the two works are complementary rather than contradictory. In this view the essay is an allegory explicated by the novel. If you think enough, the essay would imply, you deny death. The novel shows how. Specifically, the novel demonstrates that the only thinking which can guarantee survival is manipulation: thinking to exert power. Milly thought enough to live always. But she could live always because she thought enough about the image that would be left after her death, which she thought others—at least thought Densher—into picturing.

How do we make sense of these conceptions of thinking? Why did James suppose this was thinking, since manipulation is directed outward (definitionally so) and thinking is associated with what is inner (definitionally so)? Why, in James's work, is consciousness, something inner, connected to manipulation, something outer? It is as if James asked, with respect to both the essay and the novel, an almost unthinkable question: How could thought have power in the world? And as if he answered the question by asserting that thought can have power if, outside the mind and "in" the world, it breaches the boundaries between the subjective and the objective. In fact, the plot in *The Wings of the Dove* at times seems subordinate, even gratuitous, to this conclusion. For the consequence of the conclusion is that "thinking" (something inner), is, as in Spencer Brydon's case, explicitly "delivered" to some ghostly place outside the mind, where it exerts power by manipulating others' thoughts, which they mistake for their own. This, for example, Densher does when, after her death, contemplating Milly—just, we might suppose, as she wished him to—he thinks of her in an ultimate parody of possessive identification (akin to the psychoanalytic "projective identification"): "The thought was all his own." Outside the mind, thought would be free to have effects that transcend the subjective, free to work changes. Moreover, if consciousness could sur-

vive death, that would be the ultimate test of its freedom
from the self, since then consciousness would not only be
outside the self (as in the park) but also liberated from the
self. Thus thinking about death in the passages I have discussed illustrates that thinking is a complex subterfuge of
externalization.

Thinking about death is, in addition, the test case for what
thinking can do. One reason this is so is that if thinking
could reverse death, there would be no more potent demon-
stration of its efficacy. But there is a more interesting sense
in which thinking about death is the test case for the power
which James assigns to thinking. Death is the one subject
about which there is nothing *to* think. Death has no assimi-
lable content. Therefore, all you could ever do, if you tried
to address thinking to the subject of death, would be to
deny death (that is, to reverse it), there being nothing to
think about it. Then death is a double threat to thinking: it
will end all thinking one day, but even now, death cannot
be thought about because, having no unique content—no
content other than that extrapolated from this world—it
both derides thinking and curtails it, cuts thought short. The
rationale of "Is There a Life after Death?" and *The Wings of
the Dove* is, "Think enough about death and there won't be
any." But death is just what you cannot think about.

Then, too, there are more immediate, more pragmatic
problems than the contradiction to which I have pointed,
which reiterate the crucial questions: "Why is this 'thinking'? Why did James suppose it was? Why do we?" For
thinking in James's novels does not, in more mundane
terms, appear to have the properties we associate with
thinking. There would, of course, be a way to answer the
questions "Why is this thinking? Why does it look like
thinking to James and to us?" It looks like thinking because
it is a perverse attempt to have power over the things that
render us impotent. In fact, it looks a good deal like what
most of us *substitute* for thinking: it is routinized, obsessional, inescapable, predictable. It thus comes to resemble
thinking in its very mechanistic nature, in the obsessive supposition that it could wield power by being relentless. So the
very attributes that we supposed would disqualify it as
thinking also, albeit peculiarly, make it recognizable as

such.* But though, as I am suggesting, there would be grounds to explain why James's representations of consciousness resemble "thinking," there would be other grounds on which to critique "thinking," as James conceives of it.[7] This critique would have nothing to do with the lack of representational realism, per se. The critique would rather be of James's attempt to write the world into a fable where there is no difference between subjective and objective reality, no difference between thinking and exerting power by thinking. One way in which this fantasy of no distinction is entertained is, I will have illustrated, in thinking about death, where if you just think enough, and you exteriorize what you think, you eradicate the difference between subjective and objective reality. Such delusional thinking is Jamesian thinking.

In *The Sacred Fount* there is an ultimately vertiginous example of thinking as attempting to annihilate the distinction between subjective and objective reality. The example is pertinent to the issues I have been considering because the subject of *The Sacred Fount* is explicitly the narrator's thinking. To be more precise, the subject is the narrator's collusion with the thinking of *other* characters about still other characters—his attempt to make those to whom he confides his

*At James's own deathbed automatic thinking aspires to, or mimics, automatic writing. Thus William James's wife, Alice James, in January 1916 to her sons in America: "He thinks he is voyaging and visiting foreign cities, and sometimes he asks for his glasses and paper and imagines that he writes. And sometimes his hand moves over the counterpane as if writing" (quoted in Leon Edel, *The Master: 1901–1916*, vol. 5 of *The Life of Henry James* [New York: Lippincott, 1972], 559). What strikes me about Henry James's attempt to write in the throes of his disorientation is not the extravagant Napoleonic delusion of which much has been made, but rather the typical, general fact that in the last months of his life, after two strokes and in delirium, James would ask first for paper and pen and then for someone to take dictation, as if, true to the prescription elaborated in "Is There a Life after Death?", consciousness, however victimized by incoherence, had imperatively to be apprehended and imperatively to be externalized—in this case, written. To that end, James assumes the double role of author and amanuensis. In significantly broader terms, James's magical thinking about a life after death is also inevitably magical thinking about writing. The immortality he will get will exist in books, which are not only the objects of thought, but also, as much to the point, are thoughts made into objects. Hence the elaborate care in the preparation of, including the illustrations for, the New York Edition.

thoughts think as he does. In *The Sacred Fount* the narrator
thinks that either the man or the woman of each couple that
he sees exacts life by draining it from the sacred fount of the
other. The novel consists of his elaborated speculations—
made just credible enough for us to countenance—about
how to deduce (at a weekend in the country, in a house
filled with people) who is living at the expense of whom.
The theory might be mad, but it might also be only the logical conclusion of the symbiosis implicit in the notion that
one could think "for" another, could "will" the thought "of"
another, could survive death "in" the thought of another,
could therefore sacrifice life to thought—but to *another's*
thought as it has been prescribed he think it—as Milly does
for Densher. (To reiterate Kate's analysis: "'she died for you
then that you might understand her.'") Considered in these
terms, it would of course be unclear whether Densher lives
at the expense of Milly, or vice versa. ("In exchange, for
you, dearest Minny, we'll all keep your future. . . .
Twenty years hence we shall be living with your love and
longing with your eagerness and suffering with your
patience.") And this is just the sort of question—who is living at the expense of whom—that, in *The Sacred Fount*, tor-
ments the thinking of the narrator.

   The Sacred Fount, like "Is There a Life after Death?" and
The Wings of the Dove, victimizes characters by the tyranny of
thinking. But, unlike these other works, *The Sacred Fount*
prevents itself from being vulnerable to the criticism that it is
violating the boundary between subjective and objective reality. Thus the novel tyrannizes the reader as well as the
characters. It thwarts criticism because for the reader of *The
Sacred Fount* there is no way to tell the difference between
what the narrative mind thinks and whatever objective truth
there may be to what the mind thinks. Criticism is subverted
because there is no place outside the thinking mind (here
the first-person narrator) where one could assess the status
of what is being thought. Or, to put this in other terms,
since the mind has effectively annihilated its own ability to
ascertain the distinction between inside and outside, between what it supposes and what it knows, and has violated
as well *our* ability to assess such a distinction from a reliable
(that is other) place separate from that mind, then there is

no story of the world but the one the mind tells. There is no place "outside" the mind.*

The story in *The Sacred Fount* is both impossible to believe, because we can't assess its status, and impossible to dismiss, because we can't assess its status. So *The Sacred Fount* fulfills the ultimate Jamesian fantasy of the omnipotence and omnipresence of thinking or consciousness. But the completeness of the power of thinking in this fantasy—its indisputable power—has to be juxtaposed to the completeness of our inability to grasp it. For the very "no place to assess" which it has successfully arrived at also disables our recognition of it. Thinking that has so deformed itself by so confusing itself with empowerment is ultimately meaningless. And that would be the grounds of the critique of thinking in James— not that the representation of thinking is unrealistic but rather that the subversion of the boundary between the real and the willed, the objective and the subjective, in which all is ultimately only thinking, makes thinking dismissible because there is no way to understand it.

The logic of this subterfuge bears on the material I have been dealing with more directly. It does so as follows. Death disables thinking about the meaning of its own negation. To put this as strongly as James's novels sometimes do: death's power does not primarily reside in what death can do; death's power rather resides in our inability to comprehend what death can do. But, as a consequence of trying to think about death, the prohibition associated with death—death cannot be thought of—comes to be associated with the very

*This is a recognizable philosophic perception, but it is recognizable within a philosophic discourse and might be stated as follows: to try to examine the principles inside of which you are thinking means that you are outside them. But to be outside them is to be no place, or not to know where you are, for you would then be operating outside the principles you are explaining. This is just to acknowledge that such dead-endedness always happens to philosophic thought when it is thinking outside its first principles, when it is asking "What empowers me to do this?" Yet though this "no outside" is recognizable in philosophical discourse, James is not writing philosophical discourse. Yet there is a sense in which thinking in James is treated as if it were, for thought is so completely the object of representation in *The Sacred Fount* that it becomes completely the object of thought, and the narrator in that novel seems trapped in just the predicament I have described.

thinking which death repels. Thinking cannot be thought of in the sense that it cannot be understood. In *The Wings of the Dove* James's insistence on Densher's "thinking" of Milly *as* the novel's resolution and, even further, as exemplifying Densher's own moral redemption converts "thinking" from a phenomenon that is recognizable as cognition to one we cannot fathom. But if we cannot, are not able to, think about Densher's reflections on Milly after her death, we are also not permitted to think about them. For Densher's thinking of Milly after her death is made, as I have noted, both secret and sacred ("The thought was all his own"). It is made transcendent in its own right and kept unavailable to others. Thus, with respect to *The Sacred Fount*, "no way to think about thinking" means no way to assess the objectivity of what is thought. With respect to *The Wings of the Dove*, "no way to think about thinking" means that thinking has been placed in some inscrutable, even sacramentalized realm. In fact deliverance is not what happens to Milly as a consequence of death. Deliverance is rather what happens to Densher as a consequence of the thought of her death. And this exchange, of Milly's life for Densher's thought, or *this* exchange—of death as mystifying for thought as mystifying—raises inevitable questions about a magical or hallucinated transfer of power from death to thought. For if death's power comes from the fact that there is nothing to think about it, then if you impute this power to thinking itself—so that nothing to think about death becomes nothing to think about thinking—then thinking and death are made, at the least, categorically comparable. They are treated as if they had a similar status, since they can both do—that is, can both negate—the same thing. In shifting power from death (no way to think about death) to thinking itself (no way to think about thinking), there is a formal, even unassailable, resolution to the problem of power, though the cost of that resolution is incomprehension.

VII

That there is no way to evaluate the entirely unthematized counterallegory of thinking which contests the religious allegory of good and evil in *The Wings of the Dove* only means, after all, that there *is* no way to critique it. This disabling state has conventional analogues. In its defiance of limits (mortal or identic ones) the project of thinking is provisionally one of recompense, in line with that of James's nineteenth-century counterparts, Whitman and Dickinson, for example.*

James wrote of the art of consciousness, of the "interest"

*If there are literary counterparts, there are also critical analogues, other counterintuitive accounts that bear more than passing resemblance to the issues considered here, specifically Jacques Lacan's discussion of the gaze (in *The Four Fundamental Concepts of Psycho-Analysis*, ed. Jacques-Alain Miller, trans. Alan Sheridan [New York: W. W. Norton, 1978]). Lacan's terms are only analogous to my own and, as I shall explain, only to a point analogous to James's, but they provide one way of bearing down further on the extremity of thinking as picturing in James's representation.

In Lacan's topography the oppositional terms "the eye" and "the gaze" (radically simplified in my summary description) have nothing to do with the eye and the mind. They rather have to do with the way the subject sees himself, with the relation between the subject and his desire. An illusory wholeness is figured by the eye's belief that consciousness is total, a completion illustrated by the reflexive formulation, "I see myself seeing myself" (80). In this formulation, the eye, self-referential, takes all in. In another register of the unconscious, contesting the idealization that consciousness is whole, the subject constitutes his subjectivity by imagining, conversely, a split in being or a self-mutilation, whereby the object he desires is outside himself. This desired object (or this desire which projects/sees part of itself as if it *were* an object) is epitomized by the gaze. The gaze cannot be had or taken in. It is therefore associated with a lack. It cannot be taken in because it is always prior and always other; it is thus temporally and spatially indifferent to the self: "I see only from one point, but in my existence I am looked at from all sides" (72). The gaze, outside you, is what looks at you and sees nothing, or it is what looks at you and sees you as nothing. Lacan illustrates the subject's experience of the gaze by "The Ambassadors," the *trompe l'oeil* picture of Holbein's, where the beholder looking at a smudge situated between two immobile figures suddenly realizes that he is beholding a death's-head and that his own nothingness is reflected in the figure of a death's-head (85–89). The Holbein example is in fact representative, for the gaze is what the painter can always be said to put into the painting (100). The gaze traps the beholder by the lure of a totality which would complete the self that is regarding it, were such a completion not impossible, since, by definition, the gaze is imagined to be a part of the self, but that part which is external. In fact, though the painter may be said to put his gaze into the picture, what mesmerizes the beholder is not the *painter's* gaze but rather something the painter incites the beholder to see in the painting: his own alienated otherness.

The scenes I have discussed could be said to constitute different ways of predicating the relation between the eye and the gaze, between subjectivity conceived as total and subjectivity conceived as fractured, between death

of consciousness, of the "irresponsible liberties" consciousness takes "with the idea of things" (JF, 610, 611), of its
"elasticity" and "affluence" (JF, 614). In view of the feats he
attributes to it, as I have described them, he might less evasively have simply called it "power." But the stupendous
force of the claims being made for consciousness or thinking
are specifically a consequence of the obliquity of those
claims. Also of the oblique relation between thinking as externalizing and thinking as reversing. I recapitulate that connection one last time. The novel acknowledges that death
comes from the external world, and in the wake of that acknowledgment attempts to reverse it. To see that death is
external is to wish that thought could be external so that
thought could reverse death. Yet thinking about death in
James's work is ultimately the occasion for clarifying what

---

seen in a picture and death done away with when the self *becomes* the picture. Yet Lacan's scheme will not quite work for James because Lacan predicates the eye and the gaze as relational terms operating oppositionally,
whereas James's scenes (however they may *immediately* shift between similar antitheses, as I have indicated) *ultimately* insist on a definitive progression in which a split like the one described by Lacan is healed. Thus Milly,
looking at the Bronzino, is shattered by the thought of death. Milly, looking
at Strett, thinks of death again. But in the latter scene, as I have noted, she
heals the vision of brokenness by reversing the relation between death and
a picture, as it was initially figured in the scene with the Bronzino. Thus
death seen in a picture becomes the picture seen instead of death. Making
good on this chiastic discovery, in Regent's Park Milly's eye *becomes* Milly's
gaze (Milly seeing death becomes Milly reflecting it back). She converts in-
completion to omniscience, to a totality of perspectives verbally epitomized
by the conciliation of "would live" with "could live"—opposite points of
view treated as integral. If, in Lacan's words, "we are beings who are
looked at in the spectacle of the world" (75), in Regent's Park Milly turns
that around by looking at the world as if it were a spectacle.
   In *The Wings of the Dove*, then, James represents a fracture analogous to
the one described by Lacan. But unlike Lacan, James represents it as if it
could be mended, as if it were curable. To be cured, to translate the self into
that which can be seen but cannot see, as James does to Milly or as Milly
does to herself ("'She has turned her face to the wall'"), is to transform the
incomplete, mortal, mutable self into a totalized, immortalized, objective
picture of it. This picture, willed to Densher, will mesmerize him. It is what
he will come to see himself completed by. At the novel's end—to appropriate Lacan's terms in ways consonant with James's purposes—Milly, no
longer seeing at all, no longer mortal, becomes Milly as gaze, a thing to be
regarded.

thinking is in James's work. Thinking as reversing death is a way of externalizing the more general phenomenon of thinking as reversing. This is the case because although one could argue that thinking about death thematically grounds the subject of thinking as reversing (it does so because, in the novel, death is the occasion for thinking as reversing), or that thinking as reversing reaches its extreme form in relation to death, to look outside the limits of the subject would be to see, if not the same phenomenon, then a related phenomenon. It would also be to see that there is an inevitable other way to describe the phenomenon of thinking in James, one associated not with power but with revulsion at that power.

This can be illustrated by the briefest outline of the novella that stands last in *The Finer Grain*, James's last book of tales. In "The Bench of Desolation," a rewriting of sorts and in miniature of *The Golden Bowl*, characters are shown to be united over the years in a contest so bitter that one pays the other in order not to have to marry her. Although they are physically apart and psychically at war, they are conceptually entangled, since each is wholly occupied by the thought of the other. After a number of years of thus afflicting—or thus caring for—each other, they are brought face to face in a sequence of meetings which, we are led to believe, will engage them forever. In the novella's final episode they agree they cannot speak. So they mutely sit side by side, still bound by thought, this time of the immutable terms of their shared isolation. "The Bench of Desolation" is a story of perfect misery in which the characters' thoughts (of their unseverable bond when they are apart, of their unmitigated separateness when they are together) are revealed to be perfect compensation for the misery. A fable like this one disallows us from dissociating the magical, efficacious properties of thinking, even were they credible (leading, in their extreme form, to the idea that thinking can reverse death), from the obsessional properties of thinking (thinking is efficacious because it can simply, even senselessly, reverse what is present). That the sabotaging thrust of thought (its propensity to reverse) should be endorsed as if for its own sake is a counterstory also told by the novels. The story of the ambivalence about how thinking is to be conceived is revealed in the oppositional language of the passage describing Densher's contemplation—James calls it his "thought"—of "the turn [Milly] would have given her act":

> This turn had possibilities that, somehow, by wondering about them, his imagination had filled out and refined. It had made of them a revelation the loss of which was like the sight of a priceless pearl cast before his eyes—his pledge given not to save it—into the fathomless sea, or rather even it was like the sacrifice of something sentient and throbbing, something that, for the spiritual ear, might have been audible as a faint far wail. . . . He sought and guarded the stillness, so that it might prevail there till the inevitable sounds of life, once more, comparatively coarse and harsh, should smother and deaden it. . . . (2.396)

In the convolutions of that passage and in the torture of its reversals we see thinking as excrucation and thinking as its recompense—see the deadlock of thinking (how it transfixes and blocks), a deadlock not intelligible in terms of the plot or even of desire.

Thinking is compensation when associated with the reversal of death (as in *The Wings of the Dove*). Thinking prohibits compensation when associated with pure reversal (as in "The Bench of Desolation"). Yet in the passage above, such clean demarcations are conceptually blurred. If in that passage, as I have noted, thinking is excrucation *and* is its recompense, this, in its own right, asks us to see double. More: the notion that thinking rectifies suffering is savaged by a counternotion, inevitably inferred from the dis-ease of the sentences, that thinking causes it. In slightly different terms still, thinking is recompense *and* is the particular activity through which recompense is subverted. The shiftiness of these conversions, always only implicit, is always also reiterated by the passage's compulsive paradoxes, which, not directly *about* thinking, are nonetheless articulated as a specific *consequence* of it. Hence, "This turn had possibilities that, somehow, by wondering about them, his imagination had filled out and refined." In the nonchalance of the passage's "turns," for which no explanation is offered, contradictory and incommensurate conceptions of thinking (thinking as cure, thinking as cause, thinking as conduit or means of suffering) emerge as complementary ones. Thus "pure reversal" is itself too simple a designation for that aspect of ambivalence about thinking in which antithesis and tautology are only precariously distinguishable.

The last fact is distilled, even epitomized, by the respective last sentences of *The Ambassadors* and *The Wings of the Dove*, novels written in succession. " 'Then there we are!' " (the last sentence of *The Ambassadors*) reverses, it would seem, " 'We shall never be again as we were!' " (the last sentence of *The Wings of the Dove*). For thinking gets Strether nowhere; he cannot think his way out of his withdrawal from life, whereas Densher—thinking of Milly as his salvation—will never again be as he was. The sentences look and sound like opposite conclusions, since one negates existence and the other affirms it. Rather, they imply the same conclusion. They imply the same conclusion rhetorically, since " 'We shall never be again as we were' " *means* " 'Then there we are.' " And they imply the same conclusion consequentially because in both cases the effect of thinking is to disavow relations. In Strether's case thinking leads to affectless disengagement. In Densher's it leads to disengagement in the name of devotion. Yet although both sentences imply the same ending, only in *The Wings of the Dove* does "thinking blocks" get treated as "thinking saves." That is, only in *The Wings of the Dove* does James seem to invoke " 'We shall never be again as we were' " as if it were the reversal of " 'Then there we are,' " in the sense that thinking, in *The Wings of the Dove*, is represented as decisive as opposed to acquiescent. It rejects the past rather than succumbs to the present—as if these were different choices. To set these last sentences beside each other is to see thinking as empowered and thinking as eviscerated, to see representations of thinking which are radically discrepant but not quite opposed, to see thinking as intent and absolute, and thinking as recursive, to see the torque of James's thinking about thinking.

There is a final, parallel point to be made about the radical cases of thinking which I have considered here. *The Sacred Fount*, where thinking is all internal, and *The Wings of the Dove*, where thinking is all external, might be described as antithetical. Yet they in fact present different forms of the same problem. For in its most extreme form, James's representation of thinking denies the simultaneity of the internal and the subjective with the external and the objective. Thought is either all realized, as in *The Wings of the Dove*, or all idealized, as in *The Sacred Fount*. If thought in *The Wings of the Dove* is incomprehensible because it is objectified as a picture and treated as a thing, thought in *The Sacred Fount* is incomprehensible because it has no ascertainable relation to things. Thus to ask, as I did earlier, "What does it mean for thought to have power in the world?" is to pose a question which can be addressed only by acknowledging the intersection of the mind and the world. Yet in these two novels that construction cannot be so formulated because in each case James erects a dichotomy whereby thought lies on one side or on the other. Thought as psychologized implies a crossing of mind and world. Thought as pictured doesn't. Thus, as I have argued, the effect of the psychological novel, as James writes it, is to divorce thinking from psychologizing, to depsychologize it. Because in *The Wings of the Dove* thought is objectified—is, as pictured, even made material—it is perfectly clear how thought has power in the world, but to see it this way, as the novel insists we do, questions the idea, the intelligibility, of what we recognize as mental states.

If the extreme case questions the intelligibility of mental states, it—for James as seriously—also compromises the very exteriority on which the power of thinking in the late fiction depends. It does so because even in the extreme case alluded to above there remains a difference between consciousness and its object. The characterizations "all realized" or "all idealized" would seem to belie that difference. Yet both reversing (*The Wings of the Dove*) and oppositely thinking about what thinking is (*The Sacred Fount*) testify, compulsively, to the disparity of consciousness and its object, however both may be "placed" "all in the mind" or "all in the world." One could even argue that the torture of the extreme case is that being "in the same place" does not mean "being the same thing." All in the mind or all in the world only italicizes that fact, since, from either vantage, there is no way out where the difference could be checked (stopped rather than measured), it being precisely the achievement in each of these cases to have annihilated the way out.

Notes

TEXTUAL NOTE
The texts for *Roderick Hudson* and *The American* are those of the English editions published by Macmillan in 1879, the last substantive versions of the early, pre–New York Edition texts of those novels revised by James. The text for all other James novels and tales, and for the Prefaces to the novels, is the New York Edition (New York: Charles Scribner's Sons, 1907–17; reprint, 1961). Page references are to these editions.

CHAPTER ONE   INTRODUCTION BY WAY OF *THE AMERICAN SCENE*

1. The history of James criticism, from various perspectives, reiterates the understanding that, I shall argue in the first chapter, James promulgates in the Prefaces to his novels of himself as the master of psychological realism. So in an early review of 1902, "Through page after page he surveys a mind as a sick man looks at his counterpane, busy with little ridges and grooves and undulations" (F. M. Colby, "In Darkest James," *Bookman*, November 1902, reprinted in *Henry James: The Critical Heritage*, ed. Roger Gard [New York: Barnes and Noble, 1968], 339). So T. S. Eliot distinguishes between intellectual matters, with which James's novels are not concerned, and "the deeper psychology," with which they are. So André Gide and Philip Rahv see Jamesian consciousness as a kind of litmus test for personal relations, relations which exist that they might be registered in the mind's reaction to them. (Their essays, respectively, "On Henry James," "Henry James," and "Attitudes toward Henry James," are collected in *The Question of Henry James*, ed. F. W. Dupee [New York: Henry Holt, 1945; reprint, New York: Quadrangle Books, 1973].) So Ruth Bernard Yeazell's "The Syntax of Knowing" anatomizes the ways in which consciousness which is willing to know its own desire can—by what it says or withholds—come to regulate others' behavior; cast in these terms Yea-

zell's study psychologizes linguistic and epistemological questions (*Language and Knowledge in the Late Novels of Henry James* [Chicago: Univ. of Chicago Press, 1976]). In fact, surveying the criticism of James's novels, it might seem as if there were no escape from the terms of psychological realism James dictated for his readers. Even allegorical or moral interpretations of the fiction seem inevitably to rely on a psychological frame of reference, which they also construe as secondary. (See, for example, Quentin Anderson, *The American Henry James* [New Brunswick, N.J.: Rutgers Univ. Press, 1957]; Frederick Crews, *The Tragedy of Manners: Moral Drama in the Later Novels of Henry James* [New Haven: Yale Univ. Press, 1957; reprint, Hamden, Conn.: Archon Books, 1971]; Laurence B. Holland, *The Expense of Vision: Essays on the Craft of Henry James* [Princeton: Princeton Univ. Press, 1964; reprint, Baltimore: Johns Hopkins Univ. Press, 1982].) R. P. Blackmur's interest in Jamesian consciousness, as conscience, is inevitably grounded in the psychology of "the convulsive distortions afforded by living with people in any discriminating stage of consciousness at all" (*Studies in Henry James,* ed. Veronica A. Makowsky [New York: New Directions, 1983], 174), that is, in the psychopathology (my characterization) of James's everyday world.

One way out of consciousness as psychologized (above I address the question of why one might want a way out) is illustrated by a deconstructive, poststructuralist account of James's novels in which a concern with consciousness as psychologized is replaced by a concern with linguistic systems, in particular, and with signification, in general, as demonstrated in John Carlos Rowe's studies of James (especially *The Theoretical Dimensions of Henry James* [Madison: Univ. of Wisconsin Press, 1987]) or in J. Hillis Miller's discussion of the ethics of James's reading of his own novels in the Prefaces to them (*The Ethics of Reading* [New York: Columbia Univ. Press, 1987]). Another way out is exemplified by Leo Bersani's readings of James in the context of realistic conventions of the novel, especially in light of psychoanalytic understandings of these conventions. Still another way out is illustrated by Mark Seltzer's Foucauldian reading of James's politics of the novel (*Henry James and the Art of Power* [Ithaca: Cornell Univ. Press, 1984]).

An account of consciousness as psychologized understands consciousness as a phenomenon associated with subjectivity: as internal, centered, circumscribed, fixed. Conversely, a poststructuralist account (the dominant critical alternative) critiques and dismisses the idea of such a center, conceptually replacing the structure of consciousness with the structure of the sign and then proceeding to deconstruct that. In the chapters above I read James against the traditional account of consciousness as psychologized, arguing that consciousness in James's novels is not internal, not centered, not associated with subjectivity. But consciousness is not as a consequence dismissed or subordinated. Thus I suggest that in James's representation of consciousness, psychology is subverted. But the consequence of that subversion is not the deconstructive replacement of consciousness by signification, or by language more generally. In fact consciousness in James, though dissociated from psychology, doesn't disappear. It is rather revised or reconceived so as to be shown in excess of the circumstances, mental or material, that produce it. I am concerned with the nature of those revisions and the manifestations of that excess.

2. In the second chapter I examine the way in which consciousness in three early novels overwhelms and transgresses the boundaries of discrete selves, thus belying the conservative descriptions of consciousness (as centered, contained, and allied with character) advanced by the Prefaces to those novels. In the third chapter I examine the way in which consciousness is treated more like a quantity than like an entity. Moreover, it is depicted in terms of scarcity, so that one character has consciousness at another's expense or instead of another. This quantification of consciousness is dramatized in the substitutive relation between thinking and speaking in *The Golden Bowl*. One way of looking at the relation of consciousness and power, implied by these substitutions, is to say that power is dispensed by James to those who have consciousness. That's how it looks from the vantage of the Prefaces. From the vantage of a novel like *The Golden Bowl*, however, many of the characters are shown to have consciousness, though not usually at the same time. Therefore some find it preempted, usurped, depleted, or effaced by those who seem to have power in addition to having consciousness. But if one had to say whether in James's novels consciousness and power are really separate, I would say no. Consciousness is held like a sum in reserve by James and then distributed as the source of power. What makes this proposition interesting is that having consciousness is not necessarily, in a novel like *The Golden Bowl*, a guarantee of keeping it, in that if someone (Maggie) *gets* consciousness, someone else (Charlotte) *loses* it. Thus for James, in the final analysis, consciousness and power are inseparable—a fact that has bearing on another way of formulating consciousness as at once excessive and exclusive by seeing meaningful consciousness to exist alternately in thought or speech, at the command of one character or another. This way of formulating it might again appear to internalize consciousness, making it property of a self that could be said to own it. The formulation *might* suggest this but for the

emphasized instability of the placement of consciousness (in any one mode of communication or allied to any one mind), for to have more consciousness is more to risk losing it, the characteristic of excess equally applying to the amount and to the threat. Thus in these representations of consciousness there is a discrepancy between a novel's inestimable valuing of a character to whom consciousness is given and a commensurate indifference to that same character when consciousness is taken away—value, like power, attaching directly to consciousness and only indirectly to the place where it resides. In the fourth, and final, chapter I am concerned with an extreme case of excessive thinking, which also illustrates excessive consequences for thinking. Specifically I am concerned with an extreme way in which James attempts to rethink or revise what thinking is.

3. The problem of consciousness in relation to a realistic psychology is raised most fully by Leo Bersani, also the first critic to associate James with the topic of power. His amplifications of the issue—power in the subversive strategies of silence in the Jamesian text; Jamesian power in the context of realistic conventions of the novel; this power, finally, in the light of psychoanalytic and Foucauldian readings of it—make Bersani's discussions of James incomparable for the late James, as Richard Poirier's discussions are incomparable for James's early writings.

In "The Subject of Power" (*Diacritics* 7 [Fall 1977]) Bersani's argument is that the realistic novel maintains coherence and social order by expelling characters from the text whose consciousnesses it is unable to assimilate because they resist "analytic intelligibility" (8)—Milly Theale, for example. This essay of Bersani's—situated in a discussion of Foucault and Brombert, hence of repressive systems—is an explicit critique of the cost of that order. But in two essays on James ("The Jamesian Lie," in *A Future for Astyanax: Character and Desire in Literature* [Boston: Little, Brown, 1976], and "The Narrator as Center in *The Wings of the Dove*" [*Modern Fiction Studies* 6 (1960): 131–43]) the very characteristics of consciousness explicitly valued in "The Subject of Power"—its mobility, its uncontainability, its impenetrability—seem oppositely critiqued because consciousness, so portrayed, betrays the social order, being primarily associated not with freedom but with aestheticism. (This critique is reiterated in slightly different terms in *The Freudian Body: Psychoanalysis and Art* [New York: Columbia Univ. Press, 1986], 81–86.) Thus in "The Jamesian Lie" Bersani employs a poststructuralist analysis in order to uphold a psychological realism whose absence he (uncharacteristically) deplores as violative.

Bersani's analysis is exactly right in locating the problematic of

Jamesian consciousness as outside character and outside the psychological. But I would take issue with his claim about the essential meaninglessness of that dislocation. In fact, I would take issue with it in Bersani's own terms, because while he argues that characters like Maggie are unintelligible, his interpretation, despite his exasperation, reads her perfectly. The problem, then, isn't that Maggie is unintelligible but rather that the domination of consciousness which she represents is unacceptable to Bersani *because* he sees it as aesthetic, not social. For Bersani, when Jamesian consciousness is empowered outside bodies and minds, it is expelled from the text or made to be unintelligible there. In the pages above, I focus on what consciousness "outside" the mind, but still in the text, both "looks" like and *means* in four progressively extreme contexts. (One of the implications of looking at these representations of consciousness closely is to see that they repel paradigms and summarizing formulations—including, of course, my own—changing within a given text as well as from one text to another. Thinking, on behalf of which so much in James is claimed, asserts the power of its uncontainability precisely by being shifted around with respect to a moving field of contexts, hence with respect to different limits, which thinking, unpredictably, both redefines and transgresses.)

This clarified, it is crucial to add—and the reader will notice—that of all of James's critics, it is to Bersani that my own analysis of the Jamesian text, even when most different from his, is most indebted. For Bersani's irritation with "the . . . defect of James's compositional ethic" (154) makes him retaliate critically against consciousness that is empowered only (so it seems) to inflict repressive power on others. Hence what happens is something like a bypassing or dismissal of such impossible representations. This notwithstanding, it is precisely Bersani's contextualizing assessments—his decisive, sometimes savage mappings of the problematic of Jamesian consciousness—that free criticism for looking closely at it.

4. Preface to *The American Scene,* ed. Leon Edel (Bloomington and London: Indiana Univ. Press, 1968). Further references in the text will be to this edition.

5. For a superb discussion of the genre James invents in his misrepresentation of America, see Mark Seltzer, "Advertising America: *The American Scene,*" in *Henry James and the Art of Power,* 96–145. Seltzer's reading implies that James aestheticizes power (148). He therefore sees art and power as forming a continuity within *The American Scene* and implicitly between *The American Scene* and the novels. Above, I am concerned with differentiating other subversive equations (in my discussion of the equation of consciousness and power), arguing they have different consequences in the so-called travelogue and in the novels.

6. *The Complete Notebooks of Henry James*, ed. Leon Edel and Lyall H. Powers (New York: Oxford Univ. Press, 1987), 236. Further references in the text will be to this edition.

7. In the quotation from Dante, Edel and Powers transcribe the first word of the second line as *"Viene."* But the manuscript at Houghton Library clearly reads *"Venne"* (Journal VII, December 11, 1904–March 30, 1905). Thus James does not change Dante's past to present tense.

8. *Henry James Letters*, ed. Leon Edel (Cambridge, Mass.: Belknap Press, Harvard Univ. Press, 1984), 4:382–83. Further references to the *Letters* appear in the text by date, volume, and page number.

9. Another model for dissociating consciousness from a psychology would be psychoanalytic. A psychoanalytic account of consciousness is in fact both resisted and invited by the Jamesian text. For example, Freud's notion of the contingency of the conscious mind, its dynamic dependence on an unconscious to which the conscious mind is, through repression, structurally oblivious, seems assaultive to something like a Jamesian first principle: that there be nothing "outside" consciousness, at least nothing determining of consciousness, that has a constituting hold over it. In psychoanalytic terms one could describe the idea of that sufficiency as a defense or a wish, and thus as essentially immaterial to the validity of the explanation being deflected. But there are more interesting ways of describing the relation of the psychoanalytic explanation to what in James it would explain. For, as consciousness in James's fiction is represented spatially as being situated not "inside" the single self but rather "outside" "between" persons, the very idea of an unconscious located "within" the self (to which it nonetheless remains inaccessible or "other") would be, for different reasons, unacceptable, hence for different reasons unassimilable to the representations of consciousness as James's novels unfold them. Psychoanalysis would contest the position just described as follows. Consciousness as "external," even in the Jamesian sense I have described, is still *structurally* bound to the idea of an unconscious. It is so since in being "outside," albeit between persons, it is nonetheless already in that "other" position vis-à-vis what would ordinarily count as a discrete, embodied, fixed consciousness.

Another example will illustrate the tease of the psychoanalytic model in relation to the Jamesian text. In *The Wings of the Dove* we might wish psychoanalysis to elucidate the connection between thinking and reversing. For a psychoanalytic explanation would defuse the novel's assertion of magical power by identifying the source of that power. Yet the psychoanalytic critique "this is magical thinking" is identical to the novel's claim "thinking *is* magical" which invigorates Milly's and Densher's cognitive activities in *The Wings of the Dove*. Thus the psychoanalytic account whose explanatory leverage structurally depends on revealing something hidden could be seen as gratuitous because the phenomenon being explained produces the hidden account as its own *manifest* logic. Here what is at issue, then, is not the account *by* the novel as this is contested by the account *of* the novel. These are the same. What is rather at issue is the truth of the account, or rather its status. Yet from a psychoanalytic vantage nothing is at issue. For thinking or consciousness that claims to have magical power implies a redefinition of the term "consciousness" that could only be in need of psychoanalytic exegesis.

Perhaps the point to be made here is that American Freudian psychoanalysis, depending as it does on the notion of interiority, which James's texts resist in ways enumerated in the following chapters, is not the only mapping of the unconscious. The Lacanian mapping of it, which gets a firmer grip on forms of projection—specifically, on forms of projection which externalize the self as other—is taken up in passing in the fourth chapter. If the following pages do not pursue such an analysis, this is because it is precisely my argument that while James deconstructs a certain realistic notion of consciousness, the consequence of that fact is not the disappearance of consciousness, but, conversely, its existence, even its excess. Thus to carry the deconstructive activity to that point where consciousness is made to disappear is to do away with James's subject as, I argue, he has redefined it.

10. Paul Armstrong, *The Phenomenology of Henry James* (Chapel Hill: Univ. of North Carolina Press, 1983), employs phenomenology first "to connect James's interest in consciousness with his moral vision," and second "to introduce phenomenology to the humanist through figures as diverse as Heidegger, Bachelard, Sartre, Merleau-Ponty, Husserl, et al." Armstrong writes: "My reading of James provides a kind of running annotated bibliography on phenomenology" (xi). In invoking Husserl as a way of introducing my subject I mean to do precisely the opposite of "offering a phenomenological perspective on James's achievement" (viii). I rather mean to suggest that Jamesian consciousness raises questions of domination that are both apparent and repressed in Husserl's idealism.

In this context it could be argued that in my introductory remarks, by looking only at Husserl, I make a too narrow cut into phenomenology. For example, if I looked more broadly, or looked back further, I'd be looking at Hegel, who, a century before Husserl and James, was dealing with master-slave relations. But Hegel was dealing with them explicitly, whereas what interests me is the way that Husserl and James differently repress the power over others which their idealism is implicitly wielding.

11. Edmund Husserl, *Cartesian Meditations,* trans. Dorion Cairns (Dordrecht, Boston, Lancaster: Martinus Nijhoff, 1960), 155. Further references in the text will be to this edition.

12. In elucidating this constituting activity of consciousness, phenomenology is to clarify "practical living [which] is naive," for (as a consequence of that naïveté) "all those productive intentional functions of experiencing, because of which physical things are simply there, go on anonymously [and] the experiencer knows nothing about them, and likewise nothing about his productive thinking" (152–53).

13. Gaston Berger, *The Cogito in Husserl's Philosophy,* trans. Kathleen McLaughlin (Evanston: Northwestern Univ. Press, 1972), 12.

14. Noted in Berger, 36. If the objective world is derived from consciousness, objects are not "in" consciousness as an intrinsic part of it, but rather as a being there ideally, or, as Husserl would say, as a being "constituted" or "intended" by consciousness. "To intend" signifies "to mean," an equation Husserl would have gotten from Brentano, his teacher, and he in turn from Scholastic philosophy. But while for Brentano "to intend" denotes consciousness's relation to extra-mental phenomena, for Husserl it denotes any object of consciousness, italicizing the fact that to be conscious is always to be conscious *of* something. For amplifications of Husserl's notions of "intending" and "constituting," see, for example, Berger, *The Cogito in Husserl's Philosophy;* Robert Sokolowski, *The Formation of Husserl's Concept of Constitution* (The Hague: Martinus Nijhoff, 1970); Paul Ricoeur, *Husserl: An Analysis of His Phenomenology* (Evanston: Northwestern Univ. Press, 1967); Pierre Thévenaz, *What Is Phenomenology,* ed. James M. Edie (Chicago: Quadrangle Books, 1962); Jitendranath Mohanty, *Husserl and Frege* (Bloomington: Indiana Univ. Press, 1982) and "The Roots of Reflection," in *The Possibility of Transcendental Philosophy* (Dordrecht, Boston: Martinus Nijhoff, 1985); Martin Heidegger, *The Basic Problems of Phenomenology,* trans. Albert Hofstadter (Bloomington: Indiana Univ. Press, 1982); Emmanuel Levinas, *The Theory of Intuition in Husserl's Phenomenology,* trans. André Orianne (Evanston: Northwestern Univ. Press, 1973); J. Quentin Lauer, S.J., *The Triumph of Subjectivity: An Introduction to Transcendental Phenomenology* (New York: Fordham Univ. Press, 1958); and especially Jacques Derrida, *Speech and Phenomena and Other Essays on Husserl's Theory of Signs,* trans. David B. Allison (Evanston: Northwestern Univ. Press, 1973), and David Allison's introduction to that book. See also William James's chapter "Conception" (in *The Principles of Psychology,* ed. Frederick

Burkhardt and Fredson Bowers [Cambridge, Mass.: Harvard Univ. Press, 1981], 2 vols.), where ideas of consciousness as constituting objects are analogous to Husserl's.

15. The most compelling critique of Husserl is of course Derrida's in *Speech and Phenomena.* It is well exemplified by a section (pt. 3B) of Husserl's *The Crisis of European Sciences and Transcendental Phenomenology,* trans. David Carr (Evanston: Northwestern Univ. Press, 1970), 244–65. There Husserl elaborates a notion first suggested in *Cartesian Meditations*—specifically introduced in the thing-phantom passage examined above, where, not irrelevantly, the issue of a psychology is reinstated as a subject. Not irrelevantly, because it could even be argued that it is the reintroduction of the subject of psychology in the passage discussed above (a subject gotten out of the way fast at the beginning of the *Meditations*) that makes for the vertiginous moves between those ostensible two sides, as these anticipate vertiginous distinctions between psychology and phenomenology in *Crisis.* In the section in *Crisis* which I have in mind, Husserl talks about a psychological reduction comparable to the phenomenological reduction. The two are analogous, for, by a "sort of epochē within the epochē" (259), subjectivity is general, is the recognition of "mutual internality," as phenomenology attests to a "mutual externality." In Derrida's words about an analogously oxymoronic moment when the self constitutes its own self-objectification, "no language can cope with the[se] operations" (12).

16. On the subject of the alliance of James's thoughts with those of his characters, J. Hillis Miller has pointed out to me that a crucial instance of the sharing of thought—that between the narrator and the characters—is conspicuously absent from my discussions. Specifically, Miller has pointed out that I treat James in relation to his characters as if there were no narrator. This is perhaps because I see James as standing (albeit fictitiously) in an unmediated relation to his characters, almost as if in the novels—experientially, though of course not technically—the narrator becomes a screen for James's direct identification with his characters. "Direct" obviously not in point of fact, but I think in point of effect. For example, the numerous celebratory statements advanced by the narrator in the novel about Maggie Verver's revisions have, for good reason, traditionally been linked to James's celebratory statements about his own revision in the Preface to that novel. There would of course be a difference between what James says about himself and what the narrator, not bound by James's official judiciousness as an author, says about Maggie. But I understand that difference in the following way: the narrator, liberated from the authorial role imposed by

the Preface, is free to voice *James's* thoughts. *The Ambassadors* provides an instance of James's voice competing with the narrator's for proximity to his central character. For even while the narrator creates, enters into, shares Strether's thoughts, he also maintains irony toward them. Whereas James, despite the statements that profess distinction between himself and the narrator—most notably the sentence about the preference for the third-person narrator (why such a preference if not, in James's own words, to conceal the "terrible *fluidity* of self-revelation"?)—is identified at once with his character and his narrator. And this identification threatens to intervene in, if not quite to override, the relation the narrator would typically have "alone" with the character. This is just to say that partly because of James's Prefaces, in James's novels, the sharing of thoughts exists among characters, author, and narrators in an atypical way. *The Spoils of Poynton* would present yet another facet of that atypical relation in that James's unabashed advocacy of Fleda in the Preface to that novel is not commensurate with the narrator's ambivalent presentation of her. Finally, *The Bostonians* is the example that, to my mind, clarifies the (for James) normative case. It clarifies the way in which the author intervenes between narrator and character—a repositioning of the conventional way of understanding the relation of these three figures. *The Bostonians* clarifies, by itself departing from, the Jamesian normative case because with no Preface—with access to the narrator minus access to the author—readers have been uncertain about how to interpret that novel.

CHAPTER TWO   THE PREFACES, REVISION, AND IDEAS OF CONSCIOUSNESS

1. Arthur Gelb and Barbara Gelb, *O'Neill* (New York: Harper and Row, 1962), 848.

2. O'Neill's story could be complicated in the following ways. For O'Neill there was an absolute connection between the aim of production and the means of production. Thus, for a brief period, when quite young, he wrote screenplays on the typewriter—these he did not regard as serious. He could never write plays that way, however, because he did regard them as such. Nor could he dictate them. Accordingly, in 1947, he explained to Sherlee Weingarten, who offered to quit her job in the Theatre Guild to take dictation for a play which O'Neill described as "in his mind" but which he was himself incapable of writing, that "he could find the right words only with pencil and paper" (Louis Sheaffer, *O'Neill:* vol. 2, *Son and Artist* [Boston: Little, Brown, 1973], 597). "Finding the right words" is, of course, synecdochic for finding the plays, which are lodged somewhere. And the pencil—the mechanical means of

their transmission—is not trivially mechanical, since the pencil, the means of getting the words out, is also, or first, the means of locating them, of getting them conscious. Thus the means of production is tied both to the idea and to the retrieval of the idea, there being for O'Neill no interchangeability between means of production. He told a friend that "he began his day with a dozen pencils sharpened as fine as possible because this helped him to pierce through to his unconscious" (Sheaffer, *O'Neill:* vol. 1, *Son and Playwright* [Boston: Little, Brown, 1968], 265).

In 1943 Julian P. Boyd, a Princeton librarian preparing an exhibit of O'Neill's manuscripts for the Firestone Library, commented on the difference between the size of O'Neill's script in his letters and in his plays (Sheaffer, 1:540–41). O'Neill's script in the plays was always small; the Parkinson's made it smaller, for "as one grew worse with the years the other tended to diminish" (Sheaffer, 1:265). The minute writing—in time it dwindled so significantly that the person transcribing the manuscripts required a magnifying glass—was partly an attempt to control the tremor, but O'Neill also explained the size of the writing in the play manuscripts as follows: "The more concentrated and lost in myself my mind became . . . the smaller the handwriting. . . . The minute style grew on me" (Sheaffer, 1:541). When O'Neill's tremor was very bad, before he stopped being able to write at all, he would lie on his bed, on his back, and write in letters so small that virtually only Carlotta could read them. Here of course one can only speculate, but given the correspondences noted above, what is perhaps to be remarked on is the connection between writing that can barely be done with writing that can barely be read, or to place the emphasis precisely: the consonance between the diminishing ability to write/conceive the plays and the diminishing size of the letters, as if what were being revealed, or, rather, graphically represented, were the disappearing of the ability to write in the disappearing of the letters.

3. There are various adequate accounts of the movements to investigate consciousness at the turn of the century. See, for example, Ernest Jones, *The Life and Work of Sigmund Freud,* 3 vols. (New York: Basic Books, 1953–57); Henri F. Ellenberger, *The Discovery of the Unconscious: The History and Evolution of Dynamic Psychiatry* (New York: Basic Books, 1970); Frank J. Sulloway, *Freud: Biologist of the Mind* (New York: Basic Books, 1979); *Psychoanalysis, Psychotherapy and the New England Medical Scene, 1894–1944,* ed. George E. Gifford, Jr. (New York: Science History Publications, 1978); and, among primary sources, Morton Prince, *Psychotherapy and Multiple Personality: Selected Essays,* ed. Nathan G. Hale, Jr. (Cambridge, Mass.: Harvard Univ. Press, 1975); William James, *The Principles of*

Psychology and *William James on Exceptional Mental States: The 1896 Lowell Lectures,* reconstructed and edited by Eugene Taylor (Amherst: Univ. of Massachusetts Press, 1984); *The Complete Letters of Sigmund Freud to Wilhelm Fliess 1887–1904,* trans. and ed. Jeffrey Masson (Cambridge, Mass.: Belknap Press, Harvard Univ. Press, 1985); and the introductions to these primary source volumes.

4. *Letters of Freud to Fliess,* 146. Accounts of Charcot's and Janet's careers can be found in Ellenberger, 89–101 and 331–417; the account of the Bowdoin prize topic is in Prince, 3.

5. Although there is no evidence that James knew Freud's work directly, James of course knew his brother's, and one of his letters makes passing reference to Charcot. In addition, in 1911 Henry James briefly consulted James Jackson Putnam in Boston for a nervous disorder he had described in a letter to Edmund Gosse as a "black depression—the blackness of darkness and the cruellest melancholia" leading to "my terror of solitude . . . and my unfitness for society" (*Letters,* June 13, 1910, 4:556). Putnam was an early American practitioner of psychoanalysis, himself in touch with many of its founders. See *James Jackson Putnam and Psychoanalysis: Letters between Putnam and Sigmund Freud, Ernest Jones, William James, Sandor Ferenczi, and Morton Prince 1877–1917,* ed. Nathan G. Hale, Jr. (Cambridge, Mass.: Harvard Univ. Press, 1971).

6. Referring to the Prefaces, James wrote William Dean Howells on August 17, 1908: "They are, in general, a sort of plea for Criticism, for Discrimination, for Appreciation . . ." (*Letters of Henry James,* sel. and ed. Percy Lubbock [New York: Charles Scribner's Sons, 1920; reprint, Octagon Books, 1970], 2:99). Following James's cue, it is in honorific terms that the Prefaces have been spoken of. R. P. Blackmur introduces his edition of the Prefaces, *The Art of the Novel* (New York: Charles Scribner's Sons, 1934), with the following characterization: "James felt that his Prefaces represented or demonstrated an artist's consciousness and the character of his work in some detail, made an essay in general criticism which had an interest and a being aside from any connection with his own work, and that finally, they added up to a fairly exhaustive reference book on the technical aspects of the art of fiction. His judgment was correct . . ." (viii).

Since Blackmur's assessment, other critics have commented on the Prefaces. But, albeit in different contexts, they have reiterated the formal terms that initially concerned him. Thus Leo Bersani writes: "The novels are constantly in a dramatic struggle toward the security of the Prefaces" (in an earlier version of "The Jamesian Lie," *Partisan Review* 36 [1979]: 53–79). While Bersani calls attention to, without elaborating upon, the discrepancy between the writing in the novels and the writing about them, Laurence Holland's discussion insists on the thematic continuity of the two kinds of discourse, specifically focusing on the way in which similar metaphors pervade the Prefaces and the novels. John Carlos Rowe's examination of how James's Prefaces attempt to appropriate the novels' meanings adheres to the very formalist concerns Rowe is critiquing (see *The Theoretical Dimensions of Henry James*, 221–52).

Most recently J. Hillis Miller's deconstructive reading of James as a deconstructive reader ("Re-reading Revision: James and Benjamin," in *The Ethics of Reading*) argues that the "genuine" reading of the Prefaces is a misreading of the texts. In Miller's discussion of James, consciousness figures only implicitly as what James applies to the texts he rereads. Specifically, in Miller's terms consciousness of the law or thing to which the text was initially—and still is— bound asserts its superiority to any definitive text, the one that was written or the one that could be. I would argue that this ethic of reading which refers the reader (here James) to some prior "matter," "thing," or "law" which can never be pinned down, hence never associated with any particular text, provides James his implicit justification for converting one understanding of consciousness (that in the novels) to another understanding of consciousness (that in the Prefaces).

7. For examples of James's massive textual emendations, see the facsimile edition of James's textual revisions for the New York Edition of *The American* (Henry James, *The American: The Version of 1877 Revised in Autograph and Typescript for the New York Edition of 1907* [London: Scolar Press, 1976]—for which, as Rodney Dennis explains in the introduction to the facsimile, James actually worked from the corrected Macmillan reprint edition of 1883)—or Houghton Library's manuscript of *The Portrait of a Lady*, revised in autograph and typescript.

For discussion of James's textual emendations, see "Henry James 'In the Wood': Sequence and Significances of His Literary Labors, 1905–1907" (*Nineteenth-Century Fiction* 38 [March 1984]: 492–513), where Hershel Parker compiles a log of that early phase of James's work on the New York Edition when he was retouching the first three novels in the series: *Roderick Hudson, The American,* and *The Portrait of a Lady*. Parker demonstrates the important fact that James was in effect revising these novels simultaneously, and in conclusion he notes:

> On the basis of this literary log we can begin asking
> . . . questions. Rather than seeing James's late revi-
> sions of *The American* only in relation to the early texts
> of that novel, we might ask if there are significant ways

> in which the revisions of *Roderick Hudson, The Portrait of a Lady,* and *The American* (to go by the order in which the work on them was completed) are more related to each other than to their contexts in the old novels. (512–13)

As my focus on James's repeated attempts to revise conceptions of consciousness for pivotal early works suggests, I would obviously agree with Parker about the significance of examining the revised works in relation to each other—though Parker raises this question with respect to the relation of the texts of the novels, whereas, as I explain above, I am rather concerned with examining a central revisionary task as it is shared, but differently executed, by the Prefaces to the texts. (These differences would be dictated and particularized by what in a given novel James presumably supposed was in need of redefinition.) In view of the kind of revision or reinterpretation I am considering, in any given case, the particular text (early or late) of the novel considered is curiously subordinate to the more or less autonomous terms of the Preface's reconception of it, since it is precisely my point, as argued above, that the revisions James undertakes in the Prefaces to the novels cannot be negotiated or fixed by textual manipulation. In other words, what James is trying to "fix" remains more or less constant in its textual permutations. I have therefore followed the conventional practice of citing an early text for *Roderick Hudson* and *The American* and the New York Edition for James's subsequent novels (see Textual Note, p. 169).

8. Stuart Culver, in his dissertation "Henry James's *New York Edition:* The Organic Text and the Mechanics of Publication" (University of California, 1984), has pointed out that James's control of the works which would appear in a particular volume of the New York Edition, and even of the order of the volumes, was in fact at the mercy of Charles Scribner's publishing and printing schedule. This is important information, but it does not alter my observation about James's *arrangement* of his works, since James proceeded, even in his accommodations to Scribner's, as if he continued to have control of the project. Thus when he altered his initial conception to accord with his publisher's requirements, he rethought the Prefaces to adapt them to the reordering. (See, for example, the letter to Charles Scribner's of December 31, 1907 [*Letters*, 4:484].) My point here is not that the New York Edition reveals James's unmediated aesthetic vision of his novels and stories, but rather the obvious one: a collection, in any order, offers the works a contextualization inevitably different from that of their individual publication.

9. James's understanding of the process of revision is especially

idiosyncratic, and not simply in relation to the critical Prefaces. Thus, for example, to Mrs. Humphry Ward on July 26, 1899: "I'm a wretched person to *read* a novel—I begin so quickly and concomitantly, *for myself*, to write it rather—even before I know clearly what it's about! The novel I can *only* read, I can't read at all!" (*Letters*, 4:110–11). We see the consequence of James's propensity for appropriation in the following letter to William James's son, on the occasion of James's contemplation of a family memoir (it would become *Notes of a Son and Brother*). James—explaining to his nephew why revision of his brother's letters will produce a more faithful record of the man being memorialized—ventriloquizes his brother's posthumous sanction of the enterprise:

> I must nevertheless do something toward making you see [how] the editing of those earliest things, other than "rigidly," had for me a sort of exquisite inevitability. From the moment of those of my weeks in Cambridge of 1911 during which I began, by a sudden turn of talk with your Mother, to dally with the idea of a "Family Book," this idea took on for me a particular light. . . . That turn of talk was the germ, it dropped the seed. . . . it dated from those words of your Mother's, which gave me . . . a spirit and a vision as far removed as possible from my mere isolated documentation of your Father's record. . . . And when I laid hands upon the letters to use as so many touches and tones in the picture I frankly confess I seemed to see them in a better, or at all events in another light . . . than those rough and rather illiterate copies I had from you showed at their face value. I found myself again in such close relation with your Father . . . which was a passion of tenderness for doing the best thing by him that the material allowed. . . . I seemed to feel him in the room and at my elbow asking me for [this] as I worked and as he listened. It was as if he had said to me on seeing me lay my hands on the weak little relics of our common youth, "Oh but you're not going to give me away, to hand me over, in my raggedness and my poor accidents, quite unhelped, unfriended, you're going to do the very best for me you *can*, aren't you . . .?" . . . These were small things, the very smallest, they appeared to me all along the way, tiny amendments in order of words, degrees of emphasis etc., to the end that he should be more easily and engagingly readable and thereby more tasted and liked . . . there was . . . no violence done to his real identity. (*Letters*, November 15–18, 1913, 4:801–3)

I point to these two examples to indicate that we are not dealing with an ordinary understanding of textual revision. Or rather, as the last sentence of the previous letter indicated, textual revision is inseparable from the total transfiguration of identity—a conventional idea interpreted by James with unconventional liberality.

10. Although recently critics, notably Rowe and Miller, in quite different terms, have addressed revision in the theoretical sense inevitably suggested by James's massive project, no critic, to my knowledge, has then returned to the novels to assess the implication of the discrepancy between the descriptions of consciousness in the Prefaces and the representations of it in the texts for the subsequent rereading of the novels. See, however, Thomas M. Leitch, "The Editor as Hero: Henry James and the New York Edition" (*Henry James Review* 3 [Fall 1981]: 24–43) for a preliminary account of the significance of consciousness in the Prefaces and the texts of the New York Edition.

11. In the context of this discrimination, see Richard Poirier's discussion of "fixed and free" characters in James's early novels in *The Comic Sense of Henry James: A Study of the Early Novels* (New York: Oxford Univ. Press, 1967). The opposition of "fixed and free" could also crucially be applied to the very idea of character as this idea is differently endorsed by alternative passages on romance in the Preface to *The American,* as elaborated above.

12. In *Between Men: English Literature and Male Homosocial Desire* (New York: Columbia Univ. Press, 1985), Eve Kosofsky Sedgwick has adapted René Girard's notion of mediated desire to inquire into the problematic of what she calls "homosocial" bonds—defined as primary ties among men, between whom women are only "exchange"—that which permissibly draws men together. In Sedgwick's analysis the sexual and the identic are not, in fact, discrete since what men are allowed to want and who they are allowed to be are inseparable from each other. As I suggest above, however, in *Roderick Hudson* this confusion is not gender-specific, since the conflation of identic and sexual questions applies to the novel's women as well as its men, and, more to the point, does so in the same way.

13. George Eliot, *Daniel Deronda* (Harmondsworth: Penguin, 1967), 159–60.

14. An alternative response considers the confusions rather than dispensing with them and is exemplified by *The Golden Bowl.* In *The Golden Bowl* what consciousness is, what relations are (again, James's words), how the inner scene and the outer one are made to apprehend each other, the terms of the apprehension (in other words its cost), are anatomized with excruciating logic. See chapter 3.

15. These publication dates require clarification. The initial book publication of the novel in question follows the title; the subsequent date is that of its republication in the New York Edition: *Roderick Hudson* (1876, 1907); *The American* (1877, 1907); *The Portrait of a Lady* (1881, 1908); *What Maisie Knew* (1897, 1908); *The Golden Bowl* (1904, 1909). In the discussion above I see the Prefaces as a response to James's "re-perusal" of his fictions as *initially* written. But, as also noted in that discussion, any attempt to chart a development in James's attitudes will fail since the chronology points up contradictions. Thus what is to be reiterated about *The Golden Bowl*, which—unlike the Prefaces—addresses, rather than deflects attention from, the confusions of consciousness, is that it chronologically precedes the writing of the latter, italicizing the point that James's response to the confusions inherent in complex understandings of consciousness fluctuates, remaining indeterminate and equivocal.

16. *Henry James: Essays on Literature, American Writers, English Writers*, ed. Leon Edel (New York: Viking, Library of America, 1984), 53.

17. The very project undertaken by the Prefaces, and the idea of the New York Edition itself, is predicated on the supposition of sustained systematic coherence, a coherence maintained by the Prefaces' directive that we attend to the single consciousness in the novel that follows. In James's own mind, the achievement of the Edition seems connected with its success in bringing into conformity (he doesn't specify the terms of it) the earlier works. So, to Edmund Gosse on August 25, 1915:

> all my "earlier" things . . . were so intimately and interestingly revised. The edition is from that point of view really a monument (like Ozymandias) which has never had the least intelligent critical justice done it— or any sort of critical attention at all paid it—and the artistic problem involved in my scheme was a deep and exquisite one, and moreover was, as I held, very effectively solved. Only it took such time—*and* such taste— in other words such aesthetic light. No more commercially thankless job of the literary order was (Prefaces and all—*they* of a thanklessness!)—accordingly ever achieved. (*Letters*, 4:777)

On the question of James's specifically financial expectations for the New York Edition, see Michael Anesko, *"Friction with the Market": Henry James and the Profession of Authorship* (New York: Oxford Univ. Press, 1986), and Stuart Culver, "Henry James's *New York Edition*."

18. Elizabeth Ermarth, in *Realism and Consensus in the English Novel* (Princeton: Princeton Univ. Press, 1983), speaks of the collective nature of consciousness—especially the narrator's—in the realistic novel. In Ermarth's terms consciousness in the novel is a matter of "agreement," although in her discussion James is the liminal case, where coincidence breaks down. For an extraordinary discussion that challenges the conventional distinctions between narrator and character, subject and object, interior and exterior (or shows how these are socially constituted) see "Secret Subjects, Open Secrets," in D. A. Miller, *The Novel and the Police* (Berkeley and Los Angeles: Univ. of California Press, 1988). Miller is concerned with the subversion of the dichotomy between inside and outside mainly at the level of how character is made accessible (or represented) to the reader as it "'secretes' [its] subjectivity" (196). Above I am mainly concerned with how characters' consciousnesses are made accessible to each other.

19. Here the substitution of the intersubjective for the self as the locus of consciousness provides James with the grounds on which the social can be transacted. It is precisely because consciousness is not psychologized in *Maisie*, in the sense of made exclusively subjective, that the novel has "depth." The discussion above illustrates the terms of this.

20. *The Works of William James: Essays in Radical Empiricism*, ed. Frederick Burkhardt and Fredson Bowers (Cambridge, Mass.: Harvard Univ. Press, 1967), 4. Further references in the text are to this edition. "Does 'Consciousness' Exist?" and *Essays in Radical Empiricism*, in general, could be said to revise the earlier notions of consciousness expounded in *Principles of Psychology*, and especially to revise the notions articulated in "The Stream of Thought," a central chapter of that book. So, for example, in "Does 'Consciousness' Exist?" William James contemplates the relation between the object in the mind and the object in the world, whereas in the earlier *Principles* the investigation of the mind is characteristically self-reflexive, having to do with "gaps" of thought, "conclusions" to thought, "transitions" in thought, "fringes" of thought—or, to characterize these topics generally as James himself does, having to do with relations registered by thought.

Although James does not acknowledge how the concerns in the *Principles* differ from those in *Radical Empiricism*, the issues raised by the discrete problematics could even be said to distinguish the studies. For the relations of objects *in* thought and *as* thought become in *Radical Empiricism* a concern with the relation *between* objects *and* thoughts conceived nondualistically. (See, for example,

"A World of Pure Experience," where James is concerned to illustrate how virtual knowledge of Memorial Hall at Harvard University becomes actual knowledge of it.) Thus, while in *Principles* knowing is described as a process, in *Essays* it is described as a function, with no splitting between the thought and the thing. Needless to say, these claims require elaboration. Still, as implied, they reveal a pattern that might be indicated as follows. In "The Stream of Thought," the particular phenomenon repeatedly being scrutinized is the middle or part of a thought isolated specifically to illustrate either its connection to the totality or, more characteristically, its *exemplification* of the totality. In "Does 'Consciousness' Exist?" and in other essays in *Radical Empiricism*, relations in thought are themselves reconceived as only part of a subject whose totality must properly be constituted by the acknowledged relation between the object in the world and that in the mind. What these examples illustrate, therefore, is the unaddressed departure of *Essays*, published posthumously, from the assumptions of *Principles*.

For other discussions of the defamiliarized relation between objects and thoughts or, in this case, between objects and our designations for them, see Kenneth Burke, "What Are the Signs of What?" (in *Language as Symbolic Action* [Berkeley and Los Angeles: Univ. of California Press, 1966]), where there is no division between things and signs (or, in Burke's radical reversal of our ordinary understanding, "Things are signs of words"), and Richard Poirier's discussion of the significance of that proposition for Frost's poetry, in "Frost, Winnicott, Burke" (*Raritan* [Fall 1982]: 14–27). In three different contexts what is being redefined is the relation between objects and thoughts, objects and signs, objects and voice. These discussions unsettle the relation between objects and the mind so that they are in effect interpenetrated.

21. William James's conclusions are not dissimilar to the deconstructionists' (hence Lacan's reversal of Freud's "Where id is there shall ego be" to read, "Where I am it shall be"). The idea of consciousness as fully allied with the idea of the self, as Freud so allies it, or as fully emptied of the idea of the self, as the deconstructionists describe it, amounts to the same thing. It amounts to the same thing because in both cases consciousness is conceived almost exclusively in relation to subjectivity. In Henry James's novels consciousness is detached from the idea of a self (from the idea of subjectivity) and detached as well from that of interiority. William James would agree. But William James and deconstructive critics would therefore conclude that consciousness as a reified phenomenon does not exist. Henry James would argue, therefore it does.

1. These suggestions are made respectively by Yeazell, 70; Ralf Norrman (*The Insecure World of Henry James* [New York: St. Martin's Press, 1982], 129); and Carren Kaston (*Imagination and Desire in the Novels of Henry James* [New Brunswick, N.J.: Rutgers Univ. Press, 1984], 141). For an analysis which elaborates the last, prevalent point of view—that Maggie's silence is requisite for the rearrangement of the quartet—see Laurence Holland, *The Expense of Vision.*

2. I quote F. O. Matthiessen, *Henry James: The Major Phase* (New York: Oxford Univ. Press, 1944), 98, and Ruth Yeazell, 86, and characterize Leo Bersani's position in "The Jamesian Lie." Although the moral and epistemological examinations have different initial premises, they ultimately arrive at similar conclusions, much as Fanny Assingham in the novel does when she says that " 'Stupidity pushed to a certain point *is*, you know, immorality' " (1.88). Thus, representatively: "If we prefer Maggie's talk to Charlotte's, it is not that Maggie speaks honestly while Charlotte lies, but that Maggie is ultimately the superior artist—that her language makes for the most harmonious and inclusive design her world can sustain" (Yeazell, 86).

This conversion of moral deliberations to epistemological quantifications (to know most is to speak the best language) or to appreciations of artistic design, illustrated in the last quotation, is implicitly challenged by Leo Bersani's critique of the novel's realism, in the absence of which morality and epistemology cannot sensibly be considered. Bersani's assessment provides a powerful escape from the deadlock created by the moral and epistemological issues which often seem inert when characters or critics discuss them. But Bersani's passing assessment of speaking and thinking in the novel exemplifies a critical stasis similar to that which he elsewhere eschews. Thus, while he argues that "the best talk and the best thought would be [those] which resist interpretation" (139), the relation between thought and speech is not in fact fixed but, functionally if not actually, changes through the course of the novel and within particular exchanges at moments of the novel, as I explain above. This fact is crucial because it repels any single description of the relation between thinking and speaking that must be seen as developing. As a consequence, thinking and speaking are not inert ground on which Maggie or James can display their compositional resources. Rather design is the effect not the cause (and not the purpose, either) of the shifting relation between one person's speech and another person's speech, and between speech and thought. What is at stake in my description of this process is not nominal. For, however outrageously, the terms of communication are not "given" in the novel. They are rather, to a point, worked out.

Nonetheless, my position in this chapter would be closest to Bersani's. It would differ in this respect: he sees consciousness in the novel as unintelligible because it abandons the social. To the extent that I also, or ultimately, see it as such, it is because, I argue, James proposes meaning-making alternatives (neither concerned with the social as such) which, painstakingly discriminated, are then shown to have consequences whose difference is made negligible.

3. *The Complete Poetry and Prose of William Blake*, ed. David Erdman (Berkeley and Los Angeles: Univ. of California Press, 1982), 3–6.

4. Editions of *Thel* before 1904 are the originals, produced between 1789 and 1827; an 1830 essay on Blake in *London University Magazine* no. 965 which contains quotation from *Thel*; a facsimile edition of 1876; the limited edition put out by the Blake Press at Edmonton in 1885; and Yeats and Ellis's *The Works of William Blake* (London: Quaritch, 1893). As the last was considered a major publishing event of the time, it would have been unlikely for James not to have known about it, and, one could argue, also not to have seen it, though there is no evidence that he did so. Moreover, Alexander Gilchrist's *Life of William Blake*—unfinished at Gilchrist's death in 1861 but completed by Ann Gilchrist with the help of the Pre-Raphaelite Brotherhood—which initiated the Blake revolution, was published in 1863; it discusses and quotes from *Thel*. Dante Gabriel Rossetti, among others, remained involved in the expansions of the 1880 edition of that book, which includes the entire poem. Given the impact of the Gilchrist edition on the nineteenth-century canon, and given James's interest in the Pre-Raphaelites, it is reasonable to suppose that James would have seen this, though there is no proof that he did. Nor is there proof that James read Swinburne's discussion of *Thel* in the 1868 *William Blake: A Critical Essay*, for Henry James did not own this book, though he owned other Swinburne, and though Swinburne's *Blake* is a good indication of the availability of the poet's works to a post-1868 audience. On the basis of any one of these editions or critical studies, the indication that James read *Thel* is hypothetical, even weak. But it is cumulatively compelling, if for no other reason than that at the end of the century there was a major discovery of Blake by the literary establishment, and the Pre-Raphaelites, in whom James was interested, were largely instrumental in bringing it about.

I am grateful to Karen Sánchez-Eppler for her research of, and surmises about, the above material.

CHAPTER FOUR   THINKING IT OUT IN *THE WINGS OF THE DOVE*

1. In *The Wings of the Dove* James's project is less one of representing thinking than of reconceiving it. As a consequence of this revision of thinking, *The Wings of the Dove* is only superficially the moral allegory claimed by critics like Quentin Anderson (*The American Henry James*), R. P. Blackmur (*Studies in Henry James*), Frederick Crews (*The Tragedy of Manners*), Dorothea Krook (*The Ordeal of Consciousness in Henry James* [Cambridge: Cambridge Univ. Press, 1962]), and Laurence Holland (*The Expense of Vision*), and only superficially the failed realistic novel of readings by Leo Bersani ("The Jamesian Lie") and Sallie Sears (*The Negative Imagination: Form and Perspective in the Novels of Henry James* [Ithaca: Cornell Univ. Press, 1968]). Subverting the allegory of good and evil, and the unrealistic and social questions that undermine it, is the entirely unthematized counterallegory of thinking, which incapacitates traditional ways to understand it, and for which there is no comprehensible "other" level of significance. I elaborate above.

2. There are different ways to understand this. For example, Ruth Yeazell and Laurence Holland valorize a Jamesian character's ability to shape his own thinking and that of other characters, equating the designing mind, as James also does, with the artistic imagination. Conversely, for Leo Bersani the same ability demonstrates a character's betrayal of the ethical, because to conceive of the world as something to be designed by thought is to misunderstand the relation between the mind and what is exterior to it. It is always the case that specific allegiances (Holland's commitment to the ethical as defined by the artistic, and Bersani's commitment to the ethical as defined by the social) dictate disparate assessments. But in discussions of James's work these points of reference are especially arbitrary, since with respect to various passages, the phenomenological question "How is this thinking?" which ought logically to precede the evaluative question "What are the implications of thinking of this as thinking?" fails to do so. Above, I consider the difficulties that subvert the asking of that first question.

3. Eliot, Gide, and Rahv all suggest, in much the same terms, that because characters live only in connection to each other, consciousness or thinking is also relational. In the context of my discussion, the way James makes thinking relational is by confusing it with looking. For the argument that looking does not have a predominantly visual function in this particular novel, see two recent essays: Michael Moon, "Sexuality and Visual Terrorism in *The Wings of the Dove*" (*Criticism* 28 [Fall 1986]: 427–43), and Marcia Ian, "The Elaboration of Privacy in *The Wings of the Dove*" (*ELH* 51 [Spring 1984]: 107–36). Moon's essay discusses the way in which

eye games enact power relations and suppress a male homoerotic thematic; Ian's the way in which characters experience their thoughts as penetrable by others.

4. On reversal in James's work at the level of verbal strategy—specifically the chiasmus in *The Golden Bowl*—see Ralf Norrman, *The Insecure World of Henry James*, 137–85. On reversal in James's work in a larger, cultural context, see Stephen Donadio, *Nietzsche, Henry James, and the Artistic Will* (New York: Oxford Univ. Press, 1978). On the subterfuge of reversal, specifically in the context of art's masking power, see "Images of the Opposite: The Aesthetic Rewriting of Power," in Mark Seltzer, *Henry James and the Art of Power*, 146–70.

5. In *The Expense of Vision*, 285–313, with a crucial analysis for any allegorical reading of *The Wings of the Dove*, Laurence Holland discusses the two other actual pictures in the novel besides the Bronzino—Veronese's "The Supper in the House of Levi" and "The Marriage Feast at Cana"—illustrating how James draws on the two paintings to identify Milly with Mary and Christ, and Densher first with the betrayal and then with the sanctification of her. From the different vantage of the concerns discussed above, James's picturing of meaning outside, or as background to, the novel's more immediate action is parallel to that of Milly's similar externalizing of it. In James's reliance on the paintings to explicate the betrayal, meaning hangs above or outside the chapter it glosses, unintegrated with and as if overdetermining it.

6. Henry James, *Autobiography*, including *A Small Boy and Others, Notes of a Son and Brother*, and *The Middle Years*, ed. Frederick W. Dupee (New York: Criterion Books, 1956; reprint, Princeton: Princeton Univ. Press, 1983), 534. Further references in the text are to this edition.

7. What is to be remarked on about the existing critiques of Jamesian consciousness—that it is solipsistic, that it is unrealistic, that it is unsocial or amoral—is that these characterizations seem entirely accurate, even completely devastating, while simultaneously not appearing to touch (not seeming to engage with) the novels themselves. The novels remain essentially impervious to such criticism, for James never endorses the values he is accused of abandoning.

Index

Allison, David B., 176n.14
Anderson, Quentin, 170n.1, 190n.1
Anesko, Michael, 185n.17
Armstrong, Paul, 175n.10

Balzac, Honoré de, 19
Berger, Gaston, 22, 176nn.13, 14
Bersani, Leo, 170n.1, 172–73n.3, 180n.6, 188n.2, 190nn.1, 2
Blackmur, R. P., 170n.1, 180n.6, 190n.1
Blake, William, 115, 116–18, 189nn.3, 4
Brentano, Franz, 176n.14
Brombert, Victor, 172n.3
Burke, Kenneth, 187n.20

Charcot, Jean-Martin, 34, 180nn.4, 5
Colby, F. N., 169–70n.1
Consciousness. *See also* Consciousness *and* Thinking *under titles of James's works*
  conceptions of
    as differently formulated in Prefaces and novels, 36–38, 40–42, 47–53, 61–62, 63–65, 75–76, 77, 111, 171n.2, 184n.10
    in James and George Eliot, 53–55, 61, 63
    in James and Husserl, 21–22, 28, 28n, 175–76n.10
    in Henry and William James, 20–21, 77–81, 187n.21

  in Henry James, William James, and Freud, as changing, 35–36
  James as revising, 18–21, 35, 37–38, 41, 125, 172n.2, 175n.9, 190n.1
  James's, as not single or developing, 1, 2, 36, 42, 185n.15
  location of
    as all in the mind or all in the world, 26, 140–41, 144–45, 148n, 160–61, 161n, 167–68, 176n.14
    as between persons, 32–33, 34, 61–63, 71, 74–75, 77, 186n.19
    as centered, in Prefaces, 1, 36, 36n, 38, 40, 41, 46, 51, 77, 171n.2, 185n.17
    confusion about, 26, 30, 33, 42, 69–70
    and dictation, 32–34, 81–82
    as in the mind, 34, 62, 82, 152n, 160–61, 161n, 167–68, 174n.9, 178–79n.2
    as outside the mind, 1, 2, 5, 21, 32–33, 34, 43, 56–60, 62, 77–81, 81–82, 111, 124, 125, 129, 131–36, 144–45, 146, 147, 150–51, 152n, 157–58, 159, 164–65, 168, 170–71n.1, 172–73n.3, 174n.9, 190n.2
    as shifting, 41, 64–65, 68–69, 71–72, 74
    and surface, 110–11, 132
    and unconsciousness, 64n, 65, 68, 73–74, 178–79n.2
    and writing, 159n

The illustration is a reproduction of Alvin Langdon Coburn's 1906 photograph which James titled "Portland Place" and which he chose to serve as frontispiece for volume 2 of *The Golden Bowl*, the last of the twenty-four volumes of the New York Edition. James supervised the photographs, providing Coburn with detailed descriptions of the gardens, mansions, vistas, canal views, and cities he wanted photographed, and when he had nothing in mind he accompanied Coburn through London, looking for an image that would satisfy him. James wanted photographs to illustrate his novels because they were in "as different a 'medium' as possible." In the Preface to *The Golden Bowl* James wrote of Coburn's photographs that they were to be

> images always confessing themselves mere optical symbols or echoes, expressions of no particular thing in the text, but only of the type or idea of this or that thing. They were to remain at the most small pictures of our "set" stage with the actors left out; and what was above all interesting was that they were first to be constituted.
>
> This involved an amusing search which I would fain more fully commemorate. . . . On the question, for instance, of the proper preliminary compliment to the first volume of "The Golden Bowl" we easily felt that nothing would so serve as a view of the small shop in which the Bowl is first encountered.
>
> The problem thus was thrilling, for though the small shop was but a shop of the mind, of the author's projected world, in which objects are primarily related to each other, and therefore not "taken from" a particular establishment anywhere, only an image distilled and intensified, as it were, from a drop of the essence of such establishments in general, our need (since the picture was, as I have said, also completely to speak for itself) prescribed a concrete, independent, vivid instance, the instance that should oblige us by the marvel of an accidental rightness. It might so easily be wrong—by the act of being at all. . . . Just so, to conclude, it was equally obvious that for the second volume of the same fiction nothing would so nobly serve as some generalized vision of Portland Place. Both our limit and the very extent of our occasion, however, lay in the fact that, unlike wanton designers, we had, not to "create" but simply to recognise—recognise, that is, with the last fineness. The thing was to induce the vision of Portland Place *to* generalise itself. This is precisely, however, the fashion after which the prodigious city, as I have called it, does on occasion meet halfway

those forms of intelligence of it that *it* recognises. All of which meant that at a given moment the great featureless Philistine vista would itself perform a miracle, would become interesting, for a splendid atmospheric hour, as only London knows how; and that our business would be then to understand.